# JOHN MILTON,
# POET AND HUMANIST

JAMES HOLLY HANFORD

# JOHN MILTON
*poet and humanist:*
*essays by*
# JAMES HOLLY
# HANFORD

*foreword by John S. Diekhoff*

*Cleveland*
The Press of Western Reserve University
1966

# Foreword

The earliest of the essays reprinted in this volume was first published in 1910, the latest in 1925. They are collected and reprinted here because since 1910 it has not been possible to be a serious student of Milton without reading Hanford.

There is nothing obsolete in these essays. No doubt if Professor Hanford were writing these studies now instead of forty years ago, they would be somewhat different. He would draw from the Columbia *Milton* for the text of his quotations rather than from Bohn and Wright and Mitford. In "The Chronology of Milton's Private Studies" he refers us to W. T. Hales' edition of *Of Reformation* for a list of Milton's borrowings; today he would also refer us to Volume I of the Yale *Prose*, where Don M. Wolfe and William Alfred have provided ample annotation. In "The Youth of Milton" and in the other essays he would direct us to the Darbishire edition of the *Early Lives* rather than to Lockwood and Parsons. In all of the essays he would of course survey the mass of relevant scholarship produced since they were written. But that mass of scholarship would require no substantial change in these essays. The later studies would not have been written, or would themselves be very different, if Hanford had not written, however. He could write without referring to them; their authors could not without referring to him.

For the studies in this volume are a turning point and land-mark in Milton scholarship. Presenting him for an honorary degree from Western Reserve University in 1959, his friend and colleague, Lyon N. Richardson, described Professor Hanford as being himself akin to the Renaissance and identified him as

v

one of the few scholars at the beginning of the twentieth century who rescued Milton from the all-embracing arms of the Puritan tradition, from the clutching hands of eighteenth-century "sanity and order," and from nineteenth-century Romanticism. Through him, Milton became anew what he always intrinsically had been, a high soul responding to the classics and heir and partaker of the intellectual and emotional richness of the Renaissance, as well as Puritan and defender of freedom by "deeds above heroic."

It is in "Milton and the Return to Humanism" that Hanford himself defines the tendency of his work and describes the movement in Milton criticism in which he played the leading role. This seems to me the seminal essay, in which Milton is indeed rescued from the different misunderstandings of three centuries. "The mass of critical appreciation," Hanford said, "seems in large measure to have missed its mark, to have been, on the whole, perversely directed to aspects of his [Milton's] work which he himself would have deemed of secondary importance." "The real drift of the newer Miltonic study," Hanford says of the critical movement of which he is the exemplar, proposes a reinterpretation and a revaluation of *Paradise Lost*

in terms neither of sentimentalism nor of Romanticism nor of Victorian idealism but of humanism, and it seeks as a first step toward such revaluation to see Milton's philosophy as a whole by exploring his prose as well as his poetry, to set him in his right relation, not to Puritanism alone, but to the entire Renaissance, and so to realize, through a richer understanding, the significance of his work as poetic criticism of life.

In setting Milton in his right relation, Hanford and a handful of other scholars working at the same time and in the same vein not only restored Milton to his Renaissance background but reasserted his relevance to the twentieth century, "a powerful voice of guidance amid the chaos of the present day." There is extraordinary life in the dead ideas to which Raleigh thought *Paradise Lost* a monument.

There is nothing obsolete. Until I undertook to bring them together, I had not read some of these studies since the early 1930's, when I was a graduate student prudently familiarizing myself with the work of the chairman of my doctoral committee.

To read them again now has been an illuminating experience, for me and for the students in the course in Milton I have been conducting this year.

For these essays are models of scholarship. The late A. S. P. Woodhouse once described "The Youth of Milton" as the best single brief study of Milton ever written. He spoke in a moment of enthusiasm—if I remember rightly, he was presiding over the annual meeting of the Milton Society of America and was introducing Hanford, who was to speak on Milton's Italian journey. This kind of superlative is risky, of course. There are other first-rate studies of Milton, rivals for this praise, half a dozen of them in this volume. All of these essays are works of distinguished scholarship. They also illustrate Professor Hanford's extraordinary versatility. We must indeed look far for a better piece of scholarly biography than "The Youth of Milton." Although it is full of fresh insights into Milton's developing mind and character, there is no striving for novelty. Hanford always looks at the record. His insights into Milton's character spring from the record. To see how closely he has examined the record, look at "The Chronology of Milton's Private Studies." The neophyte scholar may at first be repelled by 175 footnotes in 51 pages, but as "The Youth of Milton" is a model of interpretive scholarly biography, the "Chronology" is a model both of meticulous detailed scholarship and of keen biographical interpretation. At the same time, like "The Pastoral Tradition and Milton's *Lycidas*," it is an almost frightening example of broad learning. Where is a poem better placed in its tradition than in "The Pastoral Tradition and *Lycidas*"?

What Professor Hanford did not know when he undertook the "Chronology" he found out. One may speculate—it is safer not to ask—that it was while following Milton in his private studies that Hanford got the idea of reading what Milton may have read about the art of war. Perhaps any scholar studying the *Commonplace Book* would be tempted to go beyond its items and follow Milton in his probable reading on some topic of interest. But who else, having made himself a Renaissance soldier, albeit like Milton

vii

one "that never set a squadron in the field," would from his study of military science arrive at a new critical insight into *Paradise Lost* now widely held?

The underlying idea of Milton's treatment of the conflict in Heaven is that it should be an epitome of war in general, or rather the archetype of war, according to the Platonic conception expressed by Raphael in his preliminary address to Adam. . . .

Choose whichever essay you please—"The Temptation Motive in Milton," "The Dramatic Element in *Paradise Lost*," or those already mentioned—in each there is new light on Milton as poet and as man, in each there is some critical insight that has since become commonplace.

Every student of Milton knows Hanford's *A Milton Handbook*. In its several editions since 1926 it has been the student's guide to Milton. The undergraduate studying Milton for the first time, the graduate student preparing for doctoral examinations, the professional scholar seeking a review of Milton scholarship—all depend on Hanford's *Handbook*. Up to the point of its last revision in 1946, it is a compendium of Milton scholarship.

*John Milton, Englishman,* published in 1949, is the one-volume biography to which the student or the common reader must turn for a portrait of Milton as he seems to the twentieth century. In it Hanford has modified somewhat the view of Milton he presents in these earlier essays. And he does not stop working. A study of Milton's Italian journey is in progress, and he is editing the plans for poems in the Trinity Manuscript for the Yale *Prose*. But it is these essays, written between 1910 and 1925, that changed the course of Milton criticism and made Hanford, as Lyon Richardson said, "the most discerning scholar and foremost authority of his age on Milton, his life, works, and art."

As his former student and for thirty-five years his friend, I need hardly say that I am proud that Holly Hanford has allowed me to select these essays for republication and has trusted me to introduce them.

John S. Diekhoff
Western Reserve University

viii

# Contents

# 1

## The Youth of Milton: An Interpretation of His Early Literary Development[1]

The part of Milton's life which falls between his eighteenth and his thirty-second years has never, I think, been made the subject of a special and independent critical study. Its various outward episodes—the residence at Cambridge, the retreat at Horton, the continental journey, the return to England—are presented in full detail by Masson and more interpretatively by Mark Pattison and other writers. Critical comment on the early poems, often of the most brilliant sort, of course abounds. What one misses in the discussions is a recognition of the fact that these years, comprising as they do the epoch of Milton's transition from boyhood to maturity and the first full cycle of his poetry, constitute, both from the psychological and from the literary standpoint, a unit.

Even the admirable study of the Latin poems by E. K. Rand,[2] which greatly enriches our understanding of these remarkable compositions and is so full of suggestion to the Milton student, makes no systematic attempt to integrate them with other phases of the poet's early work or to set forth in detail their significance in relation to his personality. Outwardly the Latin verse is sharply distinguished from the contemporary English poetry as belonging to a different literary tradition, and, indeed, the whole product of Milton's youthful imagination has the appearance of being highly

---

[1] Reprinted by permission from University of Michigan *Studies in Shakespeare, Milton and Donne,* New York: Macmillan, 1925.
[2] *Milton in Rustication, Studies in Philology,* April, 1922.

miscellaneous. More carefully considered, it is seen to be marked, not alone by the normal growth of his powers, but by a singularly coherent progression of experience.

The failure of Milton students generally to interpret his development in what seem to me its most essential aspects results, I believe, from an overvaluation of known outward incident and historical circumstance as determining factors in the constitution of the poetic mind. The mass of biographical detail and the still larger mass of information regarding the setting of Milton's career presented by Masson is, after all, of little avail toward an understanding of the actual unfolding of his genius. These things are, of course, not to be neglected, but they can be used only tentatively and in subordination to the all-important evidence of the poet's self-expression. Such evidence, modestly interpreted, may yield us less, but what it yields will be definite and assured, whereas conclusions based on assumptions regarding the relation between biographical incident and the subjective consciousness of the artist remain at the mercy of conjecture. Denis Saurat's important *La Pensée de Milton,* which aims to give a comprehensive map of the poet's mind, is frequently liable to objection on these grounds. A weight of inference is attached, for example, to Milton's first marriage, which, even if we possessed complete understanding of the facts, the episode will by no means bear. Another student, Heinrich Mutschmann *(Milton und das Licht)*, who approaches his subject equipped with all the paraphernalia of psychoanalysis, is shipwrecked by a wild thesis concerning Milton's supposed physical degeneracy. Finally the able and industrious Liljegren in his *Studies in Milton* stakes everything on the demonstration of two facts, that Milton did not, as he claims, meet Galileo in Italy, and that he did, as his enemies affirmed, craftily insert the Pamela prayer into the *Eikon Basilike* for the purpose of finding it there, facts sensational enough, certainly, but of purely speculative relevance even if true. The present writer, while confessing himself, in his attempt to envisage Milton's personality more clearly, indebted to these works, even to that of Mutschmann, professes to avoid their waywardness by virtue of a stricter dependence on the poet's written words.

2

The proper use of these materials involves, first of all, a careful attention to their chronology. There have been errors here which it is now possible to correct. It involves also a due proportioning of emphasis. Milton critics have in the past inclined to center attention too much on the Horton period, to the comparative neglect of that which immediately preceded it. From the standpoint of literary values such an emphasis is natural enough; but for the comprehension of the mental processes and habits which underlie his creative activity and of the moulding effects of the intellectual and imaginative forces with which he was in contact, the significance of his less mature work, of his failures, even, and of documents not literary at all may be greater than that of the Horton masterpieces.

But the Horton period itself has not, I think, been altogether rightly understood. Romantic critics like Raleigh and Moody go to great lengths in idealizing Milton's "long vacation," painting it as a moment of sweet serenity in which the poet reflects without emotional disturbance the joyous spirit of the English Renaissance. Such a view is based too exclusively on the evidence of four poems, and, with regard to these poems, it fails to take account of the effects of a studied decorum, the result of a strong personal reserve and of the strict tradition in which Milton had so carefully schooled himself, which compelled him to conceal his more instinctive emotions under a mask of formal beauty. This is generally true of the poet's early work in verse; it is particularly so of that done between 1632 and 1637. The aesthetic objectivity of the Horton poems was in considerable degree an artificial thing.

Beneath it, and in the entire body of Milton's youthful writing, we may read the evidence of disturbing experiences and intimate reactions which belong characteristically to the period of adolescence. We may read also a part, at least, of the record of Milton's awakening to the potential influences of his intellectual and artistic environment. To indicate as definitely as possible the stages in this awakening and to trace the effects of the emotional and imaginative forces thus released in him upon the developing processes of his art, is the object chiefly aimed at in the present discussion.

The record of Milton's more individual experience does not begin significantly before the period of the Latin elegies. Of his really distinctive boyhood traits we know nothing directly. Even the untimely seriousness and ambition, the deliberate purpose to fulfill expectation by becoming something good and great, are, as regards his childhood, matters of inference. We may assume him to have taken his bent thus early, but it is only later that we can study his temperament at first hand. We have Milton's own later statement to the effect that his literary talents early attracted the attention of his elders. It would be interesting to know under precisely what conditions and stimuli his first compositions were written. Given the cultural tradition of the Renaissance, it was entirely natural that he should write verses before any powerful original impulses asserted themselves in him. Latin composition was an important feature of the curriculum in all the public schools of Milton's time, a "preposterous exaction," the poet describes it in the *Tractate of Education,* "forcing the empty wits of children to compose themes, verses, and orations which are the acts of ripest judgment, and the final work of a head filled by long reading and observing, with elegant maxims and copious invention." The writing of English verse was required at Westminster and may have been at St. Paul's.

Beside this we have the special influences of Milton's home environment. It should not be forgotten that to cultivate music meant, throughout the English Renaissance, to cultivate song, and that the known compositions of Milton's father are all settings of English words. This fact presumably determines the character of Milton's first approach to poetry, and it is of far-reaching importance in its effect upon his art. Particularly suggestive, in view of the fact that the father had contributed tunes to five of the Psalms in Ravenscroft's psalter of 1621, is the preservation of two metrical Psalm paraphrases written by Milton in his sixteenth year. One surmises collaboration between the musician father and the poet son. In any case some of the sweetest of his later verses—the *Song on May Morning* and the lyrics in *Arcades* and *Comus* were composed for music. Milton's own musical training and his sense

4

of the analogy between the sister arts of music and poetry clearly underlie the conception of *L'Allegro* and *Il Penseroso*.

A less obvious result of this early influence is to be found in the aesthetic character of his enthusiasm for language. The terms in which he expresses in the poem *Ad Patrem* his gratitude to his father for his linguistic education suggest the meeting point in him of humanistic learning and the sense of beauty:

> Tuo, pater optime, sumptu
> Cum mihi Romuleae patuit facundia linguae,
> Et Latii veneres, et quae Iovis ora decebant
> Grandia magniloquis elata vocabula Graiis,
> Addere suasisti quos iactat Gallia flores,
> Et quam degeneri novus Italus ore loquelam
> Fundit, barbaricos testatus voce tumultus,
> Quaeque Palaestinus loquitur mysteria vates.[3]

His feeling for English is a home-felt delight, implying a still closer discrimination of the harmonies and ornaments of speech:

> Hail, Native Language, that by sinews weak
> Didst move my first endeavouring tongue to speak,
> And madest imperfect words with childish trips,
> Half unpronounced, slide through my infant lips,
> Driving dumb Silence from the portal door,
> Where he had mutely sat two years before. . . .
> But haste thee straight to do me once a pleasure,
> And from thy wardrobe bring thy chiefest treasure,
> Not those new-fangled toys, and trimming slight
> Which takes our late fantastics with delight;
> But cull those richest robes and gay'st attire,
> Which deepest spirits and choicest wits desire.[4]

---

[3] "When, at your cost, dear father, I had mastered the tongue of Romulus and seen all the graces of it, and had learned the noble idiom of the magniloquent Greeks, fit for the great mouth of Jove himself, you persuaded me to add to these the flowers which France boasts; and the speech which the modern Italian pours from his degenerate lips, bearing witness in every accent of the barbarian tumults; and the language in which the singers of Palestine speak their mysteries."—W. V. Moody's translation, revised by E. K. Rand, Moody, *Milton's Complete Poems*, revised edition, 1924.

[4] *At a Vacation Exercise*, vv. 1 ff. The text employed for the quotations from the English and Latin poems is W. A. Wright's, *The Poetical Works of Milton*, Cambridge, 1903.

There is no reason to suppose that these enthusiasms do not go back to the early years of Milton's schooling. They are, like the born artist's love of color, his initial gift as a poet, and they antedate the need which he later felt to find an expressive medium for those

> naked thoughts that rove about
> And loudly knock to have their passage out.

According to a statement made by Aubrey on the authority of Milton's brother Christopher he was already a poet at the age of ten and "composed many copies of verses which might well become a riper age." The anonymous biographer, who is well informed regarding Milton's early life, says that in his school days he "wrote several grave and religious poems, and paraphrased some of David's Psalms." The first of these experiments and exercises, of whatever sort they may have been, are lost, but the two Psalm paraphrases, the only pieces which survive from his school period, will serve as slightly more mature examples. They were preserved and printed in the 1645 edition of the *Poems,* not, presumably, for their own sakes but as evidences of the poet's early devotion to the Muse of his native land, and they bear accordingly the careful superscription "This and the following Psalm were done by the Author at fifteen years old." This would be in 1624, the year preceding his matriculation at the University. The choice of subject was dictated by a time when Psalm paraphrase was not merely a habit but an obsession. An illustrious line of poets had swollen the records of failure in this attempt. A pious and learned sovereign, who was not a poet, had magnanimously lent his hand. More directly responsible for Milton's endeavor in this common task were the elegant Latin versions of Buchanan, which he had doubtless studied at St. Paul's.[5]

---

[5] There are perhaps eight or ten instances in which Milton clearly owes his turn of phrase to Buchanan's rendering. Thus in v. 3 of Psalm cxxxvi, where Scripture has simply "Lord of Lords" Buchanan paraphrases "Cui domini rerum submittunt sceptra tyranni," and Milton, with a similar republican touch, "That doth the wrathful tyrants quell." Buchanan's "auricomum solem" becomes "the golden-tressed sun"; his unscriptural epithet for Og, "confisum viribus Ogum," is repeated in Milton's "large-limbed Og." In Psalm cxiv, "Pharian fields" goes back to Buchanan's "arva Phari" and the

6

Milton was to return on two later occasions to Psalm paraphrases. In 1648 he undertook to supply the need of an accurate and doctrinally sound Puritan version to supplant the Sternhold and Hopkins Psalter for congregational singing. In 1653, when he had become blind, he did the first eight Psalms (on successive days) as a combined spiritual discipline and metrical exercise, probably in anticipation of a renewal of work on the composition of *Paradise Lost*. The two early pieces differ strikingly in character from these uninspired works of his maturity. The latter are severely plain in language, and the first set, at least, as nearly literal as Milton could make them. The early versions, on the other hand, are independent poems. They are characterized by a freedom of rhythm which marks them as the products of a genuine though immature poetical enthusiasm, and their original Hebrew substance is all but lost in the ornamental phraseology which Milton adopts from the religious verse of seventeenth century England. More specifically their stylistic inspiration is Sylvester, whose rich and elaborate though somewhat undignified language apparently satisfied Milton's youthful sense of verbal beauty.[6] The choice of the 114th and 136th Psalms and the manifest enthusiasm which Milton puts into the compositions is evidence also of a deeper sympathy with the poetic substance of Sylvester, whose broad and pious sense of the greatness and goodness of God as witnessed by the excellence of created nature Milton reproduces not ineffectively. We have here the beginning of a strain in Milton's poetry the importance of which, far more than any mere consideration of style, justifies the claim of Sylvester's *DuBartas* to be counted among the permanent sources of his inspiration, a strain which reaches its culmination and full Miltonic glory in the morning hymn of Adam and Eve in the fifth book of *Paradise Lost*.

In such a passage as this Milton has, of course, far transcended

---

phrase "among their ewes," which is added to the literal rendering of v. 4, has its original in Buchanan's "ut dux gregis inter oves."

For the prevalent use of Buchanan's Latin Psalms as school texts see P. Hume Brown, *Buchanan as Humanist and Reformer*, 1890, p. 146; Foster Watson, *English Grammar Schools to 1660*, 1908, p. 472. I have no evidence that Buchanan was used at St. Paul's.

[6] See C. Dunster, *Considerations on Milton's Early Reading and the prima stamina of "Paradise Lost,"* 1800.

Sylvester's humbler muse. In it, too, more than in any attempt to reduce the Psalms to meter, does he approach their spirit, as he elaborates with his own imagery and in his own majestic idiom the great theme "The Heavens declare the glory of God." Yet the animating motive of the hymn and the quality of religious feeling manifested in it are essentially the same as in the work of his Puritan predecessor. It is an elevated and impersonal enthusiasm, having as its appropriate expression precisely the ornate magniloquence of which Sylvester is a humble and Milton the consummate master. Essentially literary in origin and developing naturally from boyhood tastes and influences this emotion and the style which attended it became characteristic of one whole phase of Milton's poetry, and of this phase the early Psalms are clear though faint precursors. With the more individual aspects of his genius, on the other hand—with such subjective experience as is embodied, for example, in the invocations in *Paradise Lost* and in the lyric parts of *Samson Agonistes,* the two paraphrases have not the slightest discernible relation.

Of analogous significance in Milton's literary biography, is the poem *On the Death of a Fair Infant Dying of a Cough,* published along with other material which he apparently had not at first considered worth printing, in the edition of 1673, and dated "Anno aetatis 17." Allowing for Milton's peculiar usage in the Latin designation of his age and assuming that the poem was composed immediately after the event which it commemorates, the death, namely, of the infant daughter of his sister Anne Philips, its date would be between December 8, 1626, and the following spring, when Milton was in his second year of residence at the University. The piece was conceived in a mood of tender grief and sympathy, not untouched with a larger sense of the mystery of death and immortality, motives toward which his mind had naturally been drawn by the ravages of the plague in London, even before they were brought home to him in a domestic sorrow. The literary influence under which his emotion characteristically shapes itself is the seventeenth century poetry of death. In style it belongs, as is evident both from its meter and its language, to the Spenserian tradition as represented particularly by Giles and Phineas

8

Fletcher. The verbal conceits which chill the feeling in all but a few stanzas show Milton in the toils of a fashion which he was later to repudiate. There are, however, beyond this, some definitely marked Miltonic traits which suggest the beginnings of a more individual style. Such expressions as "the ruined roof of shaked Olympus," the "golden-winged host," the "middle empire of the freezing air," "thy heaven-loved innocence" surely enough reveal his touch. The lovely opening anticipates the delicate perfection of the Horton poetry:

> O fairest flower, no sooner blown but blasted,
> Soft silken primrose fading timelessly,
> Summer's chief honour, if thou had'st outlasted
> Bleak Winter's force that made thy blossom dry.

We have, too, the introduction of favorite motives which he was later to employ more happily. Thus lines 38–40,

> Tell me, bright Spirit, where'er thou hoverest,
> Whether above that high first-moving sphere,
> Or in the Elysian fields (if such there were),

establish the verbal form for Lycidas, 155 ff.,

> where'er thy bones are hurled,
> Whether beyond the stormy Hebrides, . . .

and the parenthesis, "if such there were," is the first of those conscientious reservations with which Milton checks himself in his instinctive use of classical mythology. Again, the allusion to Astraea in the eighth stanza, and the mask-like imaging of Mercy and "that crowned Matron, sage white-robed truth . . . let down in cloudy throne to do the world some good," while suggesting the Fletcherian personifications, anticipate familiar passages in the poem *On the Morning of Christ's Nativity,* and the references to the guardian spirit introduce a motive to which Milton returns again and again.

These things are specifically and characteristically Miltonic. Where, however, in Stanza V, he reaches for a moment the heights of poetic utterance it is on the wings of the great tradition of Elizabethan and Jacobean song:

9

> Yet can I not persuade me thou art dead,
> Or that thy corse corrupts in earth's dark womb,
> Or that thy beauties lie in wormy bed,
> Hid from the world in a low-delved tomb.

A striking parallel to these lines is to be found in the words of Christ in Book III of *Paradise Lost:*

> Though now to Death I yield, and am his due
> All that of me can die, yet, that debt paid,
> Thou wilt not leave me in the loathsome grave,
> His prey, nor suffer my unspotted soul
> Forever with corruption there to dwell;
> But I shall rise victorious, and subdue
> My vanquisher, spoil'd of his vaunted spoil.
> Death his death's wound shall then receive, and stoop
> Inglorious, of his mortal sting disarm'd;
> I through the ample air in triumph high
> Shall lead Hell captive maugre Hell, and shew
> The powers of Darkness bound.

The poetic essence of this passage, apart from its theological implications, is something, one feels, which Milton has carried over from his youth. It shows that he could still respond with the full energy of maturity to the Christian sentiment of Donne's "Death, be not proud" or of Giles Fletcher's *Christ's Victory and Triumph*. But such moments in Milton's later work are rare. His mature spiritual life is normally ministered to by other emotions than those which associate themselves with the Resurrection, and it is only by reviving an old emotion and by falling back on his unfailing stylistic resources that he avoids the danger of mediocrity in dealing with this theme. The more striking, therefore, is its pervasiveness in the work of the Cambridge and Horton periods, where the idea of future bliss held, as we shall see, an increasingly strong and glowing appeal to his imagination.

It is, I think, significant that the poems just described stand alone among Milton's works at this period of his career. There is nothing further in English before the *Vacation Exercise* of 1628 and the *Nativity* of 1629. On the other hand, we have no less than six Latin poems dated, like the English elegy, "Anno aetatis 17," a larger number than belongs to any other single year in his life.

10

We may, perhaps, infer a deliberate postponement of further English composition in favor of an assault on the citadels of poetry in a medium dictated by the humanistic ideals of his day and rendered attractive by a growing sense of the rich beauties of Latin style.

Four of the poems, all written in the autumn of 1626, are laments occasioned by the deaths of dignitaries associated in one way or another with the University, namely, the Bishops of Winchester and Ely, alumni and former masters of Pembroke Hall, John Gostlin, the vice-chancellor, and Richard Riddle, the University beadle. The poem on the vice-chancellor is simply a meditation on the inevitableness of death, with praise of Gostlin's skill in medicine and the usual conceits regarding the failure of his art to procure him release from the common doom.

The elegies for the bishops are more elaborate and are constructed on an identical plan, having evidently been written within a short time of each other. The poet represents himself as in the act of exclaiming against Death when he is vouchsafed a vision of the abode of the blessed. In the earlier piece, *In Obitum Praesulis Wintoniensis,* Milton describes this vision in detail, painting in colorful imagery the landscape of Heaven, with its flowers, its silver streams playing over golden sands, its bejewelled angelic presences, its fanfare of celestial music. The passage anticipates both *Lycidas* and the *Epitaphium Damonis* and is the first of a series of Paradisiac pictures elaborated from antique models and enriched by the more luxuriant poetic tradition of the Renaissance, a series which culminates in the account of Eden in *Paradise Lost.* In the second piece he forebears to repeat the description of the Heaven of Heavens, but elaborates instead the journey on which he is borne by the Muse into the broad spaces of the sky, past Boötes and Orion, above the moon and the starry sphere, to the threshold of Olympus. The theme is an equally congenial one and foreshadows some of the best known and most characteristic passages in his nature poetry. The remaining elegy, *In Obitum Praeconis Academici Cantabrigiensis,* is a mere trifle, exhibiting the same conceitful humor, not untempered by kindliness, which marks the later English poems on the death of the old

11

carrier Hobson. The attitude is oddly but appropriately expressive of the sentiments of young academic gentlemen toward those minor functionaries who are ridiculed during their lives and offices only to have it faintly remembered at their passing that they were human. In style it is, like the others, laden with verbal ornament. Milton is making himself free of the realm of classic vocabulary and allusion as, in the Psalms and the English elegy, he was free of seventeenth century poetic phrase. All three pieces are largely devoid of the personal note which characterizes Milton's expression of sorrow for the loss of his sister's child. Yet one feels that he has been sincerely moved by realization of the fact of death and that it costs him no effort to accept the obligation of celebrating these successive occasions of academic mourning. Witness the sober and beautiful opening of the elegy on the Bishop of Winchester:

> Moestus eram, et tacitus, nullo comitante, sedebam,
>   Haerebantque animo tristia plura meo:
> Protinus en subiit funestae cladis imago
>   Fecit in Angliaco quam Libitina solo;
> Dum procerum ingressa est splendentes marmore turres
>   Dira sepulchrali Mors metuenda face,
> Pulsavitque auro gravidos et iaspide muros,
>   Nec metuit satrapum sternere falce greges.
> Tunc memini clarique ducis, fratrisque verendi,
>   Intempestivis ossa cremata rogis;
> Et memini Heroum quos vidit ad aethera raptos,
>   Flevit et amissos Belgia tota duces.
> At te praecipue luxi, dignissime Praesul,
>   Wintoniaeque olim gloria magna tuae.[7]

---

[7] Sad and silent I sat, comradeless; and many griefs clung about my soul. Then suddenly, behold, there arose before me an image of the deadly plague which Libitina spread on English soil, when dire Death, fearful with his sepulchral torch, entered the glorious marble towers of the great, shook the walls heavy with jasper and gold, and feared not to lay low with his scythe the host of princes. Then I thought on that illustrious duke [Duke Christian of Brunswick, a victim of the War of the Palatinate] and his worshipped brother-in-arms, whose bones were consumed on untimely pyres; and I thought on those heroes whom all Belgia saw snatched away to the skies,— saw, and wept her lost leaders. But for you chiefly I grieved, good Bishop, once the great glory of your Winchester.

Also the tenderly melancholy lines with which he brings to a close the lament for the vice-chancellor, dismissing his body to the grave and his spirit to the Elysian fields:

> Colende Praeses, membra precor tua
> Molli quiescant cespite, et ex tuo
>   Crescant rosae calthaeque busto,
>     Purpureoque hyacinthus ore.
> Sit mite de te iudicium Aeaci,
> Subrideatque Aetnaea Proserpina,
>   Interque felices perennis
>     Elysio spatiere campo! [8]

These Latin poems, then, as clearly as the English elegy, are something more than mere poetic exercises or prescriptive tasks. They spring spontaneously enough from a mood of reflective melancholy forced upon the youthful poet by the ravages of the plague, and they definitely suggest the birth in him of a more inward poetic impulse than would have been natural in his earlier boyhood. Of rather less interest is the long hexameter poem, *In Quintum Novembris,* a miniature epic, written just after the Latin elegies and describing the origin and progress of the gunpowder plot. There is perhaps a relation between this piece and the equally elaborate *Locustae* of Phineas Fletcher, but the idea of a demoniac origin of the plot was a common-place and the anti-Catholic bitterness of Milton's poem represents the prevailing and appropriate sentiment for the occasion. Thus early does the gentle and humane spirit of the youthful artist who could already invest the pain of death with beauty and send his Muse beyond the "flaming walls of space and time" receive his schooling in the harsh animosities which were for his day a necessary ingredient of patriotism and Protestant zeal. The remarkable thing is that he can throw himself so fully into the spirit of his alien theme. It is another evidence of the protean responsiveness of his genius to the

---

[8] Loved master, I pray that your limbs may rest quiet beneath the gentle sod, and that from your grave roses may spring, and marigold, and the purple-mouthed hyacinth. May Aeacus pronounce judgment mildly on you, and Proserpina, maid of Aetna, give you a smile, and may you walk forever in the Elysian fields among the blessed.

divers and even contradictory influences of the various literary traditions in which he happens from time to time to be writing. The range and character of these influences I have barely indicated. To trace them in detail would be beyond my purpose. The point to observe is that Milton's poetry, as we have thus far surveyed it, is essentially imitation, though imitation of a peculiarly generous and dynamic kind. The process of literary composition is with him in each case the result of a cultural enthusiasm which enables the poet to identify himself so completely with a literary mode that he can express himself in it freely and spontaneously without having to resort to a particular model. In the act of reproducing such a tradition Milton makes it permanently his own. The successive contacts open to him new ranges of poetic thought and expression and their influence is, as we have seen, definitely traceable in his maturest work.

It remains to consider a set of reactions of a more positive nature, reactions which belong peculiarly to the period of Milton's adolescence and which have a very different bearing on the problem of the development of his poetic personality. The first evidence of the dawn in him of an emotional experience more inwardly disturbing than the artistic melancholy which he has elaborated out of the incidents of the plague is to be found in the poem which he afterwards printed as the first of his Latin elegies. This poem, written presumably in the same spring which saw the composition of the lament for the Fair Infant, is significantly addressed to Charles Diodati, the friend who for many years served Milton as the confidant of his deepest experiences and most cherished dreams. The occasion is the incident of the poet's rustication in consequence of a quarrel with his University tutor, and *Elegy I* teaches us to look to that event as marking an important moment in the breaking down of the carefully schooled docility of Milton's boyhood. The fact of a real and fundamental change in the poet's experience is confirmed by all that we know of his relations to the University. Our fullest information comes from Christopher Milton through the biographer Aubrey, as follows: "He was a very hard student in the University and performed all his exercises there with very good applause. His first tutor there

14

was Mr. Chapell, from whom receiving some unkindness (whipped him), he was afterwards (though it seemed opposite to the rules of the college), transferred to the tuition of one Mr. Tovell, who died parson of Lutterworth." The other early biographers say nothing of any trouble, though Wood, after repeating from his authorities the statement that Milton won the admiration of all by his exercises and was esteemed to be a virtuous and sober person, adds the qualification "yet not to be ignorant of his own parts." The fact and date of the rustication are established by the elegy and Aubrey's parenthetical explanation of its cause apparently confirmed by the poet's mention of a "harsh master's threats" and "other things not to be endured by my nature." The circumstances are not difficult to reconstruct if we bear in mind the liberal environment from which Milton had just come and the atmosphere of intelligent appreciation which so evidently surrounded him at home and at school. The letters written from the University to Young and Gill [9] are evidence of the friendly relations in which he stood to these admired mentors of his boyhood. In Chapell he doubtless encountered an individual of smaller mould whose methods and attitude he resented.

Much light is thrown on Milton's situation at the University by later utterances in which he expresses a hostile point of view toward the discipline and ideals in vogue there in his time. There is contemporary evidence of still greater value. It is quite clear that he allied himself almost from the first with the group of intellectual liberals who carried on into the seventeenth century the old battle of humanistic culture against the narrow and jejune scholasticism which had taken its last refuge in the universities and which still dominated the thought and practice of the academic body as a whole. This is the basis of Milton's disparaging remarks about the students themselves in the letter already referred to. (*Alexander Gillio*, Cantabrigia, Julii 2, 1628): "Sane apud nos, quod sciam, vix unus atque alter est, qui non Philologiae, pariter et Philosophiae, prope rudis et profanus, ad Theolo-

---

[9] *The Works of John Milton in Prose and Verse*, ed. John Mitford, VII, pp. 368–371.

giam devolet implumis." [10] In the same letter he refers to certain Latin verses which he had just been writing for a friend who was Respondent in the philosophical disputation at the commencement of that year. These verses have been very plausibly identified with the poem *"Naturam non pati senium,"* which Milton included in the edition of 1645, and Masson assumes that the general subject of the disputation must have been suggested by the publication in the preceding year of George Hakewill's *Apologie or Declaration of the Power of God in the Government of the World, Consisting in an examination and Censure of the Common Errour Touching Nature's Perpetual and Universal Decay.*

The importance of Hakewill's point of view in the campaign against the vestiges of medievalism in the philosophy of the time is well recognized by the historians of thought. In championing the idea of progress against the fatalistic conception of a decline of human achievement Hakewill joins forces, as Richard Jones has recently pointed out,[11] with Francis Bacon and with the whole intellectual movement of which he was the prophet. Particularly important is his exaltation of the attainments of the moderns in such fields as mathematics, geography, and astronomy. The opposite theory of a necessary decay of nature Hakewill recognizes to be fundamentally disheartening to human endeavor: "For being once thoroughly persuaded in themselves," he writes of the maintainers of the more orthodox point of view, "that by a fatall kinde of necessitie and course of times, they are cast into those straights that notwithstanding all their striving and industrie, it is impossible they should rise to the pitch of their noble and renowned Predecessors, they begin to yield to times and to necessity, being resolved that their endeavours are all in vaine, and that they strive against the streame."

These broader issues are untouched in Milton's verses, which

---

[10] "Among us, as far as I know, there are only two or three, who without any acquaintance with criticism or philosophy, do not instantly engage with raw and untutored judgments in the study of theology."—*Milton's Prose Works,* Bohn Library edition. So throughout for the translations from the *Familiar Letters.*

[11] *The Background of the "Battle of the Books," Washington University Studies, Humanistic Series,* vol. VII (1920) , No. 2, pp. 107 ff.

deal only, in highly imaginative strains, with the alleged physical decrepitude of nature, the less fruitful theme of Hakewill's first book, and are designed as a moment of poetic ornament in a serious discussion. Even so, however, his juvenile participation in this debate on the side of the moderns, is significant in its consistency both with his humanistic inheritance and with his later attitude in theology, politics, and education. The inferences thus suggested regarding Milton's intellectual attitude are confirmed, moreover, by the position which he consistently adopts in his own academic orations, whenever the subject affords the least opportunity for the expression of his real convictions on vital issues.

In the first Prolusion,[12] dated by Masson in 1628–9, though the subject is a trifling one, Milton plainly alludes to differences in point of view which have thrown him into opposition with the majority of students and tutors. "Etenim qui possim ego vestram sperare benevolentiam, cum in hoc tanto concursu, quot oculis intueor tot ferme aspiciam infesta in me capita; adeo ut Orator venisse videor ad non exorabiles. Tantum potest ad simultates etiam in Scholis aemulatio, vel diversa Studia, vel in eisdem studiis diversa judicia sequentium."[13] The second exercise,[14] presumably somewhat later, embodies a disparagement of Aristotle in comparison with Plato, and the same point of view is represented in the undated Latin verses *De Idea Platonica quemadmodum Aristoteles intellexit*. Here Milton speaks in scorn of the unimaginative mind which cannot conceive the archetypal idea because he cannot see and touch it. With fine irony at the close he declares that if Plato expects his philosophic fancy to be received as truth he must call back the poets whom he has banished from his Republic. The third Prolusion [15] is an argument against scholasti-

---

[12] *Utrum Dies an Nox praestantior sit?*, Mitford, VII, pp. 411 ff.

[13] "For how can I hope for your good will, when, in this so great concourse, as many heads as I behold with my eyes, almost the same number do I see of visages bearing malice against me; so that I seem to have come as an *orator* to persons not *exorable*? Of so much efficacy in producing private grudges is the rivalry even in schools of those who follow different studies, or different methods in the same studies."—Masson, vol. I, p. 276.

[14] *De Sphaerarum Concentu*, Mitford, VII, pp. 421 ff.

[15] *Contra Philosophiam Scholasticam, op. cit.*, pp. 425 ff.

cism and a broad defense of the humanistic attitude and of the study of science. In the spirit of Bacon's *Novum Organum,* Milton condemns the perpetual wrangling of the schools as unfruitful either for virtue or true knowledge, and he invites the student to turn his eyes abroad upon the rich world of man and nature, ascending by degrees to the knowledge of himself and of God. His statement shows perfect comprehension of the case against the very debates in which he was himself called on to participate, and it establishes the groundwork for his entire program of future intellectual activity. The *Tractate of Education* is but an application of the method of approach advocated in this early exercise and much of *Paradise Lost* an embodiment of its results. The emphasis on physical science is particularly noteworthy. Milton can hardly be said to have possessed the true Baconian vision of man's mastery of nature by experiment and observation, but he certainly maintained throughout his life a more than ordinary interest in all branches of scientific knowledge, his deepest enthusiasm being naturally reserved for astronomy, with the most modern conceptions in which field he was, as has often been noted, thoroughly familiar.

The documents at which we have been glancing are proof, then, of the early confirmation of Milton's general intellectual point of view. They reveal the true source of all his later radicalism in humanistic culture rather than in the more specific and practical traditions of politics and religion, pointing to Erasmus and not to Luther as his progenitor. They show also the untimely establishment in him of the propagandist attitude. He consciously assumes the rôle of spokesman for a cause, playing in the little world of the University a part strikingly analogous with that which he was afterwards to adopt in public affairs. Such activities lie, of course, outside the sphere of poetry. They spring, however, from kindred sources in Milton's consciousness. No student of the poet need be told how impossible it is to separate his general opinions and purposes from his more intimate emotions, or his propagandist utterances now and later from his dominant instinct for self-portraiture and self-justification. The Latin exercises are rich in indications of Milton's early absorption in his own career, and they contain the germs of many elements in his later conception of himself as a being set apart from others and bound to cultivate himself for special uses. In the Latin portion of the exercise composed for the vacation celebration of 1628 [16] he alludes as follows to his college nickname, "The Lady," converting what was intended or thought to be intended as a disparagement into an argument of superiority. "A quibusdam audivi nuper Domina. At cur videor illis parum masculus? . . . scilicet qui Scyphos capacissimos nunquam valui pancratice haurire; aut quia manus tenenda stiva non occaluit, aut quia nunquam ad meridianum Solem supinus jacui septennis bubulcus; fortasse demum quod me virum praestiti, eo modo quo illi Ganeones: . . . at videte quam insubide, quam incogitate mihi objecerint id, quod ego jure optimo mihi vertam gloriae. Namque et ipse Demosthenes ab aemulis adversariisque parum vir dictus est. Q. itidem Hortensius omnium Oratorum post M. Tullium, clarissimus, Dionysia Psaltria appellatus est a L. Torquato." [17] That he had already begun to meditate on fame, on the kind of audience, fit though few, to which it was worth while to address himself, and on the need of long preparation for the high tasks to which he felt himself called, is evidenced in the same exercise and elsewhere in the Prolusions.

These thoughts are the materials out of which Milton is to build the ideal structure of his personality, as we have it displayed in self-sufficient grandeur in his later works. As yet the conception is too new and fragmentary to be manageable as a theme of art, but we may find in *Elegy I* an echo, however softened, of the

---

[16] *In Feriis aestivis Collegii* etc., Mitford, VII, pp. 441 ff.

[17] "By some of you I used lately to be nick-named 'The Lady.' Why seem I to them too little of a man? . . . Is it because I have never been able to quaff huge tankards lustily, or because my hands never grew hard by holding the plough, or because I never, like a seven years' herdsman, laid myself down and snored at midday; in fine, perchance, because I never proved my manhood in the same way as those debauched blackguards? . . . But see how absurdly and unreflectively they have unbraided me with that with which I on the best of grounds will turn to my glory. For Demosthenes himself was also called too little of a man by his rivals and adversaries. Quintus Hortensius, too, the most renowned of all orators after M. Tullius, was nicknamed 'a Dionysiac singing woman' by Lucius Torquatus."—Masson, I, p. 292. Milton's tone here is bantering, but one can read between the lines.

psychological processes which manifest themselves more rawly in the prose. It is thus that he refers to the incident of his banishment from Cambridge:

Me tenet urbs reflua quam Thamesis alluit unda,
    Meque nec invitum patria dulcis habet.
Iam nec arundiferum mihi cura revisere Camum,
    Nec dudum vetiti me laris angit amor.
Nuda nec arva placent, umbrasque negantia molles;
    Quam male Phoebicolis convenit ille locus!
Nec duri libet usque minas perferre Magistri,
    Caeteraque ingenio non subeunda meo.
Si sit hoc exilium patrios adiisse penates,
    Et vacuum curis otia grata sequi,
Non ego vel profugi nomen sortemve recuso,
    Laetus et exilii conditione fruor.
O utinam vates nunquam graviora tulisset
    Ille Tomitano flebilis exul agro;
Non tunc Ionio quicquam cessisset Homero,
    Neve foret victo laus tibi prima, Maro.[18]

One catches in these lines, in spite of the assumed lightness and well-bred indifference which the cultured but naïve youth wears like a borrowed garment, more than a hint of his real mood of resentment and hurt pride. Any touch of disgrace he may have felt is promptly converted to a judgment of the University as no fit place for poets and to a consciousness of satisfaction in his superior surroundings and pursuits at home. Very interesting as evidence of the kind of mental activity prompted in Milton by such an experience is the allusion to Ovid. There is obviously something here which goes beyond ordinary Renaissance practice of classical

---

[18] "That city which Thames washes with her tidal wave keeps me fast, nor does my pleasant birth-place detain me against my will. I have no wish to go back to reedy Cam; I feel no homesickness for that forbidden college room of mine. The bare fields there, niggard of pleasant shade, do not please me. How ill does that place suit with poets! I have no fancy to endure forever my stern master's threats or those other actions at which my nature rebelled. If this is "exile," to live under my father's roof and be free to use my leisure pleasantly, I will not repudiate either the outcast's name or lot, but will in all happiness enjoy this state of exile. Oh would that Ovid, sad exile in the fields of Thrace, had never suffered a worse lot! Then he would have yielded not a whit even to Ionian Homer, nor would the first praise be thine, Virgil, for he would have vanquished thee."

illustration. Milton has been meditating on the analogy between
his own little exile and the fate of Ovid until he has made a kind
of imaginative identification of himself with his Roman predecessor, as later, when the assault was intended to the city he fancied
himself a Pindar, striking reverence into the heart of the military
conqueror, and, finally, in blindness, found a solace for affliction
and an answer to his enemies by remembering:

> Those other two equall'd with me in fate,
> So were I equall'd with them in renown,
> Blind Thamyris and blind Maeonides,
> And Tiresias and Phineus, prophets old.

For Milton the fellowship of the great is at once a refuge and a
vindication. The passage in *Elegy I* is the transmutation into
poetry of the personal references in the prose oration, the passages
in *Paradise Lost* on his blindness are the verse renderings of the
replies which he made to Salmasius' tauntings in the *Second Defence.*

But these considerations by no means exhaust the importance
of the first elegy as an index to Milton's awakening emotional and
imaginative life. In his defensive retreat from the hostility of the
real world he takes refuge not alone in his reverence for the past
but in a conscious devotion to beauty in all its forms. The disfa-
vour into which he has momentarily fallen, while not taken too
seriously, has had the effect of throwing him back upon himself
and has prompted him to reveal sensations which have hitherto
found no place in his poetry. Thus, after greeting Diodati and
alluding to the cause of his sojourn in London, he launches into a
description of the enjoyments which his leisure affords him. The
poem is a less mature and more personal *L'Allegro* and *Il Penseroso* in one. He speaks briefly of his reading, then, at greater length
of attendance at the theater. Finally he turns to nature and the
spring, reserving for chief place among the objects of his enthusiasm "the maiden bands who go by like flaming stars." On this
theme he expatiates with an ardor which belies the artificial
medium in which he writes. The lines abound in images full of
enticement to the sense of youth.

21

Et decus eximium frontis, tremulosque capillos,
  Aurea quae fallax retia tendit Amor;
Pellacesque genas, ad quas hyacinthina sordet
  Purpura et ipse tui floris, Adoni, rubor! . . .
Creditur huc geminis venisse invecta columbis
  Alma pharetrigero milite cincta Venus
Huic Cnidon, et riguas Simoentis flumine valles,
  Huic Paphon, et roseam posthabitura Cypron.[19]

It was, of course, to be expected that Milton should express
himself with decorum and in an established academic mode. Sensuous desire is never with him a simple lyric force. It is from the
beginning complicated by ethical and ideal influences and
moulded in its expression by literary traditions. As, before, the
poets have been Milton's guides in the milder affections of his
youth, so now they are his tutors in the more compelling ones. For
the present his guide is clearly Ovid, to whom he twice refers in
*Elegy I* and whose stylistic example he mainly follows throughout
the poems of this group. We might infer from the elegies alone
the intense delight with which he has given himself to the study of
the *Heroïdes* and the *Amores,* and the stimulating effect which
this study has had on his awakening imagination. Fortunately,
however, there is other evidence, for Milton has given in one of
his prose works an account of his Ovidian enthusiasm, and indeed
of the whole phase of his experience which this enthusiasm ini-
tiates, an account at once so coherent and so minutely faithful as
to make it an outstanding document in the study of his early
literary development.

The passage consists of an elaborate analysis in the *Apology for
Smectymnuus* of the formation of his youthful ideals of chastity,
written in 1642 in reply to certain defamatory statements of
Bishop Hall. Although provoked by a stinging accusation and
taking the form of a piece of special pleading, Milton's utterance
is obviously much more than a merely improvised defense. It is

---

[19] "And exquisite grace of brow, and floating locks,—golden nets which
Love casts deceivingly,—inviting cheeks, to which the purple of the hyacinth,
yea, even the blush of thy flower, Adonis, is dull! Men say that hither blessed
Venus came, escorted by her quivered soldier-boy, drawn by twin doves,
willing to love London more than Cnidos, or the vales watered by the stream
of Simöis, or Paphos, or rosy Cyprus."

rather the result of a long process of introspective meditation, now summarized in a review of that part of his early creative work which he recognizes as most essentially individual in its inspiration, and serving, for those who cared more for the writer than for the controversial issue, as a kind of biographia literaria or "Growth of the Poet's Mind." The opening sentences go far toward interpreting the emotional reactions which, as we have seen, find partial expression in *Elegy I*.

I had my time, readers, as others have, who have good learning bestowed upon them, to be sent to those places where, the opinion was, it might soonest be obtained; and as the manner is, was not unstudied in those authors which are most commended. Whereof some were grave orators and historians, whose matter methought I loved indeed, but as my age then was, so I understood them; others were the smooth elegiac poets, whereof the schools are not scarce, whom both for the pleasing sound of their numerous writing, which in imitation I found most easy, and most agreeable to nature's part in me, and for their matter, which what it is there be few who know not, I was so allured to read, that no recreation came to me better welcome. For that it was then those years with me which are excused, though they be least severe, I may be saved the labour to remember ye. Whence having observed them to account it the chief glory of their wit, in that they were able to judge, to praise, and by that could esteem themselves worthiest to love those high perfections, which under one or other name they took to celebrate; I thought to myself by every instinct and presage of nature, which is not wont to be false, that what emboldened them to this task, might with such diligence as they used embolden me; and that what judgment, wit, or elegance was my share, would herein best appear, and best value itself, by how much more wisely, and with more love of virtue I should choose (let rude ears be absent) the object of not unlike praises. For albeit these thoughts to some will seem virtuous and commendable, to others only pardonable, to a third sort perhaps idle; yet the mentioning of them now will end in serious. Nor blame it, readers, in those years to propose to themselves such a reward, as the noblest dispositions above other things in this life have sometimes preferred: whereof not to be sensible when good and fair in one person meet, argues both a gross and shallow judgment, and withal an ungentle and swainish breast.[20]

We have here indicated a highly important moment in Milton's responsiveness to the stimulus of reading. The grave historians and orators, imperfectly apprehended, have left him moved by a

---

[20] *Prose Works*, Bohn edition, III, pp. 116–117.

23

cool and detached enthusiasm only; the smooth and glowing love poetry of the Roman elegists has spoken powerfully to his emotions and has roused in him the desire to exercise on similar themes the poetic talent which he is already conscious of possessing.[21] In a youth nursed in the literary traditions of the Renaissance, and, indeed, in any youth of Milton's temperament, this was entirely natural. The pagan sensuousness and romantic tone of Ovid and his fellows have put them in a quite different category from other classic writers, giving to their appeal an immediacy and force like that of contemporary poetry. It is characteristic of Milton that he should represent his enjoyment of these authors as accompanied by reflection and his creative impulse as guided by a conscious purpose and ideal. The elegists must, he thinks, have accounted it the first glory of their genius that they were able to judge of the excellence which they celebrated in verse. Their ability adequately to judge and praise these excellences was, moreover, the proof of their worthiness to love them. True glory, Milton implies (and the idea is one to which he clung throughout his life) comes not from the praises of men but from the well-grounded consciousness of inner worth. This satisfaction he will be able to enjoy in higher degree than the elegists in proportion to the superior wisdom and virtue with which he will make choice of the object of his praise.

Something of all this is clearly matter of later interpretation. In the first elegy there is little, if any, of the devotion to an ideal object implied in the prose statement. The moral reaction is negative rather than dynamic. It is evidenced in the fact that the poet allows himself no indecencies of expression and that he checks himself in his praise of the starry maidens, by announcing

---

[21] Did Milton make his excursions into the seductive region of Ovidian elegy in the regular course of school reading, as he seems to imply, or on his own initiative and privately? The *Metamorphoses* appears in all the school curricula of the time, but I find no mention of any other work of Ovid. Presumably the amatory poems would be ruled out of St. Paul's on moral grounds, and one hardly imagines even a university tutor directing a boy of sixteen to them. Milton does not mention Ovid at all among the authors to be read in his own model school. Probably he takes the *Metamorphoses* for granted.

that, while Cupid grants him immunity, he will make haste to quit their presence:

> Et vitare procul malefidae infamia Circes
> Atria, divini Molyos usus ope.

The herb moly, again employed in Milton's elaboration of the Circe myth in *Comus,* may be taken to represent the sure guid- ance of Christian ethics, to which he has hitherto owed his safety amid the strongly felt allurements of the senses. Aside from this Puritan touch (and even this has a kind of precedent in Ovid's declaration that though his verse is corrupt his life is chaste) there is nothing in the poem to suggest that Milton was as yet anything but the enthusiastic though somewhat timid disciple of his Roman predecessor in matter as in manner. The one passage in which he explicitly challenges comparison with Ovid is prompted by patriotism rather than by any philosophically based consciousness of superiority:

> Nec Pompeianas Tarpeia Musa columnas
> Iactet, et Ausoniis plena theatra stolis.
> Gloria virginibus debetur prima Britannis;
> Extera sat tibi sit foemina posse sequi.[22]

In general, then, *Elegy I* is an expression, on the one hand, of Milton's sensitive self-love, on the other of a new and intense delight in beauty, nourished by contact with the most sensuous and romantic of ancient poets and given artistic direction by the typical Renaissance ambition to "overgo" some reputed classic name in his own tongue and upon a kindred theme. These related motives are the basis of an enduring inspiration. We may trace the first of them in a poem of the succeeding year, the epistle to Thomas Young, where warm personal affection, more strongly felt no doubt in the partly hostile environment of the University, is combined with indignation at the harshness of the English church which has compelled so excellent a man to seek his sustenance

---

[22] "Let not the poet who lived by the Tarpeian rock [Ovid] boast the dames of Pompey's porch, nor the theatre full of Roman stoles. To the virgins of Britain first glory is due; suffice it, foreign woman, that thou canst follow them."

abroad. Milton's sympathy for Young is a kind of extension of the mood of defensive self-pity which we have seen implied in *Elegy I*. He reminds him that other preachers of the word—Elijah, Paul, Jesus—have been victims of persecution, as he had earlier reminded himself that Ovid, a poet, was driven into exile. Finally he gives a personal application to the motive of Psalm CXXXVI, assuring his friend that the Lord of Hosts who defended Zion will stand at his side amid the clash of battle which surrounds him. Milton writes with an accent of sincerity which leaves no doubt of the hold which the subject has taken on his emotions, but he indulges in no such aesthetic dreaming as in the first elegy and the suppressed excitement which underlies the erotic imagery of the earlier poem is entirely lacking.

It emerges again, however, in *Elegy VII*, Milton's next work, which belongs apparently to the year 1628. Here the poet picks up the theme of *Elegy I* and carries the amatory experience therein initiated to a second stage. In the first poem, as we have seen, he had made declaration of a general susceptibility to the attraction of sex and implied a fear lest, if he remained in London, Cupid might not long grant him immunity. In *Elegy VII* he represents himself as having at length enrolled perforce in the ranks of actual lovers. The deity appears to the poet in the early dawn of a spring morning, boasts of his power over men and gods, and warns him that he too shall feel it. His Muse shall not succor him, nor the serpent of healing Apollo give him aid. There follows the description of an amatory encounter—the mere exchange of glances with one among the maidens toward whom in his suburban walk he rashly allowed his eyes to rove. Her beauty pierces to the heart and the poet becomes a hopeless servant of the God whose power he has defied. In elaborating the episode Milton draws heavily upon the phraseology of ancient erotic verse, and in particular upon the allegorical and mythological love machinery of Ovid. His more immediate model is the *De Neaera* of Buchanan.[23] The Scotch poet, like Milton, represents himself as a rebel against love. The blind boy, in anger, empties his quiver against him and fills

---

[23] *Elegiarum Liber, Poemata*, Amstelaedami, p. 317.

his breast with arrows. Finding even this in vain he binds him with the tangles of Neaera's hair and leads him captive as a warning trophy for all scorners of his might. Strongly, however, as Milton's poem smells of the oil of humanism, there can be no mistaking the eager delight with which he gives himself to the spirit of his theme, importing into his verses an enthusiastic glow which is entirely absent from the elegant and pointed couplets of his original. The opening allegory of Cupid and the subsequent description of the poet's woe are academic enough and effectively conceal emotion; the lines, on the other hand, in which he narrates his springtime encounter with a nameless love sound wholly real and individual:

> Et modo qua nostri spatiantur in urbe Quirites,
>   Et modo villarum proxima rura placent.
> Turba frequens, facieque simillima turba dearum,
>   Splendida per medias itque reditque vias;
> Auctaque luce dies gemino fulgore coruscat.
>   Fallor? an et radios hinc quoque Phoebus habet?
> Haec ego non fugi spectacula grata severus,
>   Impetus et quo me fert iuvenilis agor;
> Lumina luminibus male providus obvia misi,
>   Neve oculos potui continuisse meos.
> Unam forte aliis supereminuisse notabam;
>   Principium nostri lux erat illa mali.[24]

Whether or not these verses recount an actual incident they express real and acute sensations, and the poem as a whole gives evidence of an all but complete surrender to the Ovidian attitude and mood.

An even bolder abandon characterizes *Elegy V*, the next poem in this series, written in the spring of Milton's twenty-first year. The poet greets the season and describes in ecstatic language the

---

[24] "And now I took my pleasure, sometimes in the city parks, where our citizens promenade, sometimes at neighboring country-places. Crowds of girls, with faces like to the faces of goddesses, came and went radiantly through the walks; the day brightened with a double splendor. Surely, the sun himself stole his beams from their faces. I was not stern with myself; I did not flee from the gracious spectacle, but let myself be led wherever youthful impulse directed. Rashly I sent my gaze to meet theirs; I could not control my eyes. Then by chance I noted one supreme above the others, and the light of her eyes was the beginning of my ills."

sensation of a returning impulse in his breast. The spring it is which has given him his genius and the spring shall be celebrated in his song. What follows is strikingly pagan in tone and luxuriant in imagery. Earth bares her rich breast to the love of Phoebus. Cupid wanders about the world stirring all Earth's children to follow her example. Venus rises with restored youth as from the warm sea. The youths cry "Hymen" throughout the marbled cities. Throngs of golden-girdled maidens go forth yearning for love. At nightfall Sylvanus and the Satyrs wanton in the fields; Pan riots, and Faunus pursues the Oread, who hides in order that she may be found.

In subject and general conception this piece, like *Elegy VII*, depends upon a poem of Buchanan, the *Majae Calendae,* printed in the *Elegiarum Liber*.[25] There are resemblances also in detail. Thus Buchanan as well as Milton alludes to the rejuvenation of Venus, depicts Cupid as furbishing his arrows and rekindling his torch, and describes the rout of all Earth's sons and daughters under the impulse of desire:

> Applauduntque deo pueri, innuptaeque puellae
> Queis rudis in vacuo pectore flamma calet.
> Plaudit utrique deo quicquid creat humidus aer,
> Quicquid alit tellus, aequora quicquid alunt.

In Buchanan, however, the love theme is subsidiary and there is nothing to correspond to Milton's description of the effect of the coming of spring on his own inspiration as a poet. The difference is essential and stamps Milton's work as a directly personal utterance, the fullest expression we have yet encountered of the motives and yearnings which dominated his imagination at this time.

We may pause at this point to consider the significance of the fact that these very intimate reactions should take place under the influence of classical rather than of English poetry and should come to expression in Latin rather than in the poet's mother tongue. It has already been noted that Milton seems in his second academic year to have abandoned for the time being his early experimentation in English verse, presumably a result of the humanistic tendency to undervalue the vernacular as a source of

---

[25] *Poemata,* p. 301.

serious culture. There were additional reasons why he should have employed the learned medium in the poems which we have just considered. The element of Puritanism in his early environment had bred in him a timidity and sense of shame which inhibited his open utterance of any but the most decorous and approved, or in some cases, the most trivial sentiments. To give rein to sensuousness in the vernacular was to range oneself with a group of unacceptable licentious rhymsters. To do so in Latin was to follow the tradition of the honored classics and of the eminently respectable learned moderns, like Buchanan, who had imitated them. Against this somewhat pedantic attitude stood Milton's patriotism and his natural instinct for expression in his mother tongue, and ultimately these forces triumphed over his humanistic predispositions and freed him to pour himself out in English. His feelings on the subject are recorded in the enthusiastic apostrophe to his native language from which quotation has already been made. This piece, an English digression in a Latin vacation exercise, was composed during the Easter term of 1628, a year earlier than the fifth Latin elegy, and it is natural to associate Milton's renewed consciousness of the claims of English verse with the access of creative power which he describes in the latter poem. We may connect it also with more mature and serious meditation on his vocation as a poet, clear evidence of which appears in these pieces for the first time. In *Elegy V* Milton characterizes his poetic insight in terms which manifestly anticipate his later consciousness of the kind of task to which he felt himself called:

> Iam mihi mens liquidi raptatur in ardua caeli,
>> Perque vagas nubes corpore liber eo;
> Perque umbras, perque antra feror, penetralia vatum;
>> Et mihi fana patent interiora Deum;
> Intuiturque animus toto quid agatur Olympo,
>> Nec fugiunt oculos Tartara caeca meos.
> Quid tam grande sonat distento spiritus ore?
>> Quid parit haec rabies, quid sacer iste furor? [26]

---

[26] Now my spirit is rapt into the skyey steeps, and freed from the flesh I walk through the wandering clouds; through the shades I go, and the caverns, inmost prophetic sanctuaries; and the inner fanes of the gods lie open to me. My soul sees all that comes to pass in Olympus, and the darks of Hades escape not my vision. What lofty song does my soul intend, as it stands with lips apart? what does this madness bring to birth, this sacred fury?

In the *Vacation Exercise* there is an expansion, in similar terms, of the same idea:

> Yet I had rather, if I were to choose,
> Thy service in some graver subject use,
> Such as may make thee search thy coffers round,
> Before thou clothe my fancy in fit sound;
> Such where the deep transported mind may soar
> Above the wheeling poles, and at Heaven's door
> Look in, and see each blissful deity
> How he before the thunderous throne doth lie,
> Listening to what unshorn Apollo sings
> To the touch of golden wires, while Hebe brings
> Immortal nectar to her kingly sire;
> Then, passing through the spheres of watchful fire,
> And misty regions of wide air next under,
> And hills of snow and lofts of piled thunder,
> May tell at length how green-eyed Neptune raves,
> In Heaven's defiance mustering all his waves;
> Then sing of secret things that came to pass
> When bedlam Nature in her cradle was;
> And last of kings and queens and heroes old,
> Such as the wise Demodocus once told
> In solemn songs at King Alcinous' feast,
> While sad Ulysses' soul and all the rest
> Are held with his melodious harmony,
> In willing chains and sweet captivity.

The fruits of Milton's declared intention to return seriously to English composition were delayed for some six months after the writing of the *Vacation Exercise*. There exist the English *Song on May Morning* and the sonnet *O Nightingale!* both of which I should ascribe to the period of the Latin elegies, and, indeed, specifically to the spring of 1629.[27] The first is a purified lyric comment on the theme of *Elegy V*, its contrast with the latter poem in style and mood being due to Milton's momentary reversion to the spirit of Elizabethan song. In the sonnet the opening lines are a direct translation from the Latin, and the conclusion embodies a

---

[27] The argument, so far as the sonnet is concerned, is given in detail in my article *The Arrangement and Dates of Milton's Sonnets, Modern Philology,* Jan., 1921. The position which I have assigned to the Song is made probable by its relation to *Elegy V*.

declaration of the rôle which Milton has consciously adopted in accordance with his own feelings and his devotion to his Roman models:

> Whether the Muse or Love call thee his mate,
> Both them I serve, and of their train am I.

The sonnet is not, however, itself Ovidian in tone. Neither is it, like the song, Elizabethan. It suggests rather the direct influence of Italian models and represents a transition on Milton's part to a new set of foreign poetic allegiances, responding to and helping to determine an important change in literary mood.

Such a transition is duly recorded in Milton's account of himself in the *Apology for Smectymnuus.* The significance of the passage, the first sentence of which has already been quoted, appears to have been overlooked entirely by the poet's biographers and critics:

For blame it not, readers, in those years to propose to themselves such a reward as the noblest dispositions above other things in this life have sometimes preferred; whereof not to be sensible when good and fair in one person meet argues both a gross and shallow judgment, and withal an ungentle and swainish breast. For by the firm settling of these persuasions I became, to my best memory, so much a proficient, that if I found those authors anywhere speaking unworthy things of themselves or unchaste of those names which before they had extolled, this effect it wrought on me, from that time forward their art I still applauded, but the men I deplored; and above them all preferred the two famous renowners of Beatrice and Laura, who never write but honor of them to whom they devote their verse, displaying sublime and pure thoughts, without transgression.

Milton associates the change in his literary point of view with his ambition and his personal idealism, making it an inevitable outcome of the resolve to be the highest that his mind perceived. He becomes an adept in rejecting the grosser enticements of the flesh, and his literary taste responds to the conscious exercise of his judgment. Dante and Petrarch are the poetic embodiments of his new aspirations. In these poets, as in the Romans, he finds illustrations of the devotion of genius to the praise of beauty, but he finds them also inflamed by a pure idealism in the light of which the limitations of their predecessors may be judged. The art of the

Romans he still, like a good humanist, judges superior, the men themselves far lower in a spiritual scale. His own path is clear. He will continue to rival the pagans in their perfection of outward form, but he will follow the Christians in the purity and elevation of their conceptions. This is the formula for Milton's youthful poetic aspirations. It was later transformed to suit with a more mature idea of his true objects, but it was never abandoned. We may well question, however, whether, in viewing his early romantic yearnings and aesthetic enthusiasms as an aspect of the higher aspirations of the soul, Milton is not reading retrospectively into his experience the ideas of a later time. Such a process is a familiar one in the literary history of the Renaissance. We have its prototype in Dante's spiritual interpretations in the *Vita Nuova* of sonnets many of which were written in a purely mundane mood. The most, then, that we can infer from the passage quoted is that Dante and Petrarch came in turn to supplant Ovid as objects of Milton's literary discipleship. The results of this new allegiance are indicated in the sonnet *O Nightingale!* and more directly in the Italian poems which immediately follow it in the edition of 1645.

The assumption that these pieces must have been composed in Italy has hitherto obscured their significance in the scheme of Milton's early work. They are to be read as documents in the history of the phase of Milton's emotional and imaginative life which begins when he first enrolls himself as a lover and which definitely ends, as we shall see, before he took up his residence at Horton. I should date them immediately after *Elegy V* and the English Sonnet, i.e., between the spring of 1629 and the winter of 1629–30.[28]

The Italian sequence is, like the first elegy, addressed to Diodati and is ostensibly devoted to the praise of a foreign lady named Emilia, whom Milton has apparently met in London and whose

---

[28] This is in accord with the consensus of recent scholarly opinion. See John Smart, *Milton's Sonnets:* also D. H. Stevens, *The Order of Milton's Sonnets, Modern Philology,* April, 1919, and my own study cited above. No error has done more to obscure Milton's early poetical development than the assumption that the Italian poems must have been written during Milton's continental journey.

servant he proclaims himself in language of extravagant compliment to be. These poems are manifestly Petrarchan. Milton is still more interested in himself and his verses than he is in the object of his praise. In the second sonnet and the canzone he gracefully elaborates the image of himself endeavoring to transplant the flower of Italian speech into an alien soil surrounded by the ridicule of uncomprehending English youths who bid him pluck the laurels which await him in his mother tongue. His answer is that his lady tells him "This is the language of which Love himself is boastful." In the third sonnet he confesses to Diodati his former scorn of love has yielded. In the last poem in the series he tells that his heart is bold and constant, armed in adamant, secure against the attacks of force or envy, raised above vulgar fears and hopes, eager for every excellence and devoted to the Muses; it is less firm in its susceptibility to love alone. Even such a one, it will be remembered, is Adam,

> in all enjoyments else
> Superior and unmoved, here only weak
> Against the charm of beauty's powerful glance.

Elsewhere he praises the lady's gentle spirit and dark-eyed beauty. She is possessed of more languages than one, and her song draws the moon down from its sphere. In such degree only do the poems express enthusiasm for a feminine embodiment of the good and fair. It was, of course, to be expected that this amatory verse should contain nothing inconsistent with the standards of conduct and taste which Milton had set for himself. What we miss is such sublimation of emotional experience as might have resulted if Milton's spirit had really been enkindled at this time by the *Vita Nuova* and the lyric poetry of the *dolce stil,* as he had a little earlier been enkindled by the Roman elegies. But though he mentions Dante it is evidently only Petrarch who really avails him, and the religion of love, which glows in Dante with transcendent fervor, is pale and conventionalized in his successor. This religion in its sincerity is not for Milton. In the Italian sonnets he has, indeed, rid himself of sensuousness, but only by means of a temporary abstraction of his art from his actual emotional experience.

33

The higher mood, when it comes to him at this stage in his development, will be born of an ethical reaction, for Milton is at heart a humanist and a Protestant and his acceptance of the point of view of courtly and romantic love is, after all, a *tour de force*.

For the first clear indication in his creative work of such an ethical reaction we are prepared by the next passage in the prose statement. The change in attitude is again connected with his purpose and ambitions as a poet. The suggestions as to the character of his thoughts on this subject which we have noted in the *Vacation Exercise* and in *Elegy V* are now explicitly confirmed.

And long it was not after [he continues] when I was confirmed in this opinion, that he who would not be frustrate of his hope to write well hereafter in laudable things, ought himself to be a true poem; that is a composition and pattern of the best and honorablest things; not presuming to sing praises of heroic men, or famous cities, unless he have in himself the experience and practice of all that which is praiseworthy.

Milton's language suggests that the confirmation of his convictions regarding the relation between personal conduct and poetic achievement and the accompanying resolution to devote himself to something higher and more serious than amatory lyrics marks a definite stage in his inner history. We can fix the moment of this change with considerable precision, for its first fruits in his poetry are to be found in the sixth Latin elegy, written at the Christmas season of 1629, some six months later than *Elegy V*. The poet addresses Diodati, "who, sending the author some verses from the country at Christmas time, asked him to excuse their mediocrity, on the ground that they were composed amid the distractions of the festival season." Milton expostulates at the implication that revelry is not propitious to poetry, citing to the contrary the examples of Ovid, Anacreon, Pindar, and Horace. Bacchus and Erato, Ceres and Venus, are the patrons of elegy, and feasting, wine, and love its proper sources of inspiration. With the epic poet it is different. He must live austerely like an ascetic. His life must be pure. He is like a priest who ministers at the altars of the gods. In conclusion Milton tells what he himself is writing—an ode on the Nativity as a birthday gift to Christ.

The formula here given for the discipline of the epic poet is, allowing for the more exalted language of poetry, so precisely identical with that of the statement in the *Apology* as to make it clear that Milton is in the latter statement looking back to and thinking in terms of his meditation of 1629. We may infer that the Latin utterance represents a definite resolution regarding his life work. It is natural to associate such a resolution with the poet's coming of age on December 9 of the same year. He was apparently in the habit of taking account of himself at various anniversaries of his life, witness the *Sonnet on His Being Arrived at the Age of Twenty-three* and the one to Skinner on the third anniversary of his blindness. The thought that he was now in the technical sense a man may well have prompted him to look upon his earlier performance as belonging to the past, and the coincidence of his birthday with the Christmas season explains the mood in which he took up the subject of the Nativity.

The poem itself, as all critics have recognized, strikes a new note in the poetry of Milton. Belonging in its general tradition to the sober vein to which he had already declared allegiance in the English poems and exhibiting, like them, the influence of the Spenserian school, it quite transcends the earlier poems in elevation and poetic fervor. We feel that here, for the first time, we have the genuine and characteristic reaction of Milton's personality upon a serious religious object. He contemplates the event, not at all with the loving surrender of a Catholic poet to its human sweetness, but with an austere intellectualized emotion stirred in him by the idea of its moral significance. Christ is, for him, not a babe, nor indeed a person at all, but a symbol of purity and truth, that truth which "came once into the world with her divine Master, and was a perfect shape most glorious to look on." The pagan deities are multiform ugliness of error, put to rout by the god-like simplicity of Christ as shadows by the sun. The poet completely identifies himself with his conception and this identification calls forth all his imaginative and expressive powers. However much Milton's precise theological ideas may have changed in later life and his ethical sense become enriched with the content of experience, his attitude retains to the end the form which it assumes in the *Nativity* ode. The poem is the lyric prelude of *Paradise Lost* and in an exacter sense of *Paradise Regained*.

I have, I think, said enough to suggest that the moment in Milton's literary life represented by *Elegy VI* and the *Nativity* is something more than a passing mood. It remains to consider how consistently he maintained this lofty and severe position.

Obviously we need look for no such complete break with the past as would result from a sudden religious conversion, nor even for the kind of outward change of profession for which not a few of his seventeenth century predecessors and contemporaries in English verse gave precedent. Milton never felt the need of clothing his Muse in a mourning garment. He remains to the end what he had always been, a humanist, and his ultimate exclusive adherence to religious themes is the result of a long development. His work after 1629 is still eclectic in its inspiration and full of variety. The poem on Shakespeare, the two epitaphs on the university carrier, and the elegy on the Marchioness of Winchester belong to the immediately succeeding years. These works exhibit a fresh range of contact with earlier English verse. Largely abandoning the manner of the Fletchers and definitely rejecting the "new-fangled toys and trimming slight" of the metaphysical school, Milton enrolls himself among the sons of Ben. *On Shakespeare* and the two Hobson poems (1630 and 1631) are in the vein of seventeenth century epigram. The elegy for the Marchioness (1631) is his first essay in octosyllabic couplets, a measure which carries with it the pure and classic style of the Jonsonian lyric:

> Gentle Lady, may thy grave,
> Peace and quiet ever have!
> After this thy travail sore,
> Sweet rest seize thee ever more.

The spirit of the earlier elegy, *On a Fair Infant,* finds an echo in the tender delicacy with which Milton celebrates this gentle mother's death in child-bed, likening her to the biblical Rachel,

> Who, after years of barrenness,
> The highly favored Joseph bore
> To him who served for her before,
> And at her next birth, much like thee,
> Through pangs fled to felicity,

but the poetic mode has changed. A direct suggestion for the poem appears to have come from William Browne's celebrated *Epitaph on the Countess Dowager of Pembroke.*[29] Compare the two openings:

> Under this marble hearse
> Lies the subject of all verse:
> Sidney's sister, Pembroke's mother,

and Milton's

> This rich marble doth inter
> The honored wife of Winchester,
> A viscount's daughter, an earl's heir.

The last lines of Browne's lyric similarly supplied Milton with the conceit upon which he constructed the poem on Shakespeare:

> Marble piles let no man raise
> To her name: for after days
> Some kind woman born as she,
> Reading this, like Niobe
> Shall turn marble, and become
> Both her mourner and her tomb.

> What needs my Shakespeare for his honored bones,
> The labour of an age in piled stones. . . .
> Then thou, our fancy of itself bereaving
> Dost make us marble with too much conceiving;
> And so sepulchred in such pomp dost lie,
> As kings for such a tomb would wish to die.

These poems, then, give evidence of Milton's continued delight in the pure artistry of verse and of his willingness to give himself even after the earnest declaration of *Elegy VI* to various more or less impersonal aesthetic moods. There are, however, clear indications of a conscious change in the main direction of his literary purposes from this time on. The seven Latin elegies represent, as we have seen, the serious fruit of Milton's early ambition to enter the lists with the great names of literature, the choice of Ovid as a model being dictated by the example of Buchanan, by his own sympathetic taste, and by a sense of the appropriateness of the

---

[29] The lines, as given in the text, had appeared in the fourth edition of Camden's *Remains* (1629), p. 336. See *Athenaeum*, Aug. 11, 1906, p. 159.

material to youth. Having attained his goal he promptly abandons it in favor of the higher seriousness of epic poetry. His progress, as Professor Rand points out, is strikingly parallel with that of Virgil, whose poetry passes through various stages from the atmosphere of Alexandria to that of Augustan Rome. Of this parallel Milton himself was fully aware. The idea of it must already have been present in his mind when he wrote the poem *On the Morning of Christ's Nativity*, as a true messianic eclogue, corresponding to the Roman poet's prophecy of the Golden Age which was to follow upon the birth of a son to Pollio and matching that utterance in its already half-epic exaltation. The materials of Milton's future poetry are as yet but vaguely defined, but his mind is plainly set toward the mysteries of Heaven and Hell and the deeds of "pious heroes and leaders part divine." The spell of Petrarch allures him only momentarily from his true path. In taking formal farewell of the elegiac mood he takes farewell of all amatory trifling. At any rate he no longer appears in the rôle of a romantic lover, and a postscript appended to the Latin poems dismisses the whole experience as belonging to a bygone phase.

> Haec ego mente olim laeva, studioque supino,
> Nequitiae posui vana trophaea meae.
> Scilicet abreptum sic me malus impulit error,
> Indocilisque aetas prava magistra fuit;
> Donec Socraticos umbrosa Academia rivos
> Praebuit, admissum dedocuitque iugum.
> Protinus, extinctis ex illo tempore flammis,
> Cincta rigent multo pectora nostra gelu;
> Unde suis frigus metuit puer ipse sagittis,
> Et Diomedeam vim timet ipsa Venus.[30]

That we do not find Milton turning at once to epic verse is not surprising. For a work designed to rank his name with greater

---

[30] These vain trophies of my idleness I set up in time past, in unbalanced mood and with lax endeavor. Vicious error hurried me astray, and my untaught years were an ill mistress to me; until the shady Academe [*i.e., Plato's philosophy*] offered me its Socratic streams, and loosened from my neck the yoke to which I had submitted. At once all these youthful flames became extinct, and since then my breast is rigid with accumulated ice; whence Cupid himself fears freezing for his arrows, and Venus dreads my Diomedean strength.

ones than Ovid he naturally felt himself, at the age of twenty-one, unready. Instead, he proposes, apparently, a series of lofty religious poems celebrating the successive events in the life of Christ and the festivals of the Christian calendar. Of these the *Nativity* was triumphantly completed, and a poem on *The Passion* earnestly begun at the Easter season of the following year. His failure to complete this piece illustrates the breakdown of his higher inspiration when the theme found no responsive echo in his own experience. The crucifixion, neither now nor later, had the slightest hold on his emotions. That Milton did not fully recognize the conditions of the successful exercise of his poetic faculty is suggested by the character of the note appended to the *Passion*,[31] and also, perhaps, by the fact that he appears still to have cherished the plan of a series of poems on the events as late as the Horton period, when he wrote the complete but uninspired piece *Upon the Circumcision* (see below).

We have, I think, in Milton's inability to satisfy with anything like the fullness of success which he had attained in the elegies the ideal which he had set for himself in 1629 the true explanation of his feeling of immaturity and failure confessed in the noble sonnet *On His Being Arrived at the Age of Twenty-three*. Milton did not, when he wrote these lines, "forget the Latin poems," as Moody suggests. He remembered them all too well. Nor could he have been dissatisfied with anything in the mere technique of his achievement in English verse. The idea that he was thinking of Thomas Randolph as one of the spirits more timely happy than himself is patently absurd, for there was nothing in the work of Randolph or any contemporary poet that Milton could have envied. The Roman epic poet Lucan or even Sir Philip Sidney would be a more plausible suggestion, if we must assume that Milton had any particular person in mind. But his sense of a lack of inward ripeness was primarily with reference to his own ideals and it could have been dissipated only by a successful beginning at epic poetry, which he had not, so far as we know, attempted, or by the maintenance through a number of similar works of the

---

[31] "This Subject the Author finding to be above the years he had when he wrote it, and nothing satisfied with what was begun, left it unfinished."

level of high seriousness which he had momentarily attained in the poem on the Nativity. The result of his dissatisfaction appears to have been the resolution to wait patiently for this time, withdrawing his energies for the present from serious composition and devoting himself to intellectual, moral, and aesthetic self-cultivation. Not until after his Italian journey, i.e. in 1639–40, did Milton deliberately set forth to vindicate his "inward ripeness" by attempting to realize the next stage in his literary plans.

The intervening years of his residence at Horton I am disposed to regard as scarcely less epochal than the earlier period at the University. Though the foundations of his culture were firmly established and the controlling ideas and motives of his life already operative, his transition to full intellectual maturity had not yet taken place; and the divergent or contradictory elements in his consciousness remained to be fused by the tremendous energy of Milton's mind into philosophic and aesthetic wholeness. Among the all too scanty documents which enable us to trace Milton's spiritual development in the years under discussion the manuscript letter to an unknown friend, written apparently near the beginning of the Horton period, bears emphatic testimony to the strain of moral earnestness which found expression in *Elegy VI* and the sonnet *On His Being Arrived at the Age of Twenty-three*. This elaborate piece of self-analysis in the more explicit medium of prose represents, like Milton's earlier and later vindicatory utterances, the fruits of a process of serious self-examination regarding his way of life. It was his habit, as we have observed, to call upon his powers of expression as a means of confirming himself in a course of action to which his nature and his reason counselled him. The tone of confident assurance which this letter shares with other similar pronouncements is, I am inclined to believe, primarily a form of utterance and may cover real uncertainty and debate.

Such a debate would naturally have preceded Milton's decision to postpone or abandon his proposed entry into the church and settle down for a period of independent study on his father's country estate. The actual literary expression of his purposes and meditations was apparently occasioned by the expostulation of a serious-minded friend, who took it upon himself to be the prompter of the youthful poet's conscience. This friend (whom we may assume to have been a divine) had evidently warned Milton that the hours of the day were passing and had suggested that he was allowing his love of study to become a form of idleness and self-indulgence. In reply, Milton admits that study as a mere gratification of curiosity is not praiseworthy, but he feels assured that this weakness cannot be ascribed to him. The love of learning alone, he says, would not suffice to weigh against the motives which would naturally urge him toward an active life. These motives he analyzes with characteristic thoroughness: they are the need of providing for a family and home; the desire of fame; the consciousness that God demands our employment of the talent which is lodged in us. His real reason, he concludes, viewing the matter quite objectively, is precisely that he may more thoroughly prepare himself to render up a true account. He is, he adds, the more inclined to this course because he has noted a certain belatedness in himself, as recorded in the sonnet written on the occasion of this twenty-third birthday. The sonnet is included in the letter and indeed the prose composition has somewhat the air of an artistic setting for the poetical gem. It is even possible that the expostulating friend is a figment of Milton's imagination. At any rate, what he is primarily doing is giving expression to the recurrent mood of earnestness which had already come to constitute a profound and essential element in his emotional experience.

It is odd but characteristic that Milton should, in this statement, say nothing whatever regarding his literary purposes and ambitions. No reader previously unacquainted with his thoughts on this subject could possibly infer them from the letter, the plain implication of the language being that he intends, when he is ready, to labor in the vineyard as a minister. It is possible, of course, that in the suggestion about a congregation and preaching Milton was maintaining a mental reservation, having already determined to interpret his ministry in terms of the poetic enunciation of divine truth. More probably he had not yet altogether abandoned the plan of entering the church. In any case there is a misleading suppression of a part of his full mind, which we may regard as a characteristic manifestation of Miltonic strategy. The friend is representative of the normal judgment of the world. He is not, therefore, an intimate of the inner shrine of Milton's purposes and, since he presumably holds the common inadequate view of art, would misunderstand and condemn a confession of the important place which poetry occupied in his thought. In his undergraduate days Milton had freely enough proclaimed his interest to the circle of his academic contemporaries. Since he had come to take a more serious view of himself he had reserved his confidences, communicating them privately to the entirely sympathetic Diodati, and now, with an apologia based on the true and elevated conception of poetry, to his father.

The charming Latin epistle *Ad Patrem* was probably written contemporaneously with the English letter at the beginning of the Horton period, and it should be set beside the latter statement as completing the representation of Milton's point of view at this time. The contrast between the two is striking. In the Latin epistle Milton surrenders himself entirely to his enthusiasm for self-cultivation and creative art. We hear nothing of his intention to enter the church, nothing of the need of rendering account of the "one talent which 'tis death to hide." Milton extolls poetry as a worthy object of highest endeavor, drawing his arguments from the tradition of Renaissance criticism so nobly embodied in Sidney's *Apology for Poetry,* and he appeals to his father on the strength of his own devotion to a sister art to continue to indulge the son in his pursuit of knowledge and in his conception of himself as "a part though the humblest of the gifted throng." That Milton does not directly give expression to his dominant ethical motive while he is hymning his delight in the Muses for their own sakes is an illustration of the characteristic zeal which leads him to suppress one part of his consciousness while another is momentarily engaging his attention. But even here the implications of his idealism are present. He will not mix obscurely with the dull rabble or join forces with the profane. The poetry which he praises is that which chants the exploits of heroes, and chaos, and the broad-laid foundations of the world. The viewpoint is essentially that of *Elegy VI,* though the emphasis has changed with the occasion.

We are now prepared to consider in detail the poetic fruitage of the Horton era. It was probably at the very beginning of the period, before the date of the English letter to a friend, that he composed the famous pair of lyrics, *L'Allegro* and *Il Penseroso.* Indeed, it is quite possible that they go back to some vacation interval in his university life. The uncertainty somewhat disturbs the precision of our study of Milton's early literary career. In any case, however, the poems can hardly belong to the period of the fifth elegy and the *Song on May Morning.* They resemble these pieces, to be sure, in their enthusiastic expression of Milton's joy in beauty, but they exhibit a conscious particularity in the development of the aesthetic motive which may be taken to imply a later and more complex attitude. It is as if Milton had deliberately set out to imprison the essence of his literary culture without admixture of more personal ideals and to survey systematically the whole range of his aesthetic pleasures. Whether this was done in his last years at the University, along with the poem on Shakespeare and the elegy on the Marchioness of Winchester, or in the first exhilaration of his release from the academic environment, among the fresh delights of Horton, does not much matter.

The true bearing of the companion pieces is best understood by comparison with *Elegy I.* In the Latin poem, as we have seen, Milton combines the recitation of his intellectual and artistic delights with an account of his reaction against the University and a confession of his susceptibility to love. The passage on the theater does not separate comedy from tragedy; the expression of his enthusiasm for nature is not elaborated and passes quickly into a rhapsody on the English maidens. In *L'Allegro* and *Il Penseroso,* taking rather more than a hint from Burton, Milton amuses himself by analyzing his aesthetic reactions and classifying them in two contrasting modes. There is, of course, no question of two individuals. *L'Allegro* and *Il Penseroso* are equally Milton. To interpret the fiction otherwise is to assume that a cultivated lover of music may care only for the scherzo movement of symphonies, or that a nature enthusiast takes pleasure in sombre but not in cheerful landscapes or a trained play-goer in tragedy to the exclusion of comedy. It is to deny, in short, the catholicity of Milton's taste, the very thing that the poems are designed to illustrate and do illustrate.

Equally absurd is Moody's description of the poems as a kind of summing up of two possible attitudes toward life, which Milton, while feeling the appeal of each, must have recognized the practical impossibility of combining, or his suggestion that *Il Penseroso* reflects the advancing shades of Puritanism and, in Milton, the giving way of the exuberance of youth to the sobriety of manhood. In point of fact *Il Penseroso* is quite as much Elizabethan in mood as *L'Allegro* and as little touched with Puritanism, while the cheerfulness of the latter poem is anything but the exuberance of youth. The two pieces taken together are, indeed, the evidence of a carefully disciplined and completely self-possessed maturity of aesthetic cultivation and of a mind free for the moment from temperamental bias of any sort. The poems are studiously objective, even the effects of his reading being represented as elements in an impersonal experience. The element of sex, moreover, is carefully excluded. The choirs of maidens who usurped the landscape in *Elegy I* are here kept at a becoming distance. The passing reference to neat-handed Phillis, and the "store of ladies whose bright eyes rain influence," with the vaguer surmise of a possible beauty in a distant tower, are but pleasurable additions to an undisturbed sense of visible and meditated loveliness.

But Milton's sojourn in the realm of purely idyllic beauty could not, given his nature and education, be very long. For him the writing of poems like *L'Allegro* and *Il Penseroso*, however exquisite the result, was in a sense a *tour de force*. We may assume that after a year or so, at most, of aesthetic leisure on his father's estate he would have felt the need of a return to more serious and purposeful endeavor. The English letter, which I have already analyzed and which we may now fit more exactly into its place in the Horton era, reflects such a moment in his thought. The fact that Milton at this time began to set down his compositions in the

Cambridge manuscript may also be significant. A little later (c. 1636), as we shall see, he embarked on a more consistent course of study than the discursive and dilettante readings recorded in *L'Allegro* and *Il Penseroso*, and started to accumulate notes toward a philosophy of life in the *Commonplace Book*. In poetry he returns for a brief interval to the sober vein of the *Nativity*.

I have already noted his attempt to continue the devotional strain of that poem in the odes on the Passion and the Circumcision. Both these pieces are undated. The first of them most probably succeeded the *Nativity* at the following Easter season. It is tempting to assume that the poem on the Circumcision came between them on the appropriate occasion in January, 1629–30. But this is almost certainly not the case. For though the piece is allied in theme to the *Nativity*, in form and style it is closely associated with the verses *At a Solemn Music* and *On Time*, and all three belong to a later date in Milton's literary career. The evidence of the Cambridge manuscript is, I believe, decisive on this point. In that document, *At a Solemn Music*, in three drafts, immediately precedes the *Letter to a Friend*, and the poems *On Time* and *Upon the Circumcision* follow it. Then comes *Comus*, establishing a *terminus ad quem* in 1634. The letter and the three companion odes are not much earlier; they would, indeed, belong to the same year if Masson's date for *Arcades*, which precedes them in the manuscript, is to be trusted. The poems represent a new experiment in English verse of the more solemn sort. *On Time* has its kinship in idea with the English letter and the sonnet *On His Being Arrived at the Age of Twenty-three*, but in place of the mood of disturbed self-searching reflected in those utterances, it is expressive of deep religious and contemplative joy, the chords of which Milton had already touched in the *Nativity*:

> Then long Eternity shall greet our bliss
> With an individual kiss,
> And joy shall overtake us in a flood;
> When everything that is divinely good,
> And perfectly divine,
> With Truth, and Peace, and Love shall ever shine
> About the supreme throne

45

> Of him to whose happy-making sight alone
> When once our heavenly-guided soul shall climb,
> Then, all this earthly grossness quit,
> Attired with stars we shall for ever sit,
> Triumphing over Death, and Chance, and Thee, O Time.

Similar imagery and an identical emotion pervade the poem *At a Solemn Music*. Both works are dignified and noble compositions, deeply felt and phrased in beauty. They are more mature in style than the *Nativity*, but come short of it in metrical felicity and in poetic fervor. The more vital forces of Milton's personality are not engaged in them. *Upon the Circumcision* is less fortunate. Milton strives to frame his thoughts to sadness in remembrance of Christ's sacrifice, symbolically suggested according to religious convention by the event which he commemorates, but the Muse withholds her wonted blessing on his endeavor. Only in the opening, where the poet is dealing momentarily with his native theme of the celestial song which attended the birth of Christ, does he achieve real beauty of feeling and expression:

> Ye flaming powers, and winged Warriors bright,
> That erst with music and triumphant song,
> First heard by happy watchful shepherds' ear,
> So sweetly sung your joy the clouds along,
> Through the soft silence of the listening night. . . .

The succeeding lines show, to my judgment, a falling off of inspiration.

With these comparatively slight and experimental pieces Milton apparently abandons any further attempt to express the religious mood in verse. But two poems of any sort, *Comus* and *Lycidas*, were written during the remaining four or more years of the Horton period and both of these were composed for definite occasions at the request of others. At the opening of *Lycidas* Milton alludes to his feeling of unreadiness and to the resolution which he had apparently cherished of waiting for his ultimate inspiration before writing again at all:

> Yet once more, O ye Laurels, and once more,
> Ye Myrtles brown, with ivy never sere,
> I come to pluck your berries harsh and crude,

And with forced fingers rude
Shatter your leaves before the mellowing year.
Bitter constraint and sad occasion dear
Compels me to disturb your season due.

The occasional character of these poems does not, however, diminish their significance. They are, indeed, the great masterpieces of Milton's youth, springing from the deepest sources of his inspiration. They reveal, moreover, new influences of more far-reaching importance in the moulding of his inner life than the delightful but unserious children of the Muse who had dominated his art in the composition of *L'Allegro, Il Penseroso,* and *Arcades.* The key is again provided by Milton's autobiographical statement in the *Apology for Smectymnuus:*

Next (for hear me out now readers, that I may tel ye whither my younger feet wandered), I betook me to those fables and romances, which recount in solemn cantos the deeds of knighthood founded by our victorious kings, and from hence in renown all over Christendom. There I read it in the oath of every knight that he should defend to the expense of his best blood, if so befell him, the honour and chastity of virgin or matron; from whence even then I learned what a noble virtue chastity must be, to the defence of which so many worthies, by such a dear adventure of themselves, had sworn. And if I found in the story afterward, any of them, by word or deed, breaking that oath, I judged it the same fault of the poet, as that which is attributed to Homer, to have written indecent things of the gods. Only this my mind gave me, that every free and gentle spirit, without that oath, ought to be born a knight, nor needed to expect the gilt spur, or the laying of a sword upon his shoulder to stir him both by his counsel and his arms, to secure and protect the weakness of any attempted chastity. So that even these books, which to many others have been the fuel of wantonness and loose living, I cannot think how, unless by divine indulgence, proved to me so many incitements, as you have heard, to the love and steadfast observation of that virtue which abhors the society of the bordellos.

The interest of this passage as an index to Milton's enthusiasm for the literature of romance and as a revelation of the intense subjective passion with which he read, is obvious. One is reminded of the phrase about "dinging a book a quoit's distance from him" in *Areopagitica.* Considered from the point of view of our detailed analysis of the poet's early literary development the statement bears a more particular significance. The plain implication of the context is that these imaginative wanderings of his youthful feet belong not to an indefinite period, and certainly not to his boyhood, but to the epoch which immediately succeeded his devotion to Dante and Petrarch and his resolution to shape his career toward the highest forms of poetry. In view of the reliability of Milton's account thus far the presumption is in favor of an equal precision in his statement at this point. Let us consider the passage more closely with a view to determining the exact character of the literary reference.

The general terms of the description apply well enough to the *Morte d'Arthur,* a book, certainly, in which the high vows of knighthood are both taken and broken and which has often enough been "fuel of wantonness," but it is not Malory who would have inflamed a young idealist with the love of chastity and it is not his work of which Milton is thinking as marking an epoch in his development as a poet. Much more plausibly it is the romantic poets of the Renaissance—Boiardo and Ariosto among the Italians, and particularly Spenser who would first have come to his attention and first aroused his enthusiasm for their subject matter, leading to a subsequent exploration of the more authentic legends in medieval romance and chronicle. The single phrase "solemn cantos" is sufficient to determine the fact that Milton had the *Faerie Queene* specifically in mind. We may compare the later expression in *Areopagitica,* "our sage and serious Spenser" and the reference in *Il Penseroso,*

> Or if aught else great bards beside
> In *sage and solemn* tune have sung
> Of turneys and enchantments drear
> Where more is meant than meets the ear.

Now the time at which Milton first made the acquaintance of Spenser or the Italians is uncertain. The allusions to Ariosto in the *Commonplace Book* belong between circa 1634 and 1637 and may well represent a first extensive study in this period, following upon the earlier occupation with Dante and Petrarch. The *Faerie Queene* Milton must, one would suppose, have read before. We may, however, safely infer from the quoted passage that, no matter how early he may have felt the interest and charm of Spenser, the influence of his lofty and serious cantos as a powerful stimulus to his emotions was first deeply felt at the point in his development which we have now reached. It is in consonance with such an assumption that there are in Milton no allusions to Spenser and no marked trace of his influence in anything written before the Horton period. In a poet as susceptible of literary influence as Milton has shown himself to be, this would be strange indeed if he had already been profoundly stirred by the enthusiasm which he describes. Striking too is the fact that in his first statements regarding his plans for epic he should give no hint of his later intention to deal with Arthurian material. It seems probable that his purposes were shaped in this direction by his study of the Italians and by his acceptance of Spenser as his English master.

The proof that Milton's statement does actually mark the moment of a new allegiance and that this moment coincides with the beginning of the Horton period is to be found in the English poems themselves. His adoption at this time of the pastoral mode is in accord with the precedent of Spenser as well as with that of Virgil. The clear allusion to the *Faerie Queene* in *Il Penseroso* I have already quoted. It is, however, when we come to *Comus* that we feel for the first time the full effects of the impregnation of Milton's thought with the poetic idealism of his great Elizabethan predecessor. We are prepared by the terms of Milton's description to find the relation here dynamic and essential. The extraordinary degree to which Spenser actually affected Milton's art I shall consider in a moment. For the present the important thing to observe is that he carried to the *Faerie Queene,* by his own confession, the same highly serious and subjective attitude which he had brought to his earlier reading, finding in his exaltation of chastity something to which his own nature and mood responded with unusual power, and that this response belongs definitely to a phase of his emotional idealism for which he had not yet found a satisfactory expression. If the way of thinking and judging in the passage from the *Apology* seems rather immature for the age of twenty-two or thereabouts, this only harmonizes with our general impression of Milton's temperament and with what he appears to have felt about himself. It remains, of course, quite possible that such ascetic dreamings go back in their origin to an earlier period, for Milton is not fixing a chronology but describing the stages in a development, and we need believe only that these influences and this experience first reached their full fruition in the Horton period. This consideration applies also to Milton's further statement regarding his contact with Platonic philosophy, which it is desirable to quote before undertaking the analysis of *Comus*.

Thus from the laureate fraternity of poets [he goes on], riper years and the ceaseless round of studies led me to the shady spaces of philosophy; but chiefly to the divine volumes of Plato and his equal Xenophon: where if I should tell ye what I learned of chastity and love, I mean of that which is truly so, whose charming cup is only virtue, which she bears in her hand to those who are worthy (the rest are cheated with a thick intoxicating potion, which a certain sorceress, the abuser of love's name carries about) and how the first and chiefest office of love ends in the soul, producing those two happy twins of her divine generation, knowledge and virtue. With such abstracted sublimities as these, it might be worth your listening, readers, as I may one day hope to have ye in a still time, when there shall be no chiding.

The actual beginnings of Milton's study of Plato go back to his school days. The passionate assimilation of the doctrine of love and virtue is evidently the work of his later youth. The dialogue uppermost in his thoughts is the *Symposium*, which he has evidently been studying along with the parallel account in Xenophon's work of the same name in the Horton period, perhaps for the first time. It is significant that he makes his new interest follow and grow out of his reading of poetry. That a poet should be a poet's guide to emotional Platonism is very natural. That Spenser should have been the guide of Milton is particularly so. For the later born poet found in his predecessor not only his own serious love of virtue combined with a fine responsiveness to sensuous beauty, but the embodiment of the Platonic philosophy with which he was already acquainted, touched after the fashion of the Renaissance with the romantic charm of sex. The two influences are henceforth one. They combine in *Comus* to give a quality of poetic inspiration wholly new in Milton's work, a fusion of the ecstasies of sense and spirit which the poet has hitherto been unable to obtain.

The myth of Circe had long been established as a Platonic symbol of the degradation of the soul through sensuality [32] and as such had attracted Milton as early as the first Latin elegy. It had received imaginative transformation and adaptation to the Christian ideal of sexual purity at the hands of Spenser in the second book of the *Faerie Queene*. The reference in *Areopagitica* shows the impression which the allegory of the Bower of Bliss had left on Milton's mind.[33] It seemed to him the prime illustration of the superior power of poetry to enforce a moral truth, a principle on which his own subsequent practice of the art was to take its stand. The appropriateness of the material to the masque was obvious.[34] Very naturally, therefore, he chose the motive as a vehicle for the expression of those inmost thoughts and feelings which had gradually grown clear and dominant in his consciousness. The classical framework of the myth is, as might be expected, adhered to more closely by Milton than by Spenser, or rather he definitely attaches his own invention to it where Spenser transforms the original to the substance of his dream. The embodiment of Platonic thought, moreover, is specific, appearing in particular passages, very strikingly in the famous one on chastity, and in the poem as a whole. Milton has taken evident pains to point the allegory and to make his fiction wear the aspect of a Platonic myth. Take, for example, the following exposition of the symbolism of Circe's cup,

> which as they taste
> (For most do taste through fond intemperate thirst),
> Soon as the potion works, their human countenance,
> The express resemblance of the gods, is changed
> Into some brutish form of wolf or bear,
> Or ounce or tiger, hog, or bearded goat,
> All other parts remaining as they were.

---

[32] For example, in Heraclitus Ponticus, *Allegoriae in Homeri Fabulas de Diis,* a copy of which has come down to us bearing Milton's signature and the date 1637. See Sotheby, *Ramblings,* p. 125.

[33] ". . . which was the reason why our sage and serious poet Spenser, whom I dare be known to think a better teacher than Scotus or Aquinas, describing true temperance under the person of Guion, brings him in with his palmer through the cave of Mammon and the bower of earthly bliss, that he might see and know, and yet abstain."

[34] The Circe myth had been employed in Browne's *Inner Temple Masque,* presented Jan. 13, 1614.

51

And they, so perfect is their misery,
Not once perceive their foul disfigurement,
But boast themselves more comely than before,
And all their friends and native home forget.

Incidentally he moralizes, after the fashion of Plato and his follow-ers, the stories of Diana and Minerva, and that of Cupid and Psyche, creating a genealogy analogous to that of Love in the *Symposium*.

All this is the fruit of Milton's conscious classicism. It is, how-ever, to Spenser that *Comus* is most deeply indebted in its poetic essence. In his elaboration of the fiction, as in the quality of his emotion, Milton has been influenced by his master's romantic allegory of chastity in the third book of the *Faerie Queene*. This is clearest, so far as plot incident is concerned, in the parallel be-tween the rescue of Amoret in Book III and the freeing of the Lady at the close of *Comus*. In both works the enchanter is surprised as he stands before his enthralled victim endeavoring to subdue her will to his lust. In Spenser the rescuer (Britomart) strikes him down, but is told that only he can undo the spell which he has worked. She then forces him "his charms back to reverse." In Milton the brothers, after having put Comus to flight, are informed by Thyrsis that they should have secured him as the instrument of the Lady's release.

Without his rod reversed
And backward mutters of dissevering power
We cannot free the Lady that sits here.

The identity of phrase and of idea is quite conclusive of Milton's indebtedness at this point. He undoubtedly received modifying suggestions for the plot from other sources, but nothing so essen-tial as he derived from the *Faerie Queene*. The relationship here is one which extends to the fundamental philosophy and poetic method.

It is not by any means confined to this one episode. Britomart, the central figure in Book III, is Spenser's symbol of what Milton calls the sun-clad power of chastity. The martial conception un-derlies such passages as *Comus*, 440 ff. The idea that chastity draws down Heaven to its defense, which is the dominant motive in the whole of *Comus,* is set forth by Spenser in the episode of Proteus's rescue of Florimel attacked by the lustful fisherman, with the poet's comment, so much in the spirit of certain passages in *Comus,*

> See how the heavens, of voluntary grace
> And sovereign favour towards chastity
> Doe succor send to her distressed cace.
> So much high God doth innocence embrace.

A more specific suggestion came to Milton from the description of the Garden of Adonis in Canto VI. I have already alluded to his introduction of Cupid and Psyche, with the mention of their allegorical descendants, Youth and Joy, as an instance of his Platonizing mythography. The immediate pattern of Milton's description is Spenser, who introduces as symbols of the Platonic creative principle first Venus and Adonis, then Cupid and Psyche, endowing the last two with a daughter, Pleasure. To the detail of Milton's curious application of this material I shall return in another connection. Enough has been said to confirm the assumption that *Comus* was written under the dominating poetic influence of Spenser, as surely, though not as exclusively, as the Latin elegies were written under the spell of Ovid and the Italian sonnets under that of Petrarch. Imitative, on the other hand, *Comus* certainly is not, for the unique personality of Milton is stamped upon the whole composition and the accent of his poetic idiom is heard everywhere. Milton could thus acknowledge his indebtedness as to a revered and beloved teacher, without feeling that his originality had been subjugated. He evidently considered his relationship to be analogous to that which Spenser had himself maintained toward Chaucer, and as the Elizabethan poet had delighted to express his gratitude to his predecessor under the name of Tityrus, so Milton pays graceful tribute to Spenser as Meliboeus,[35]

> The soothest shepherd that ere piped in plains.

---

[35] In support of this identification see J. F. Bense, " 'Meliboeus old' in Milton's 'Comus,' " *Neophilologus,* I, pp. 62–64.

I am not disposed to attach exaggerated importance to Milton's confession to Dryden in his old age that Spenser was his "original." If the phrase is taken to mean that Spenser, more than any other poet, enabled Milton to interpret his genius to itself and to find a medium for his emotions at a crucial moment in his development, it says no more than truth. It is true also that Milton continued in Spenser's debt throughout his career and that, as Professor Greenlaw has ably shown,[36] the poetic fabric of *Paradise Lost* owes vastly more to the *Faerie Queene* and the *Four Hymns* than is apparent on the surface. Of all this Milton was clearly mindful. His own genius was, however, after all, radically different from Spenser's and his culture was too wide and the influences under which it operated too complex to allow him to remain, like the Fletchers, a Spenserian. The idea of poetical sonship, which Milton possibly suggested to Dryden in the conversation about his own poetic origins, was a fiction prompted by gratitude and by the precedent of Spenser's own adoption of the only earlier English poet who was in any sense his equal as the one from whom he had derived his lineage.

With the principle of chastity Milton in *Comus* largely settled his account. The intensity with which he seized upon this virtue as the center and test of his ethical idealism is explained by the strength of his own romantic passion, a passion which is still the chief motive force of his imaginative life. Occasional passages give direct and moving expression to Milton's wider ethical convictions, but it is "the sage and serious doctrine of virginity" that holds the center of his thought and the mood of the poem contrasts strikingly with the glowing but mature enthusiasm of *Paradise Lost*. As a matter of fact *Comus* appears to reflect a partial suppression of the poet's sensuous excitement rather than its supersedence or complete conversion. For Milton this could be no resting-place, however happy the immediate poetic product.

I have said that the poem settled Milton's account with chastity. The subject, indeed, continued to occupy him as late as 1642 when he penned the passage in the *Apology* and, as I believe,

---

[36] *Studies in Philology*, XIV, pp. 196–218.

until his marriage, but it no longer forced itself upon his creative art. What *Comus* did not do was to end the mood of youthful excitement by giving full imaginative expression to Milton's emotional life. Such an expression demanded not the exaltation of a negative virtue, but some more fervid celebration of the mystery of love, such as he apparently still had in mind when he promised to edify his readers with a representation of these abstracted sublimities at a time when there should be no chiding. A sort of fulfillment of this vague promise is, as we shall see, contained in *Paradise Lost,* but when Milton ultimately came to gather up in the epic the ripe fruit of his experience his attitude had undergone great changes, and the form in which he embodied the mystery of love bore a much modified relation to these promptings of his youth. It is rather to the documents of the later Horton period itself that we should look for the more immediate traces of Milton's idealized passion.

There needs no resort to psychological theory to show that the very restraints which Milton imposed upon himself intensified the sensuous impulses of his nature or to make clear the influence of these impulses on his reflective and imaginative processes. The very fervor with which he seizes upon the doctrines and imagery of the *Symposium* is evidence of his intoxication with something more glowing than purity as an abstract and negative ideal. He is compelled in the revelation of his new experience to repudiate the amatory phase recorded in the elegies, and he does so, not by destroying these children of his more sensuous Muse, but by carefully dating the elegies and appending to them the engaging postscript already quoted.

But the banishment of the earthly Aphrodite is only one phase of Milton's new philosophical discipleship. In the teaching of his master, friendship, the friendship of the good, is the human motive force and basis of the devotion of the soul to its ultimate divine object. With Platonic love in its romantic form Milton had, as we have seen, already experimented immaturely and unsuccessfully in the Italian sonnets. The tradition, while not without its appeal to him, was essentially foreign to his temperament. It was associated, too, in his own day with things and persons that he condemned, for the doctrine of Platonic love had received a new lease of life at the court of Henrietta Maria, where it had become more than ever a mask of triviality and corruption.[37] In contact now with the pure source which these vagaries had perverted Milton needed no longer dally with a false ideal. He substituted consciously and deliberately the principle of friendship, attaching new meaning to a sentiment which had already played a part in the experience of his boyhood and youth. It is not without significance that the first prose letters to his early acquaintance, Charles Diodati, which Milton cared to preserve and publish, should date from the year 1637 or that the only important poems to be composed between that year and 1641, *Lycidas* and the *Epitaphium Damonis,* should be elegies to the memory of dead friends. The earlier exchange of verse epistles with Diodati had apparently ceased some eight years before, and Milton seems to imply that letters of any sort and even meetings had recently become infrequent. The renewal of the old intimacy was evidently initiated by Milton. "Jam istuc demum plane video te agere," he writes on September 2, 1637, " ut obstinato silentio nos aliquando pervincas; quod si ita est, euga habe tibi istam gloriolam, en scribimus priores." He has, he continues, taken pains to inquire after Diodati's welfare from his brother, and, having been accidentally informed that his friend was in town, he had hastened to his lodgings only to find them vacant. The letter is one of warm importunity, prompted by a desire of closer community of understanding and affection. "Quare," he concludes, "quod sine tuo incommodo fiat, advola ocyus et aliquo in loco te siste, qui locus mitiorem spem praebeat, posse quoquo modo fieri ut aliquoties inter nos saltem visamus, quod utinam nobis non aliter esses vicinus, rusticanus atque es urbicus." [38] Diodati evidently replied to this appeal by a letter in which he wished Milton health six

---

[37] See Jefferson Fletcher, *The Religion of Beauty in Woman,* pp. 166 ff.

[38] "I clearly see that you are determined not to be overcome in silence; if this be so, you shall have the palm of victory, for I will write first. . . . Wherefore as soon as you can do it without inconvenience to yourself, I beseech you to take up your quarters where we may at least be able to visit one another; for I hope you would not be a different neighbor to us in the country from what you are in town."

hundred times. The poet in turn, on September 23 of the same year, writes a long letter in which he opens himself without reserve. The document is as remarkable a Miltonic revelation as we have met. It reflects as in a mirror a whole phase of the Renaissance—the attempt of high souls to make the spiritual discipline of Platonic philosophy a reality, to relive an imagined antiquity in a finer way than any humanist who was not also a poet could comprehend. It is the more heroic in that Milton in his generation stands alone as the last of a giant race. His idealism harks back to the days of Ficino and Pico and the Platonic academy of Lorenzo dei Medici.

There can be no mistaking the change which has come over his attitude since his earlier verse epistles. His former pleasant companionship, brooded upon in absence, has taken on the character, on his side at least, of a fully developed Platonic relationship. He has, apparently, not had the many letters for which he hoped, but his old regard has suffered not the slightest diminution. "Non enim in Epistolarum ac Salutationum momentis veram amicitiam volo, quae omnia ficta esse possunt; sed altis animi radicibus niti utrinque et sustinere se; coeptamque sinceris, et sanctis rationibus, etiamsi mutua cessarent officia, per omnem tamen vitam suspicione et culpa vacare: ad quem fovendam non tam scripto sit opus, quam viva invicem virtutum recordatione. Nec continuo, ut tu non scripseris, non erit quo illud suppleri officium possit, scribit vicem tuam apud me tua probitas verasque literas intimis sensibus meis exarat, scribit morum simplicitas, et recti amor; scribit ingenium etiam tuum, haudquaquam quotidianum, et majorem in modum te mihi commendat." [39] The contrast between these and

---

[39] "For I do not think that true friendship consists in the frequency of letters or in professions of regard, which may be counterfeited; but it is so deeply rooted in the heart and affections, as to support itself against the rudest blast; and when it originates in sincerity and virtue, it may remain through life without suspicion and without blame, even when there is no longer any reciprocal interchange of kindness. For the cherishing aliment of such a friendship as this there is not so much need of letters as of a lively recollection of each other's virtues. And though you may not have written there is something that may supply the omission: your probity writes to me in your stead; it is a letter written on the innermost membrane of your heart; the simplicity of your manners, and the rectitude of your principles, serve as correspondents in your place; your genius, which is above the common level,

earlier expressions of Milton's regard for Diodati is striking. In 1629 he had addressed him as a pleasant reveller from whose way of life his own more serious aspirations were beginning to withdraw him. Now he hails him as the embodiment of the Platonic good and fair, making their friendship a part of the loftiest meditations of his soul. "Ego enim," he continues, "ne nimis minitere, tui similes impossible est quin amem, nam de caetero quidem quid de me statuerit Deus nescio, illud certe; δεινόν μοι ἔρωτα, εἴπερ τῷ ἄλλῳ τοῦ καλοῦ ἐνέσταξε. Nec tanto Ceres labore, ut in fabulis est, Liberam fertur quaesivisse filiam, quanto ego hanc τοῦ καλοῦ ἰδέαν, veluti pulcherrimam quandam imaginem, per omnes rerum formas et facies: ( πολλαί γάρ μορφαί τῶν Δαιμονίων ) dies noctesque indagare soleo, et quasi certis quibusdam vestigiis ducentem sector Unde fit, ut qui, spretis quae vulgus prava rerum aestimatione opinatur, id sentire et loqui et esse audet; quod summa per omne aevum sapientia optimum esse docuit, illi me protinus, sicubi reperiam, necessitate quadam adjungam." As of old he rounds out his flight with a communication of his own poetic aspirations: "Quid cogitem quaeris; ita me bonus Deus, immortalitatem. Quid agam vero? πτεροφυῶ, et volare meditor: sed tenellis admodum adhuc pennis evehit se noster Pegasus, humile sapiamus." [39]

This letter, then, is Milton's fullest and most direct expression of the philosophic aspect of the Platonic enthusiasm which reached its height toward the close of the Horton period. Such an

---

writes, and serves in a still greater degree to endear you to me. . . . But, lest you indulge in an excess of menace, I must inform you, that I cannot help loving those who are like you; for whatever the deity may have bestowed on me in other respects he has certainly inspired me, if any ever were inspired, with a passion for the good and fair. Nor did Ceres, according to the fable, ever seek her daughter Proserpine with such unceasing solicitude, as I have sought this idea of the beautiful in all the forms and appearances of things (for many are the forms of the divine). I am wont day and night to continue my search; and I follow in the way in which you go before. Hence, I feel an irresistible impulse to cultivate the friendship of him who, despising the prejudices and false conceptions of the vulgar, dares to think, to speak, and to be that which the highest wisdom has in every age taught to be the best. . . . Do you ask what I am meditating? By the help of Heaven an immortality of fame. But what am I doing? I am letting my wings grow, and preparing to fly; but my Pegasus has not yet feathers enough to soar aloft in the fields of air."
—Bohn translation, with modifications.

expression was appropriate to the cooler element of prose. In the exactly contemporary elegy *Lycidas* (it is dated November, 1637, in the Cambridge manuscript) and the somewhat later *Epitaphium Damonis,* where Milton is again the poet, with his singing robes about him, his rapture is loftier and more intense. It is commonly and I think rightly assumed concerning the first of these works that Milton had enjoyed no particularly close intimacy with Edward King, its subject. The mood is one of reflective melancholy and tender pathos rather than of poignant sorrow, though the latter note is not altogether lacking. There is no direct statement of Platonic doctrine, but the idea of a pure and inspiring friendship, founded in virtue and associating itself with the most elevated self-communion, underlies the whole poem and is in conformity with the present aspect of Milton's experience. The digressions on fame and the clergy, which are really not digressions at all, together with the concluding utterances regarding immortality, are expressions of Milton's deepest thoughts upon the central topic of the aspirations, ideals, and destiny of the poet.

In the *Epitaphium* the accent of personal grief is keener and the reflective element less pronounced. The immediacy of his sense of loss throws Milton back upon the mood of intimacy and affection which had characterized his early association with Diodati and had survived the process of Platonic idealization. The old habit of communicating his poetic plans in Latin to the sympathetic ear of Diodati is pathetically continued in the passage in which Milton describes his attempt at an Arthurian epic. The external conventions of the pastoral are adhered to even more rigidly than in *Lycidas,* but the deep emotion which inspired the poem burns through them at every point.

The culmination of this emotion in the close of the *Epitaphium* involves a moment in Milton's imaginative life which has not yet been introduced into this discussion, the result of an infusion into his consciousness of one element of Christian mysticism. The subject may best be introduced by quoting the final paragraph of Milton's prose apologia:

Last of all, not in time, but as perfection is last, that care was ever had of me, with my earliest capacity, not to be negligently trained in the precepts of the Christian religion: this that I have hitherto related, hath been to shew, that though Christianity had been but slightly taught me, yet a certain reservedness of natural disposition, and moral discipline, learnt out of the noblest philosophy, was enough to keep me in disdain of far less incontinence than this of the bordello. But having had the doctrine of holy scripture unfolding those chaste and high mysteries, with timeliest care infused, that "the body is for the Lord and the Lord for the body;" thus also I argued to myself, that if unchastity in a woman, whom St. Paul terms the glory of man, be such a scandal and dishonour, then certainly in a man, who is both the image and glory of God, it must, though commonly not so thought, be much more deflowering and dishonourable; in that he sins both against his own body, which is the perfecter sex, and his own glory, which is in the woman; and, that which is worst, against the image and glory of God, which is in himself. Nor did I slumber over that place expressing such high rewards of ever accompanying the Lamb, with those celestial songs to others inapprehensible, but not to those who were not defiled with women, which doubtless means fornication; for marriage must not be called a defilement.

It is, then, in the precepts of religion that Milton finally grounds his habit of restraint in matters of sex. The careful Christian discipline of his childhood and its fundamental importance in determining his actual conduct might, of course, even without his declaration, have been taken for granted. What primarily interests us in the foregoing passage, however, is its revelation of the intensity with which he seized upon certain New Testament passages and assimilated their doctrine and still more their imagery to the substance of his own poetic thought. We have here a new source of inspiration the results of which may be clearly traced in his creative work. The teaching of St. Paul is for him a "chaste and high mystery" of divine authority, which supersedes, though it is not discordant with, the inspired utterances of Diotima. The Platonic principle of the supremacy of soul has its religious counterpart and intelligible fulfillment in the pronouncement "the body is for the Lord and the Lord for the body." Thus in the passage from *Comus,* "So dear to Heaven is saintly chastity," the framework of Platonic idealism is fitted with a specific ethical and Christian content. The second scriptural passage which Milton "did not slumber over" and which he here adduces as the climax of his meditation, carries us still further. The "place" is Revelation, xiv. 1 ff.: "And I looked, and, lo, a

Lamb stood on the mount Sion, and with him an hundred forty and four thousand, having his father's name written in their foreheads. . . . And I heard a voice from Heaven as the voice of many waters and as the voice of a great thunder: and I heard the voice of harpers harping with their harps: And they sung as it were a new song before the throne, and before the four beasts and the elders: and no man could learn that song but the hundred and forty and four thousand which were redeemed from the earth. These are they which were not defiled with women; for they are virgins. These are they which follow the Lamb whithersoever he goeth."

It would be a great mistake to dismiss Milton's reference as a merely casual employment of Scripture in the usual manner of the seventeenth century controversialist. His avowal of special interest in it falls in with too much that we know to be characteristic of his state of mind in the period now under discussion. We have, for example, indications from other sources that Milton shared, in some degree at least, the predilection of his time for the shadowy semi-religious borderland between philosophy and occultism represented by the Cabala and the Hermetic books.[40] His contact with materials of this sort certainly dates from the Horton period and it is naturally associated with his Platonic studies. Thus the passage in *Il Penseroso* in which he describes his nightly readings is true to the practice of his time in its emphasis on the more dubious Neoplatonic speculations. It is not the authentic spirit of Plato which must be unsphered to reveal

> What worlds or what vast regions hold
> The mortal mind that hath forsook
> Her mansion in this fleshly nook;

and to tell

> Of those demons that are found
> In fire, air, flood, or under ground,
> Whose power hath a true consent
> With planet, or with element,

---

[40] "thrice-great Hermes," *Il Penseroso*, v. 88.

but the spirits of Hermes, Iamblichus, and Michael Psellus. It was evidently not for nothing that the poet was a coeval of Henry More. There is, to be sure, no reason to suppose that he ever committed himself seriously to the intellectual extravagance of his fellow alumnus and the little group of inspired fanatics who surrounded him. And so often in his experience the imaginative impulses which fundamentally made him a poet encountered in Milton intellectual inhibitions which prevented him from surrendering himself to them without reserve. Though for that separate and limited part of Milton represented by *Il Penseroso* the speculations of Hermes might join with the translunary dreams of Plato and the enchantments drear of Spenser in affording a fascinating realm for curiosity to explore, he could hardly allow in these fantastic writings more than a small residuum of truth to challenge his more sober thought.

With the apocalyptic parts of Scripture the case was different. Even Plato and Spenser must yield precedence to inspired authority, in whose prophetic rapture a more daring and untrammeled expression was the garment of a profounder and more authentic truth. There is evidence enough of the position of importance occupied by the Book of Revelation in his thought. He adduces it in the introduction to *Samson Agonistes* in support of his thesis as to the dignity of drama, referring to the commentary of Paraeus, where the work is analyzed into scenes and choruses. The same point had been made by him over twenty years before in *Reason of Church Government*. We must remember also that it was in Revelation that Milton found the chief scriptural authority for the war of the angels,[41] with mystic and philosophic implications of which he shows himself to be conscious in his own treatment of the theme. Doubtless he was already meditating on those passages during the Horton period and glorying in their majesty and strangeness. His sense of their significance would have deepened with the years, and, in the end, enriched and elaborated by farbrought associations, they became the center of his imaginative activity. The appeal of the symbolic image of the Lamb and the

---

[41] Rev., xii. 3–17.

throng of virgins was more immediate and intense. It clearly belongs to the passing phase of emotion which we have associated with Milton's adolescence, now drawing to a close.

The passage did not, of course, stand alone in his thought. It was connected with the general idea of Heavenly love and the mystic marriage of the soul with God, an idea which was deeply interfused with Christian tradition and appears to have enjoyed a special popularity in the religious writing of Milton's own day. How profoundly this conception, with its ecstatic biblical expressions, impressed itself on Milton's imagination and how intricately it associated itself with Platonic forms and their Spenserian embodiments may best be understood by a comparative consideration of the three outstanding poems already mentioned as the sole fruit of Milton's creative powers between the years 1634 and 1640, namely, *Comus, Lycidas,* and the *Epitaphium Damonis.*

In the Spirit's Epilogue in *Comus* Milton sings of Paradise. The language is highly esoteric as well as exquisitely poetic, and Milton expressly calls attention in the parenthesis, "List mortals, if your ears be true," to the hidden spiritual meaning. The bliss proposed is that of Heavenly love as the ineffable compensation for a life devoted to the ideal of chastity, the representative and touchstone of all the virtues. In adopting Spenser's image of the Garden of Adonis Milton entirely changes its application, adapting it to his allegory of virtue and its reward, and impregnating the whole with mystical emotion, the rapt ecstacy of apocalyptic vision. The pagan image of the love of a mortal youth for a goddess draws insensibly nearer to the truth in the reversed symbol of the union of the God of love himself with Psyche, the human soul, and if Milton's classic taste prevents him from concluding with an allusion to the Lamb and his eternal bride it is because there is no need.

In the last lines of *Lycidas,* written three years later, the imagery is explicitly Christian:

> So Lycidas sunk low, but mounted high,
> Through the dear might of Him that walked the waves,
> Where, other groves and other streams along,
> With nectar pure his oozy locks he laves,

And hears the unexpressive nuptial song,
In the blest kingdoms meek of joy and love.

The nuptial music heard by Lycidas is the new song before the throne of the one hundred and forty and four thousand virgins of Revelation, the "celestial song to others inapprehensible but not to those who were not defiled with women" of Milton's own description.

Finally in the conclusion of the *Epitaphium,* again after an interval of three years, Milton throws off all restraint and concealment of expression (the mask of Latin being in itself a sufficient drapery) and indulges his imagination in a description of the joys of Heavenly love which reaches a point of sensuous intensity far beyond anything we have hitherto encountered in his verse. The first part of the passage is an elaboration of the description in *Comus:*

> Parte alia polus omnipatens, et magnus Olympus:
> Quis putet? hic quoque Amor, pictaeque in nube pharetrae
> Arma corusca, faces, et spicula tincta pyropo;
> Nec tenues animas, pectusque ignobile vulgi,
> Hinc ferit; at circum flammantia lumina torquens,
> Semper in erectum spargit sua tela per orbes
> Impiger, et pronos nunquam collimat ad ictus:
> Hinc mentes ardere sacrae, formaeque deorum.[42]

What follows has its parallel rather in the quoted lines from *Lycidas;* almost every motive, indeed, in the consolation with which Milton brings his lament for Edward King to a close being represented with a greater fervor in the account of the apotheosis of Diodati. It is necessary to give here only the final explicit description of the mystic marriage:

> Quod tibi purpureus pudor, et sine labe iuventus
> Grata fuit, quod nulla tori libata voluptas,

---

[42] "In another place is the mighty stretch of sky where Olympus lies open to view. Yes, and Love is there, too; in clouds his quiver is pictured, his shining arms, his torch, his arrows tipped with fiery bronze. But he does not aim upon our earth at light minds, at the herd of vulgar souls. No; he rolls his flaming eyes and steadfastly sends his arrows upward through the orbs of heaven, never aiming a downward stroke. Under his fire the souls of the blessed burn, and the bodies of the gods."

En! etiam tibi virginei servantur honores!
Ipse, caput nitidum cinctus rutilante corona,
Laetaque frondentis gestans umbracula palmae
Aeternum perages immortales hymenaeos,
Cantus ubi, choreisque furit lyra mista beatis,
Festa Sionaeo bacchantur et Orgia thyrso.[43]

It is evident in this astonishing passage that the native sense
impulses which first awakened Milton to the beauty of the spring
and woman have lost nothing of their power. A part only of his
passion has been absorbed in the real experience of friendship;
the rest is transmuted into an imaginative and religious rapture
which allies him for the moment with the tradition of Catholic
Christianity. It does so, to be sure, only outwardly, for there is
fundamental disparity between his essentially humanistic attitude
and the devout asceticism of the Middle Ages. He belongs by
temper and inheritance to the Renaissance. Symbolism in his
hands becomes concrete and glowing imagery and the Christian
meaning is transfused with the spirit as it is assimilated to the
language of Pagan poetry.

With the *Epitaphium Damonis* Milton's early poetic productivity comes to an end. In its last phase it has been the product of
the cloistral and contemplative period at Horton, though the
mood itself has survived the Italian journey and, as the passage in
the *Apology for Smectymnuus* indicates, the beginnings of his
active life as a teacher and controversialist. What further fruitage
it might have had we cannot tell, but there is little likelihood that
the peculiar form of emotional excitement embodied in the *Epitaphium* would have continued long. The whole phase of his experience recapitulated in the *Apology* was essentially youthful and
transitory, though Milton's intellectual precocity, his aesthetic discipline, and his almost infallible good taste made its expressions
wear a certain deceptive air of maturity. Having served their purpose as the chief inspiration of his Muse when he was still in the

---

[43] "Because thy cheek kept its rosy blush and thy youth its stainlessness,
because thou knewest not the joy of marriage, lo, for thy virginal spirit
virginal honors are reserved. Thy bright head crowned with light, and glad
palms in thy hand, thou dost ever act and act again the immortal nuptials,
there where singing is, and the lyre mixes madly with the chorals beatific, and
the wild orgies rage under the thyrsus of Sion."

main unable to give utterance to his profounder moral and intellectual consciousness, these emotions yielded to time, though not without leaving a permanent impress upon his genius.

Meanwhile Milton's cultural interests were broadening and his purposes in art and life defining themselves more sharply. In abandoning his intention to enter the church he had envisaged another form of public service more congenial to his taste and more consonant with his thirst for an immortality of fame. To fulfill this purpose it was necessary for him to equip himself with understanding of the world of men and affairs, and in particular to gain a sound basis for the formulation of his views on the great issues which were beginning to agitate the public mind of his time. Accordingly we find him embarking about the year 1635 on a course of modern historical study, beginning with the authorities on the later Roman empire, and progressing through the Byzantine writers, the Greek and Latin fathers, the medieval chroniclers of Italy, France, and England, down to the historians of the Reformation and contemporary affairs. Books of public policy and law were included in the program, as were also biography, memoirs, and treatises, ancient and modern, on the art of war. The detail of this reading is recorded in the *Commonplace Book,* where Milton made references to individual passages in his authors and copied out under appropriate headings many excerpts and observations. It is fortunately possible, as I have shown elsewhere,[44] to date many of the entries with considerable exactness, and, in particular, to set apart from the rest the entire body of materials which belong to the Horton period.

This latter group is of the greatest importance as an index to the interests and tendencies which find only scanty echoes in his earlier poetry. A considerable number of the entries reflect the contemporary interest in questions of ecclesiastical custom and in the precedents and authorities regarding them, with a marked predilection for evidence in support of the more liberal Reformation practice. The Puritanism, or more properly the liberalism, of Milton was evidently of very early growth. A note on Constan-

---

[44] In "The Chronology of Milton's Private Studies," the second essay in this volume.

tine's giving the clergy immunity from civil office and one praising
the modesty of princes who refuse to meddle in matters of religion
show his fundamental convictions regarding the relations of
church and state to have been already in process of formation.
Even more striking are the political entries, which contain the
gist of Milton's whole republicanism. In the earliest stratum a
broad interest is manifested in the relation of prince and subject,
as in the following: "Ad subditos suos scribens. Constantinus
magnus nec alio nomine quam fratres appellat." In a slightly later
group of entries (still within the Horton period) the political materials are more obviously related to the issues of the day. Thus the
title "Rex" is begun, with entries relative to the deification of the
Roman emperors, and that of "Subditus," with two notes giving
instances of Papal release of subjects from allegiance to a sovereign. The setting down of the title "Census et Vectigal" is evidently connected with interest in the illegal exactions of Charles.
And finally one note is definitely republican: "Severus Sulpitius
ait regium nomen semper liberis gentibus fere invisum." Were it
not for the unquestionable evidence of the manuscript we should
have been inclined, I think, to ascribe this last citation rather to
the period of the tract *Of the Tenure of Kings and Magistrates*
(1649) than to that of *Lycidas*. To the earlier period, however, it
certainly belongs and it is, with the rest, conclusive evidence of
the degree to which Milton had matured his thought on public
questions before he found himself actually surrounded by the
influences which determined his public career. The Horton entries as a whole give definition to Milton's subsequent mention of
"many studious and contemplative years altogether spent in the
search for civil and religious knowledge" and to his description of
himself as having from his youth "studied the distinctions between civil and religious rights."

The convictions thus formed came ultimately to be as intimate
an element in Milton's consciousness and as available to him for
poetic expression as the introspective activities of which we have
been tracing the effects on his creative work. They did so in the
degree to which they became associated with his personal life and
ideals and with his conception of his function as a poet. Thus the

outburst against the clergy in *Lycidas,* the first great passage in which he voices his convictions on' an issue of the day, owes its emotional intensity to the fact that it is, in reality, a justification of his decision not to enter the church and a vindication of his idea that he could fulfill an analogous function more effectively in his own way. It is significant that neither in this passage nor in anything else written during his early years does Milton give utterance to the passion for political and intellectual freedom which became one of the supreme inspiring motives of his eloquence. His opinions on the subject were, as we have seen, already fixed, but nothing had yet happened to bring it home to him in the form of personal desire. Later, when he found himself hampered in his own activities by the restraint of a narrow authority and a narrow law, his impersonal convictions were converted into passion and achieved memorable expression in prose and verse. It is not surprising that, looking back from that later viewpoint, he should have forgotten that his feelings had not always been the same, and should have substituted for the mixed motives which kept him out of the church the single determination not to subscribe himself slave.

To say this much is not, of course, to say that the issues to which Milton devoted his life meant nothing to him until they became personal; it is simply to affirm the principle that the gap between mere intellectual and moral sincerity and poetic sincerity is a wide one and that Milton came only gradually into his full imaginative inheritance. The processes by which the infusion of his ethical and political ideals with personal emotion is accomplished, and, conversely, the process by which the promptings of desire are converted into universal truth—these processes are the fundamental facts of Milton's development. The difference between his earlier and later work is due simply to a shift in the center of his experience and to a consequent widening of his grasp of the moral issues which confront mankind. The increasing maturity of his ideas is reflected in the richer and more harmonious conception which he now adopts of his work as a poet—a conception which at length completely reconciles his need of ministering to men as a teacher of the truth with his desire to create beauty and with his passion for fame. Speaking again in the *Reason of Church Government* ( 1641) of his plans for epic and dramatic poetry, he concludes with the following analysis of the function of the poet-teacher:

These abilities, wheresoever they be found, are the inspired gift of God, rarely bestowed, but yet to some (though most abuse) in every nation; and are of power, beside the office of a pulpit, to inbreed and cherish in a great people the seeds of virtue and public civility, to allay the perturbations of the mind, and set the affections in right tune; to celebrate in glorious and lofty hymns the throne and equipage of God's almightiness, and what he works, and what he suffers to be wrought with high providence in his church; to sing victorious agonies of martyrs and saints, the deeds and triumphs of just and pious nations, doing valiantly through faith against the enemies of Christ; to deplore the general relapse of kingdoms and states from justice and God's true worship. Lastly, whatsoever in religion is holy and sublime, in virtue amiable and grave, whatsoever hath passion or admiration in all the changes of that which is called fortune from without, or the wily subtleties and refluxes of man's thoughts from within; all these things with a solid and treatable smoothness to paint out and describe, teaching over the whole book of sanctity and virtue, through all the instances of example, with such delight to those especially of soft and delicious temper, who will not look upon truth herself, unless they see her elegantly dressed; that whereas the paths of honesty and good life appear now rugged and difficult, though they be indeed easy and pleasant, they will then appear easy and pleasant, though they were rugged and difficult indeed.

Though this passage was written a year before the retrospective discussion in the *Apology,* it better represents Milton's mature aims at the outset of his career of public service, and the form of the ideal which was actually to dominate his creative activity henceforth. The poet no longer speaks privately to the aspirations of the individual, but to the public conscience of mankind. While he still cherishes for himself and for the few who can receive it the esoteric doctrine of chastity and true love, his immediate attention is bent, with all the tremendous energy of his spirit, upon the broader theme of "virtue and public civility," "justice and God's true worship," "the rugged and difficult paths of honesty and true life." He advocates public festivals, "as in those famous governments of old," where, not only in pulpits but at set and solemn panurgies, in theaters and porches, the people may be led, by wise and artful recitations, combining recreation with instruction, to the practice of justice, temperance and fortitude. The function which he here proposes to himself is thus essentially a public one, analogous, on the one hand, to that of the prophets of Israel and on the other to that of the orators of Greece and Rome. In the imagination of such a task Milton's ambitions take the form of a loftier enthusiasm than the desire to rival an Ovid or even a Spenser, and though he is still questioning "what king or knight before the conquest might be chosen in whom to lay the pattern" of a Christian hero, it is easy to see that such a theme will fail to satisfy his present more comprehensive purposes. From the standpoint of the present discussion we may affirm that the emotions of love and friendship have given way to that of patriotism as the dominant motive of Milton's expressive power. His passion for individual perfection henceforth clothes itself in zeal for public righteousness and his vision is more often directed toward outward objects and events.

There is no real break, however, in the continuity of his inner life. Whenever Milton is attacked, as he was by Bishop Hall, he becomes acutely introspective. Affliction also has the natural effect of turning his imagination upon the world of his own moral and religious consciousness. Such utterances as the autobiographical statements in the *Second Defense,* the lyric parts of *Paradise Lost,* and the sonnets are the result. In these expressions we have the full fruit of Milton's mature lyric emotion, so far as it is generated by conscious superiority of personality and moral ideals. The mood is that of the *Sonnet on His Being Arrived at the Age of Twenty-three,* intensified by a sharper sense of the opposition of circumstance and enriched by a profounder religious feeling.

The development of his thought of sex is more complicated. To follow it we must return again to the end of the Horton period when Milton was beginning to regard the chapter of his youth as closed. The change is marked by a turning of his thoughts toward the philosophy of marriage, a direction clearly indicated by certain entries in the *Commonplace Book* which belong to the later Horton period. These entries cite the testimony of various authors regarding the practice of marriage among the apostles and the clergy of the early church. Milton is evidently satisfying himself that marriage is no defilement even for a priest, and, inferentially, that his own not inferior priesthood of poetry does not demand a state of celibacy. One sentence from Justin Martyr is to the effect that the Jews countenanced polygamy "propter varia mysteria sub ea latentia," a curious bit of evidence of Milton's early interest in the vagaries of radical Protestantism. In the *De Doctrina Christiana,* written a whole generation later, he is at pains to show that polygamy is countenanced by Scripture and is not abhorrent to reason. I am not disposed to take this strain in Milton's thought too seriously. It is for him a kind of *a fortiori* directed against the lingering tendency of men like Laud to return to an attitude regarding marriage which did violence at once to Milton's instinct and to his reason, and which he felt to be unscriptural and unprotestant. For him the married state was divinely instituted and without the shadow of a stain. His militant enthusiasm on the subject is recorded poetically in the famous passage in *Paradise Lost:*

> Nor turn'd, I ween,
> Adam from his fair spouse, nor Eve the rites
> Mysterious of connubial love refused:
> Whatever hypocrites austerely talk
> Of purity, and place, and innocence,
> Defaming as impure what God declares
> Pure, and commands to some, leaves free to all.
> Our Maker bids increase; who bids abstain
> But our destroyer, foe to God and Man?
> Hail, wedded Love, mysterious law, true source
> Of human offspring, sole propriety
> In Paradise of all things common else! . . .
> Far be it that I should write thee sin or blame,
> Or think thee unbefitting holiest place.

In Milton's matured philosophy there was, of course, no inconsistency between the praise of purity and the praise of married love. Yet it is apparent that his mood has changed since the publication of *Comus.* His moral sense no longer throws him into opposition with nature; his idealism takes the form of a glorification of the true and humane conception of love as a spiritual and religious companionship, where the satisfaction of the senses has merely an instrumental though a necessary function. Milton thus makes his personal convictions an element in his public message of reform. Such is the motive of the divorce pamphlets, and such is the theme of a considerable portion of *Paradise Lost*. In the passage cited Milton not only defends marriage against asceticism and exalts it in both its physical and its spiritual aspects as a divine mystery, but inveighs against mere sensuality, the domination of passion, the subjection of reason to desire. His direct antagonism to the romantic ideal of love here reaches its culmination and he repudiates as false the whole chivalric conception:

> Here Love his golden shafts employs, here lights
> His constant lamp, and waves his purple wings,
> Reigns here and revels: not in the bought smile
> Of harlots, loveless, joyless, unendear'd,
> Casual fruition; nor in court-amours,
> Mix'd dance, or wanton mask, or midnight ball,
> Or serenate, which the starved lover sings
> To his proud fair, best quitted with disdain.

This motive underlies his insistence on the subordination of Eve. The expression "He for God only, she for God in him" exactly reverses the attitude of the medieval and the Petrarchan lover, whose deification of woman, when it is not actually the mask of sensuality, does violence to the facts and is in all cases full of danger. It is this attitude in Adam to which Eve appeals when she has sinned, and in his momentary adoption of it Adam falls. The doctrine is that of *Comus* in its ethical rather than its ascetic aspect. We recognize in Eve the enchantress Circe and the enchanter Comus, but we perceive that what is exacted of Adam is the control of his instinct, not its denial. What survives of the Platonic view of love, now domesticated and happily wedded to the Christian teaching of St. Paul, is to be found in Raphael's words to Adam in Book VIII:

> What higher in her society thou find'st
> Attractive, human, rational, love still;
> In loving thou dost well; in passion not,

> Wherein true love consists not. Love refines
> The thoughts, and heart enlarges; hath his seat
> In Reason, and is judicious; is the scale
> By which to heavenly love thou may'st ascend,
> Not sunk in carnal pleasure; for which cause
> Among the beasts no mate for thee was found.

Even here, however, Milton feels it necessary to modify the ascetic implications in the angel's too uncompromising statement. He does so in Adam's half-abashed reply:

> Neither her outside form'd so fair, nor aught
> In procreation common to all kinds
> (Though higher of the genial bed by far,
> And with mysterious reverence, I deem)
> So much delights me as those graceful acts,
> Those thousand decencies, that daily flow
> From all her words and actions, mix'd with love
> And sweet compliance, which declare unfeign'd
> Union of mind, or in us both one soul;

and in the interested inquiry whether angels love and in what fashion. This opens the way for a final statement of the doctrine of paradisiac love. The passage, which ranks as one of the prime curiosities of Milton's angelology, is as follows:

> To whom the Angel, with a smile that glow'd
> Celestial rosy red, love's proper hue,
> Answer'd: "Let it suffice thee that thou know'st
> Us happy, and without love no happiness.
> Whatever pure thou in the body enjoy'st
> (And pure thou were created) we enjoy
> In eminence, and obstacle find none
> Of membrane, joint, or limb, exclusive bars;
> Easier than air with air, if Spirits embrace,
> Total they mix, union of pure with pure
> Desiring; nor restrained conveyance need
> As flesh to mix with flesh, or soul with soul."

The idea here is obviously the same that we have met at the close of *Comus*, *Lycidas* and the *Epitaphium*. But it now presents itself in different terms. The heavenly marriage, instead of being the "bliss to die with dim descried" of the human Psyche which has preserved herself free from earthly stain, is rather the celestial

73

counterpart of an experience already known on earth, and the rapture which had attached itself to the contemplation of the mystic garden of Adonis is transferred to the lower but more comprehensible mysteries of the Garden of Eden.

With this final integration of his sensuous and ideal experience Milton's poetic evolution may be said to be complete. The sequence of his development, while it could hardly have been predicted with assurance, represents a normal and logical unfolding of his unique and powerful personality from youth to maturity under the influence of literary and philosophic culture. It was not, of course, unaffected by his personal circumstances and the outward events of his career. But these incidents and circumstances, even such intimate and moving ones as his marriage with Mary Powell, his blindness, the death of his second wife, while they were of immense importance in quickening his emotions and in furnishing him with occasions for the exercise of his philosophy and faith, were in no case the factors which determined the main direction of his creative effort. The same may be said of his years of public service. The struggles of the Commonwealth and Milton's share in them are clearly enough reflected in *Paradise Lost,* but there is no sound basis for the supposition that the poem differs in its general intention from what it would have been if Milton had written it in 1642. If, then, we continue to look to the conditions and events of Milton's later life for much of the substance and fiber of his major works, it is in the records of his youth that we must seek the essential bent of his genius and the primary moulding forces of his imagination. The great initial impulses of his nature, as these impulses were stimulated and guided by a succession of ideal influences, remain the all-important motives of his poetic art.

NOTE.—It is pointed out to me by Mr. Harris Fletcher of the University of Michigan that the verse epistle to Thomas Young (*Elegy IV*), dated by Milton "anno aetatis 18" and discussed on pages 25–26 of the present study as presumably belonging to the year 1627, was actually written in March, 1625 (*cf.* Stern, *Milton und seine Zeit,* I. 29–30, and note). It therefore antedates *Elegy I* and suggests that the first stages of the process of self-realization which I have described go back to a period earlier than the beginnings of his University career.

# 2

## The Chronology of Milton's Private Studies[1]

The remarkable autograph manuscript discovered in 1874 by A. J. Horwood among the papers of Sir Frederick Graham of Netherby is one of the basic documents for the study of Milton. It furnishes a list of some ninety authors, many of them by no means obvious, whom Milton knew; it indicates a large number of specific passages which he found interesting; and, finally, it contains, either explicitly or by implication, a host of opinions and ideas, consideration of which affords a new insight into the workings of his mind. The Commonplace Book is, indeed, an important key to Milton's intellectual activity, and as such it merits a more careful critical consideration and a wider application than it has yet received. The facsimile published by the Royal Society of Literature[2] in 1876 rendered the document accessible in its original form, and Horwood's edition for the Camden Society[3] attempted a solution of some of the fundamental problems which must be dealt with before the note book can be put to fruitful use. But Horwood unfortunately did his work with little care and left it incomplete in many particulars. His text in the revised edition is reasonably accurate, but the editorial work is in the highest degree unsatisfactory. The editor did not undertake the necessary labor of identifying all the works and authors cited, nor did he always distinguish between those quoted by Milton at first

---

[1] Reprinted by permission from *PMLA*, XXXVI, 1921.
[2] *A Common-Place Book of John Milton*, reproduced from the original manuscript, London, 1876.
[3] *A Common-Place Book of John Milton*, edited by Alfred J. Horwood, London, 1876 (Camden Society) ; revised edition, 1877.

and at second hand. His list of parallels from Milton's published writings is scanty, and he has failed to supply other obvious apparatus.

The most serious barrier, however, to any extensive application of the Commonplace Book to the study of Milton has been the absence of certainty regarding the dates of the entries. They are not set down in chronological order, like the materials in the Cambridge Manuscript, and it is impossible from the printed text to form any idea when the separate entries were made. This is obviously a matter of the utmost importance if we wish to learn more from these entries than that Milton read such and such an author and was interested in such and such a passage or idea at some undetermined period of his life. Horwood points out a few indications of date in the case of individual entries, and occasional assertions have been made on the unsafe basis of the contents of the notes as to the periods to which they belong. It does not seem to have occurred to any student to make a more thorough application of the available evidence, especially that afforded by the manuscript itself, and to see how far it is possible to go toward a chronology of the entire body of material.

In studying the Commonplace Book recently with a view to taking a fuller account of the contribution made by it to our knowledge of Milton, the writer was led to experiment with the solution of this problem. The results, though by no means so complete as one could wish, are definite enough to justify a positive denial of certain current assumptions based on the inaccurate observations [4] of Horwood, and to suggest new conclusions of considerable importance. In the present paper I have undertaken, after discussing the criteria for dating the entries and describing the general method employed, to present a chronological analysis of the Commonplace Book and to indicate the bearing of the material, when so ordered, on the history of Milton's mind, reserv-

---

[4] Horwood's statement that some of the writing (*i.e.,* the first and third entries on page 197) is in the hand of Daniel Skinner has been repeated without question by almost every writer who has had occasion to refer to the Commonplace Book. This identification is absolutely unsound, as anyone who cares to compare the scribal entries with Skinner's genuine handwriting can easily determine. (See pages 99–100, below.)

ing for later studies various miscellaneous questions which present themselves. Incidentally, I have added an expanded and corrected list of the authors and, wherever possible, of the editions referred to, in the hope that attention may be directed anew to many lines of investigation suggested by the document and that a more adequate working basis may be provided for its use.[5]

It is evident at a glance that the notes in the Commonplace Book were made at various times by a number of different persons. Distinction may at once be made between the entries in Milton's autograph and those in other hands. Of the latter, some (the minority) were evidently dictated by him. They follow the exact form established by Milton himself, and some of the handwriting is, as will be shown, identical with that of amanuenses whom he is known to have employed. One set of entries was certainly not dictated by him. These are in a hand identified by Horwood as that of Sir Richard Graham, Lord Preston, who apparently acquired the volume after Milton's death. They are evidently the work of a person who, taking advantage of Milton's method and materials, continued the collection for his own purposes. This is proved by many small differences in the manner of entry, by the emergence of opinions and interests at variance with Milton's, and finally by the reference to an edition of Machiavelli published in 1675 (p. 177). Setting aside these entries, therefore, as not belonging to the document as Milton left it, we may divide the remaining material into notes inserted by Milton himself while he still had his eyesight and others dictated by him to the various amanuenses who assisted him in or before his blindness.

---

[5] For the paleographical part of the investigation I have used in the first instance the autotype facsimile of the Commonplace Book. Observations based on this have, however, been tested with the original in the British Museum by Miss E. Margaret Thompson, who has also determined for me some doubtful points on the basis of differences in ink not adequately reproduced in the facsimile. Various other reproductions of the writing of Milton and his scribes and most of the originals available in America have also been employed. The edition of Milton's prose referred to is that of Mitford. It has proved impossible to trust the statements regarding Milton's autograph and the writing of his amanuenses made by earlier investigators in this field, though I have often benefited by their suggestions. I am greatly indebted to the keen observation and wide experience of Professor Carleton Brown, who very generously assisted me in the initial stages of my study.

The earliest date for the dictated entries cannot be determined on this ground with absolute certainty, for there is evidence that Milton made occasional use of scribes long before 1652, the year in which his blindness became complete. But the data afforded by the Cambridge MS. and other Miltonic documents is such as to establish a pretty strong presumption that any material in the hand of an amanuensis was written after about 1650.[6]

A second highly important step in the classification of the entries is made possible by a change which Milton adopted in his handwriting during his Italian journey (1638–9). In the majority of the autograph entries he uses the Italic form of the letter "e," in others the Greek form, and this he does, save in a few instances to be discussed later, with absolute consistency.[7] The same phenomenon is to be observed in the Cambridge MS. and in all other

---

[6] Phillips alludes to Milton's practice of dictating to his students passages from the Divines as a part of their Sunday exercises. In *Apology,* 1641/2, Milton speaks of reading good authors "or causing them to be read." The sonnet "Captain or Colonel or Knight at Arms," 1642, in the Cambridge Manuscript appears in a scribal hand, with revision of the title by Milton himself. Finally, the inscription in the album of Christopher Arnold, 1651, is in the hand of an amanuensis, with Milton's personal signature.

All this, however, does not show that Milton was in the habit of employing assistance for the writing of ordinary notes or for recording his compositions in prose or verse until the period of his partial or total blindness. Indeed, the Cambridge MS. appears to prove the contrary. All the later sonnets in that document before that to Cromwell, 1652, are in Milton's hand, the last being the Fairfax sonnet of 1648, though several of them were copied after 1652 for the press by scribes. Besides the Cambridge MS. materials the latest specimens of Milton's autograph, except signatures, are: a list of his treatises from 1641 to 1648 (Sotheby, *Ramblings,* 119); a letter to Dati, 1647 (New York Public Library); a receipt from Robert Warcup, 1647 (Dreer collection, Philadelphia); and entries in the Family Bible (*Milton Facsimiles,* published by the British Museum), made in 1646 and 1650. In the last mentioned document Milton has written also the first words of an entry of 1652, which is continued by an amanuensis.

[7] Horwood attempts to distinguish between the strata of Milton's autograph entries on the basis of general appearance, but his consequent division of them into "large and small writing" proves upon examination to be inaccurate. The size of the writing is dependent on circumstances. The early writing is usually smaller, but it is the formation of the letter "e" which constitutes the chief criterion, and of this Horwood makes no use. It is noted in Sotheby's *Ramblings in Elucidation of the Autograph of Milton,* and is applied by Masson to the Cambridge MS. The fact has not been used hitherto in relation to the Commonplace Book, nor have other specimens of Milton's writing been examined with reference to this point.

specimens of Milton's handwriting. In the Cambridge MS. the text of the poems written during the Horton period (1632–8) employs the Greek "$\epsilon$" with not more than a half-dozen exceptions; while the notes of dramatic subjects and the autograph sonnets (written after 1639) contain, except in the case of capitals and the superscript "e" in "ȳ," not a single instance of this formation of the letter. Sotheby issues a warning to those who would determine the date of an autograph from the formation of a single letter, but Milton's uncommon consistency in this, as in so many matters, leaves no doubt as to the general validity of the test. The first example of the later hand is the inscription in the autograph book of the Carduini family,[8] dated June 10, 1639, where the Italic "e" is employed in the two quotations and the signature, and in all his subsequent writing Milton adheres uniformly to this practice. In the writing before 1638–9, he occasionally slips into the use of an Italic "e," but he does this so rarely that the uniform use of this character in any piece of writing consisting of more than a word or two constitutes a reasonably certain test of its having been written after his departure for Italy (April, 1638), while the use of a Greek "$\epsilon$" even sporadically is practically conclusive evidence of a date prior to that time.[9]

---

[8] In the possession of the Harvard College Library.

[9] An apparent contradiction is to be found in the annotations made by Milton in the several volumes of classic authors which have come down to us from his Library—the Euripides, from which Sotheby gives a page of specimens, and the Pindar in the Harvard College Library. (The Lycophron, which I have had the privilege of examining through the courtesy of its owner, Mr. Alfred White of Brooklyn, uses consistently the Greek "$\epsilon$.") In these sets of notes the "c's" seem to be freely mixed. The explanation is, in part, at least, that Milton returned from time to time to these volumes, the first notes in which were made before 1639. In the Pindar one extensive set of entries having the Italic "e" consists of quotations from a single author, Eustathius, and these are evidently later additions. The two page index at the end contains no single instance of Italic "e." The situation appears to be the same with the Euripides. It is certainly so in the corrections to the minor poems, which again might seem like an invalidation of the criterion. Thus in Lycidas the correction of "glimmering" to "opening," or "burnished" to "westring," and the note inserted after the title, "In this monodie" etc., all of which use consistently the later "e," were made after the publication of the first edition in 1638, presumably just before the publication of the 1645 edition of the poems. This kind of explanation removes a large proportion of the apparent irregularities. There remain some cases of the Italic "e" in the text of the minor poems, a considerable number in the Pindar, and several in

We have, then, manuscript data for dividing Milton's reading notes into three chronological groups. It is possible to go further and to determine in many cases the order within the groups. Close inspection of the autotype shows that Milton invariably made the heading at the top of the page at the same time that he recorded the first entry under it, and that this first entry was in every case but one [10] put at the top of the page contiguously with the heading. The remaining entries were made at the same writing or later. It is often possible to distinguish by the handwriting strata of notes clearly separated by intervals of time. On page 109, for example, the first and ninth blocks of entries (the first and twelfth in Horwood) are brought out to an even margin and bear every evidence of having been written under the same conditions. They are obviously earlier than the other entries on the page, which were filled in singly or in groups in the remaining spaces, some care being taken to have each additional note placed near the one to which it is most closely related in idea. These evidences of stratification in the entries extend, as we shall see, beyond the single page.

Taking this kind of evidence as a basis, and applying such other simple manuscript tests (crowding, etc.) as will at once suggest themselves, we may now inquire how far the analysis will carry us toward a complete and significant chronology of the entries, and whether the order of the notes affords a reliable index of the order in which the authors cited were read by Milton. The evidence here is rather complex and the detail must be reserved for presentation later. But it will be clear, I think, that the Commonplace Book exhibits a quite unexpected simplicity of method, and that it is possible to make it serve as a rough guide to one large department of Milton's reading. It is to be observed that Milton did not record in the volume notes from works to which he must

---

one correction to *Lycidas* which was certainly made before 1638. One post-1639 entry in the Commonplace Book, moreover, has two exceptional instances of Greek "ε." The letter is written rather large and is in each case separated from the initial letter of the word as if a capital (see last entry on p. 183).

[10] P. 249, where an amanuensis wrote the heading at the top of page and began the entry in the middle, the space between being later filled in by Lord Preston.

constantly have been referring. There are only three quotations from the classics and none at all from Scripture. Nor did he ordinarily, as we shall see, use it for materials gathered in the immediate process of research, but rather as a permanent aid to his thought and memory. The great majority of the entries were obviously made in the course of Milton's general reading in certain fields. The method employed was apparently to mark the significant passages and from time to time to write up a series of notes based on them under appropriate headings in the Commonplace Book. Often he appears to have used several authors simultaneously, as, for example, in studying the history of England, and here we find a mingling of references to various works in the same note. Sometimes, too, a passage considered as worth recording recalled another in some work previously read. But the passage so recalled is apt to be from an author whom Milton had been through very recently, and this process is not carried far enough to invalidate the general assumption that the chronological position of one note relative to others indicates the position of the work to which it refers in the scheme of Milton's reading and the place of the entire body of notes from that author in the chronology of the Commonplace Book. The surprising thing is that the evidence is so seldom contradictory in this regard. There are, moreover, various ways of checking the results, as indicated in particular cases below.

For the actual dating of the notes and the reading in the first two periods there is material in the dates of publication of the works or editions used by Milton,[11] and in allusions in Milton's other works. The latter are especially conclusive when they are to

---

[11] The edition can usually be ascertained only when Milton gives page references. In many cases he cites book and chapter. With the assistance of Miss E. Margaret Thompson, working in the British Museum, I have succeeded in identifying, in all but a few instances, editions to which Milton's page references apply. Where the pagination of several duplicate issues answers to Milton's pages I have so stated. All editions available to Milton, of which copies are to be found in the British Museum or in the Harvard College Library, have been examined.

[Other editions, not in the British Museum or Harvard, have been identified by Ruth Mohl, *The Complete Prose Works of John Milton*, Vol. I, ed. Don M. Wolfe, New Haven: Yale University Press, 1953, pp. 344–513. *JSD*.]

passages cited in the Commonplace Book. An exhaustive application of data of this sort is obviously impossible until the question of Milton's use of materials from the authors cited has been fully worked out. The present study must therefore be regarded as to this extent incomplete.

For the third period of Milton's life (c. 1650–1674), that which followed his partial or total loss of sight, we have the data for grouping the various sets of entries in the handwriting of the different scribes to whom they were dictated. The whole question of Milton's use of amanuenses is here involved, and unfortunately the facts are far from clear. It seems quite certain, however, that the old idea of their being members of his family is untenable. The evidence of the extant documents, against the statements of the biographers, is remarkably consistent for a series of scribes working for him in successive periods. This is borne out by the Cambridge MS. and other scribal material so far as we can date it, and by the Commonplace Book itself. Owing to the scanty number of the dictated entries there is little indication in the manuscript of the relative position of the groups. But several of the hands can be identified as belonging to scribes whose work appears in other Milton items of known date, and the conclusions as to chronology suggested by these identifications can sometimes be checked by other data.

The analysis, with the detailed observations on which it is based, follows. In order to simplify the presentation, it has been necessary to relegate all modifications of the general classification of the entries by authors, together with the citation of Milton's editions, to foot-notes. In cases, however, where entries from one work appear in more than one of the larger chronological divisions, the title is repeated. The order within the smaller groups is not especially significant, but I have endeavored to suggest by the arrangement the relation which different works bore to each other in Milton's program of study, from the standpoint of subject matter, sometimes, also, to indicate roughly the probable chronological relation of the notes. The grouping itself is meant to be uninfluenced by conjecture, though I have often been guided in my observations by the inherent probabilities of the case. The numbers in parentheses refer to the pages of the Commonplace Book.

### AUTHORS ENTERED BEFORE 1639 (ALL IN MILTON'S HAND)

## First Group

These entries are in a small, neatly printed hand; they were evidently made with great care and attention to uniformity. It is possible to distinguish them at a glance from all other writing in the volume. With the exceptions noted below the "e" is formed in the Greek fashion. The nearest approach to this style in other autograph material is the index to the Pindar (presumably written in 1634), but the writing bears a general resemblance to the script used throughout the early poems in the Cambridge MS., the latter being, however, hastier and more current. References from Socrates and Eusebius are frequently combined in the same note. There is no way of determining the order in which the authors included in this group were used. The notes may well have been made in large part at a single sitting. Wherever there is opportunity of testing them in relation to others, the position of the group as the earliest in the volume is confirmed.

The earliest allusions in Milton's published works to authorities in this group are in *Of Reformation* (1641), where, as also throughout the later prose, the church historians, Eusebius and Socrates, are heavily drawn on, sometimes with reference to the specific passages cited in the Commonplace Book.[12] Procopius is first referred to in *Doctrine and Discipline* (1643).

1. Eusebius, Historia Ecclesiastica (53,[13] 105, 109, 177).

2. Eusebius, Vita Constantini (55, 181).

3. Socrates Scholasticus, Historia Ecclesiastica (53, 55, 61, 109, 151, 181).

---

[12] See W. T. Hale's edition of the tract *Of Reformation, Yale Studies in English,* Introduction, for a discussion and list of Milton's borrowings.

[13] This entry, a mere citation added to the note from Socrates (No. 3), is in a different style and has two instances of Italic "e." The incident referred to is elaborated in *Areopagitica,* P. W., II, p. 409.

4. Historia Miscella [14] (181).

5. Procopius, De Bello Persico [15] (151, 230).

*Second Group (later than Group I)*

The writing here is much less uniform than that of the Group I entries, and at least three strata are discernible: (a) the notes from historical authors (including Sigonius, Gregoras, Cantacuzenus, and Nicephoras), written rather carefully after the general manner of the Group I entries but easily distinguishable from them; (b) the notes from Dante, Boccaccio, and Prudentius, similar to (a) in general appearance but in a lighter ink; (c) most of the references to the fathers, hastily written with a coarse pen and black ink. The three styles, together with that of Group I, are very clearly illustrated on pages 181–2. The Dante-Boccaccio-Prudentius group (b) is determined by page 182 to be later than the Sigonius group (a). The manuscript seems to provide no certain criterion for deciding the chronological position of the entries from the fathers (c).

Suggestions as to the date of the studies here represented are afforded by Milton's use of an edition of Severus published in 1635, and by the statement in a letter to Diodati, dated September, 1637, that he had finished a course of reading in later Greek history and in the period of Italian history covered by Sigonius (see below, p. 107). He speaks in Epistle VIII (Florence, September 10, 1638) of his delight in feasting on Dante. It has been argued, though inconclusively, that the influence of the Divine Comedy is to be found in "Lycidas" (1637). See Oscar Kuhns, "Dante's Influence on Milton," *Modern Language Notes*, XIII, 1–11. Milton shows thorough familiarity with the works referred to of Cyprian, Ignatius, Tertullian, Justin, Severus, Cedrenus, and

---

[14] This is an anonymous compilation in 24 books, based on the *Historia Romana* of Paulus Diaconus. Milton's page references fit "Historiae Miscellae a Paulo Aquilegiensi Diacono Lib. XXIV, editi ab Henrico Canisio Noviosnago I. C.". . . Ingolstadii . . . 1603.

[15] The Persian War constitutes the first two books of Procopius' *Historiae*. Milton's references are to the editio princeps, edited by Hoeschel, Augsburg, 1607.

Sigonius in the tract *Of Reformation* (1641), occasionally citing one of the passages referred to in the Commonplace Book.[16]

    6. Sulpicius Severus, Historia Sacra [17] (150,[18] 182 [19]).

    7. Evagrius, Historia Ecclesiastica (220).

    8. Sigonius, De Occidentali Imperio (182 [19]).

    9. Sigonius, De Regno Italiae [20] (183, 220, 240).

    10. Gregoras Nicephoras, Historia Byzantina [21] (181, 220, 240).

    11. Cantacuzenus (John VI), Historia Byzantina [22] (240).

    12. Dante, Divina Comedia: [23] Inferno (12, 16, 70, 160); Paradiso (111).

    13. Dante, Canzone IV [24] (191).

    14. Prudentius, Liber Peristephanon (191 [25]).

    15. Boccaccio, Vita di Dante [26] (182 [27]).

---

[16] See Hale, *loc. cit.*

[17] Milton's references fit the Elzevir edition, Leyden, 1635.

[18] These notes have several instances of Italic "e."

[19] This note begins a second page under the title "Rex," the first having been already nearly filled with entries from the Group I authors.

[20] Milton's references fit the edition published by Wechel at Frankfurt in 1575 and the duplicate edition published by the heirs of Wechel at Frankfurt in 1591, fol.

[21] The early editions of Gregoras contain only the first eleven books, covering the period from 1204 to the accession of John VI in 1341. The remaining thirteen were added in the Paris folio of 1702.

[22] Milton must have used the Latin translation of Cantacuzenus by Jacobus Pontanus, 1603. The Greek text remained unedited until 1645.

[23] The edition is fixed by the reference on page 160, which cites Canto XI and "Daniell. in eum locum," i.e. "*Dante,* con l'espositione di M. Bernardino Daniello da Lucca sopra la sua Comedia," Venezia, 1568. This is the oɪʃly edition of Daniello's commentary.

[24] This is the Canzone on Nobility, prefixed to the fourth book of the *Convivio.*

[25] Obviously entered contemporaneously with note from Dante (No. 13).

[26] Unless Milton is citing Boccaccio at second hand from some unmentioned source he must have used the editio princeps, published by Sermartelli, Florence, 1576. He remarks that the incident of the burning of the *De Monarchia* was suppressed in later editions of the *Vita,* which he may therefore also have known. If this is a second hand quotation it is the only one made in the Commonplace Book without reference to its immediate source. [See Ruth Mohl, *op. cit.,* p. 438, n. 4. JSD.]

[27] This entry was clearly set down at a later time than the note from Sigonius (No. 8).

16. Ariosto, Orlando Furioso (151 [28]).

17. Clement of Alexandria, Stromata [29] (71, 109).

18. Clement of Alexandria, Paedagogus (106).

19. Cyprian, Tractatus de Disciplina et Habitu Virginum (106).

20. Cyprian, Epistolae (109).

21. Cyprian, De Spectaculis (241).

22. Ignatius, Epistolae [30] (109).

23. Tertullian, De Spectaculis (4,[31] 241 [31]).

24. Tertullian, De Jejuniis (13).

25. Tertullian, Apologetica (181).

26. Justin Martyr,[32] Tryphon (109 [33]).

27. Justin Martyr, Apologia pro Christianis (182 [34]).

28. Cedrenus, Compendium Historiarum [35] (109 [36]).

29. Sozomen, Historia Ecclesiastica (109 [37]).

---

[28] Italic "e" used four times in this entry. The note was apparently made with a different pen from the Dante group (Nos. 12–14).

[29] Milton's references to Clement all fit the edition of the *Opera* published by Carolus Morellus, Paris, 1629, reissued in duplicate by Mathaeus Guillemot, Paris, 1641. These editions contain annotations by Fredericus Sylburgius and material from other commentaries.

[30] Milton's references fit the Geneva edition of Ignatius, published in 1623, "cum XII exercitationibus in eundem Ignatium pro antiquitate Catholica adversus Baronium et Bellarminum auctore Nicolao Videlio, professore in Academia Genevensi et verbi divini ministro."

[31] These two entries and the following from the *De Jejuniis* constitute the most considerable portion of the notebook in which Milton mixes the Greek and Italic "e." There can be little doubt that the entries belong before 1639 and constitute a chronological unit with the other materials from the fathers. Milton cites the edition of Rigaltius. This would be the first Rigaltius edition, published at Paris, c. 1634, presumably identical in pagination with the second, Paris, 1641, which answers to Milton's page references. No copy of this first edition is accessible to me.

[32] Milton used the Cologne ed. of the *Opera,* 1636.

[33] This note must have been made with the Ignatius-Clement-Cyprian group above it (Nos. 17–22).

[34] This note is apparently contemporaneous with the entries from Sigonius, De Imperio (No. 8) and from Boccaccio (No. 15.). The writing does not show the characteristics of the other entries from the fathers and cannot therefore be used as a test of the chronological position of the group.

[35] Milton apparently used the Bâsle ed. of 1566.

[36] This entry, a mere citation, appears to have been added to the Eusebius note (No. 1) when the entries which follow were made from the Ignatius-Clement-Justin group (Nos. 17, 22, 26).

[37] This entry has the Italic "e" and may belong after 1639. It has, however,

AUTHORS ENTERED BETWEEN 1639 AND 1652 (ALL IN
MILTON'S HAND)

## First Group

The entries here and in the later groups in this division have
uniformly the Italic "e." Lactantius (No. 30) is twice associated
with Tertullian (No. 23), but close inspection of the writing will
show that in both cases the Lactantius entry belongs to a later
stratum (pages 4, 241). On page 14 Milton has combined a
Lactantius citation with a reference to the sodomy of King Mem-
pricius "in fabulis nostris," but the latter note is a recollection of
Geoffrey of Monmouth (II, 6), read in the Horton period, and is
not from the chronicle history reading represented in Group II.
Elsewhere the Lactantius entries are entirely separate from the
others, and the notes from Malmesbury and Holinshed on pages
14 and 173 are obviously of later date than those from Lactantius
on the same page. Similarly the Savonarola entry (No. 33) on
page 179 is evidently earlier than the items from the chronicles
which follow it.

Lactantius is first explicitly cited in *Of Reformation* (1641),
but there is reason to suppose that Milton may have been familiar
with the *Institutes* at a much earlier period.[38]

30. Lactantius, De Ira Dei (4).
31. Lactantius, De Opificio Dei (18).

---

all the appearance of having been set down with those from the fathers on
this page.

[38] See Osgood, *American Journal of Philology*, Jan.–March, 1920; also A. F.
Leach, "Milton as Schoolboy and Schoolmaster," *Proceedings of the British
Academy*, 1907–8, pp. 305 and 307. Professor Osgood's parallels between the
*Institutes* and the "Nativity Ode" seem to me conclusive of direct indebtedness. Cf. also Cook's citations from *Institutes*, II, 16, in connection with the
stanzas about the cessation of oracles, *Transactions of the Connecticut Academy*, xv. In Mr. Leach's extract from Colet, where Lactantius is prescribed
among other Christian authors for study in St. Paul's school, the poem on the
Phoenix and not, as the writer assumed, the prose may be meant. However,
Lactantius, as the "Christian Cicero" was much esteemed and his genuine
writings may well have been studied by the advanced students at St. Paul's. Of
Milton's general familiarity with Lactantius and of his large indebtedness to
him there can be no doubt. See below, p. 111.

32. Lactantius, Divinae Institutiones (4, 5, 14, 178, 241).

33. Savonarola, Tratto delle Revelatione della Reformatione della Chiesa [39] (179).

### Second Group (later than Group I)

The references in this section show many varieties of Milton's handwriting and were evidently made at various times. The entries from Speed, Holinshed, Malmesbury, and Stow (Nos. 35–38) are so linked together that it is apparent that Milton was using these authors in close conjunction with one another when they were set down. A few Holinshed and Speed entries appear in later strata; so also do the notes from Sarpi (No. 49), Camden (No. 44), and the earlier books of Girard and Thuanus (Nos. 50–51). A chronological distinction might here be made, but it would be difficult to define it exactly on the grounds which I have adopted for this analysis. I have indicated some of the detail in the notes. A few detached entries are added when they seem quite certainly to be earlier than or contemporary with entries from other authors in this group. But for clearness in presentation of the sequence other more doubtful miscellaneous entries, also those which can be related to this group only on evidence other than paleographical, even when their chronology is quite certain, are reserved for individual treatment later.

From Milton's familiarity with English history displayed in *Of Reformation* (1641), where Camden, Holinshed, Speed, Hayward, and Sir Thomas Smith are directly or indirectly quoted,[40] we may infer the study represented by the titles in this group to have been well advanced by the summer of 1641. The same conclusion is suggested by the fact that Malmesbury, Holinshed, Stow, and Speed are associated also in the notes for British tragedies in the Cambridge MS., which are ascribed by Masson on

---

[39] The Latin editions are entitled *Compendium Revelationum* etc. Milton cites the Italian text, giving a page number. The edition printed at Florence in 1495 is without pagination. He must therefore have used some later reprint.

[40] Hale, *loc. cit.* Hale notes that while Speed and Holinshed are nowhere cited their phraseology is reproduced in several places. Bede is first cited in *Of Prelatical Episcopacy* (1641).

various grounds to the twelve months (1639–40) immediately following Milton's return from Italy and which presumably grew out of the same study. What proportion of the notes in the Commonplace Book stood complete in 1641 is more doubtful, certainly the majority of those in the Holinshed-Speed-Stow-Malmesbury group. A note from Sir Thomas Smith (No. 39) is clearly echoed in *Of Reformation*[41] (1641) and the Camden entry on page 245 (No. 44) cites passages of which Milton makes use in the same pamphlet (Hale, *loc. cit.*). The Sleidanus note on page 76 (No. 46) is worked up in *Apology* (1641/2) (P. W., III, 260). Since most of the notes from this author were clearly written with the same pen we may feel assured that Milton had gone carefully through the work before writing his tract. The Camden notes as a whole are later than those from Holinshed etc., while those from Sarpi (No. 49), which seem from the writing to have been set down at one time, are later still. Fortunately we can date the Sarpi entries with considerable definiteness. The passage on divorce (p. 112) and the one on dispensations from the law (p. 189) are made use of in the second edition of *Doctrine and Discipline of Divorce,* published before February 2, 1643/4, but not in the first, published before August 1, 1643. Milton would almost certainly have embodied them in his first pamphlet had he noted them before he wrote it, for he was eager for support of his theory. Furthermore, the note on freedom of the press (p. 184) is employed in *Areopagitica,* November, 1644. Milton knew something of Sarpi, to be sure, as early as 1641, for he refers to him in *Reason of Church Government,* though in a manner which leaves it doubtful if he had read him,[42] and it is possible that the Sarpi entries actually belong to the years 1640–1. At any rate, a *terminus ad quem* in 1643 is conclusively established for the elaborate body of notes in Group II, since in no case can one of them be shown to be later than an entry from Sarpi. It is to be observed that the divorce entries first appear in the Sarpi group, except for one not very

---

[41] Prose Works, I, p. 56. Cf. second note from Smith on p. 182.

[42] "You know, Sir, what was the judgment of Padre Paulo, the great Venetian antagonist of the Pope, for it is extant in the hands of many men." P. W. I, p. 41. Sarpi's prophecy of the civil war in England, to which he refers, would, of course, be a matter of common knowledge.

explicit citation to Camden (p. 197), which may, of course, be later than the bulk of the chronicle notes.

34. Bede, Historia Ecclesiastica [43] (57).

35. William of Malmesbury, De Gestis Regum Anglicorum [44] (14, 53, 72,[45] 73,[46] 184, 185).

36. Stow, Annales, or a General Chronicle of England [47] (15, 57,[48] 72, 109, 179,[49] 180, 181, 184, 185, 220, 242).

37. Holinshed, Chronicles of England, Scotland, and Ireland [50] (17, 19, 72, 74, 109, 110, 178, 179, 181, 182, 183, 185,[51] 186,[52] 220, 221, 242, 243, 244).

38. Speed, History of Great Britain [53] (53, 72, 74, 109, 160, 179, 180, 183, 185, 186, 187, 220, 221, 242, 245).

39. Sir Thomas Smith, Commonwealth of England (182,[54] 185).

40. Aristotle, Ethics (182 [55]).

41. Lambard, Archeion, or a Commentary upon the High Courts of Justice in England [56] (179, 183 [57]).

---

[43] For an edition of Bede presumably used by Milton see Gildas (No. 83).

[44] Milton's references agree with the edition of *De Gestis* in Saville's *Rerum Anglicarum post Bedam Scriptores,* London, 1596, and with a second folio of the same, Frankfurt, 1601.

[45] Contemporaneous with entries from Holinshed (No. 37), Stow (No. 36), and Speed (No. 38). Elsewhere Malmesbury is regularly cited with the parallel passage in Stow.

[46] Malmesbury is not mentioned in this note but the anecdote is referred to him in Milton's *History of Britain,* P. W. III, p. 224.

[47] Milton used the London folio of 1615 or the same as reissued in duplicate with additions in 1631.

[48] This entry is probably later than that from Bede (No. 34).

[49] Later than note from Savonarola and apparently contemporaneous with one from Holinshed (No. 37).

[50] Milton's references fit the three volume London folio of 1587.

[51] Crowded before and therefore later than the entry from Sir Thomas Smith (No. 39).

[52] Contemporaneous with entry from Girard (No. 50) and with Holinshed note on page 242.

[53] Milton's references fit the second edition, London, 1623, fol.

[54] The first and second entries from Smith seem to have been made with the Holinshed notes. The third is apparently earlier than the entry from Machiavelli (No. 43) at the foot of the page.

[55] A marginal jotting contemporaneous with third entry from Smith (No. 39).

[56] Horwood erroneously takes Milton's reference to be to the *Archeionomia,* a collection of early English laws.

[57] Simultaneous with Holinshed note (eleventh entry on this page).

42. DuChesne, Histoire Generale d'Angleterre, d'Ecosse, et d'Irlande [58] (109,[59] 220 [60]).

43. Machiavelli, Arte della Guerra [61] (177,[62] 182).

44. Camden, Annales Rerum Anglicarum et Hibernicarum Regnante Elizabetha [63] (6, 109,[64] 177, 181,[65] 186,[66] 188, 220,[67] 242, 245).

45. Hayward, The Life and Reign of King Edward the Sixth [68] (245 [69]).

46. Sleidanus, De Statu Religionis et Reipublica Carolo Quinto Caesare [70][71] (18,[72] 55, 76, 181,[73] 185, 243,[74] 244,[75] 246).

47. Ascam, Toxophilus (245 [76]).

48. Jovius (Paolo Giovio), Historia sui Temporis [77] (13,[78] 181,[78] 242,[79] 247).

---

[58] Milton's references answer to the pages of the second edition, Paris, 1634, fol., also to those of the third, Paris, 1641.

[59] Earlier than Camden (No. 44).

[60] Added to note from Holinshed (No. 37) at a later writing.

[61] Milton's references are to the edition of the *Arte* printed in *Tutte le opere di Nicolo Machiavelli* . . . 1550.

[62] Earlier than entry from Thuanus, Book 29, crowded before it (See No. 51).

[63] Milton's references fit William Stansby's edition, London, 1615.

[64] Later than note from DuChesne (No. 42).

[65] Written after the Holinshed entry to which it is attached, being in a paler ink.

[66] Apparently later than Holinshed entry.

[67] The Camden entries were apparently added on this page after it had been nearly filled with long citations from Holinshed (No. 37).

[68] Milton used the first edition, London, 1630.

[69] Apparently entered with the Speed-Ascam-Camden entries on this page.

[70] Milton's page references agree with none of the Latin editions in the British Museum or in Harvard College Library, nor with the English translation of 1560.

[71] Most of the entries from Sleidanus appear in a faded ink and were evidently written in at one time.

[72] Later than Lactantius (No. 31).

[73] At a different time from and probably later than the two Cuspinian entries (No. 61). Note ink and spacing.

[74] Later than Holinshed (No. 37).

[75] Earlier than the Thuanus-Sarpi group (Nos. 49–51).

[76] Contemporaneous with citations from Speed and Camden (Nos. 38, 44).

[77] Milton's references agree with the pagination of none of the editions available in the Harvard College Library or the British Museum.

[78] Added to Holinshed entries, being in a paler ink.

[79] Later than Holinshed entry.

49. Sarpi (Paolo Servita), Istoria del Concilio Tridentino [80] (109, 112, 179,[81] 184,[82] 189, 244 [83]).

50. Girard (Book 1 only. See below, No. 53).

51. Thuanus (Earlier books only. See below, No. 52).

### Third Group (later than Group II)

The extensive set of entries from Comines, Girard, and Thuanus bears obvious marks of having been written, in the main, at one time. The writing is made with a particularly fine pen and is immediately distinguishable on the pages where it occurs. Moreover, the entries from these authors usually appear in close conjunction. To this set may be attached with reasonable assurance the isolated entry from Gilles (No. 55) on page 53. There is abundant evidence for dating the notes in this hand later than those in Group II. A study of the consecutive pages 109–116 with regard to the content of the entries will alone suffice to establish the sequence of these groups. Milton began page 109, "Matrimonium," and page 111, "De Liberis Educandis," before 1639. He next (*i. e.*, after the Italian journey) inscribed the title "Concubinatus," with an entry from Holinshed on the page which had been left blank between. He then entered the title, "De Servis," with three notes from Justinian on page 113. Later he began to fill the blank page 112 (now the nearest to "Matrimonium") with three entries from Sarpi under the new heading, "De Divortio." Still later, apparently, he added on page 112 the two entries from Leunclavius and the reference to Bodin, and, at one sitting, the notes from the Group III authorities, continuing them on page 114, which had begun with the citation from Raleigh and those from the earlier books of Thuanus after page 109 was well filled with entries from Group II.

---

[80] Milton's extracts are from the Italian edition, "Istoria . . . di Pietro Soave," London, 1619. Hales, in his edition of *Areopagitica*, Oxford Press, p. 82, cites Nathaniel Brent's English translation, London, 1620, which Milton may, of course, also have known.

[81] Later than Holinshed entry, being crowded before it.

[82] Later than Malmesbury-Stow entry at top of page (Nos. 35–36).

[83] Later than Holinshed (No. 37) and Sleidanus (No. 46) and contemporaneous with entry from Thuanus, Book 21 (No. 51). The second Sarpi entry on this page is earlier than the note from Thuanus, Book 57.

These remarks apply to all the Comines entries and to those from Books 3–6 of Girard and Books 71–2 of Thuanus. The entries from Girard, Book 1, and most of those from the earlier books of Thuanus are associated with the authors in Group II and are evidently earlier (see notes). The divorce entries all occur in the later set of notes.

A definite dating of Group III is made possible by the publication of Gilles' *History of the Waldensians* in 1644 and by the fact that the divorce materials from Thuanus are first used in *The Judgment of Martin Bucer* (1644). Had Milton noted them before that year, he would almost certainly have embodied them in the second edition of *Doctrine and Discipline* (1643/4). This confirms the conclusion suggested by the facts about the Sarpi entries that the Group II notes stood complete by 1643. Girard is first cited in *Tenure of Kings* (1648/9) where materials from Thuanus are also used, Gilles in *Of Civil Power* (1659). "Girard and the French histories" are referred to in *Defensio* (1650).

52. Thuanus (Jacques Auguste de Thou), Historia sui Temporis [84] (14, 17,[85] 53, 110, 112, 114,[86] 115,[87] 177,[88] 182,[89] 183,[90] 184,[91] 185,[92] 186,[93] 188,[94] 244 [95]).

53. Girard (Bernard, Sieur du Haillan), L'Histoire de

---

[84] Milton used the Geneva edition, 5 vols. fol., 1620.

[85] Book 12. Apparently simultaneous with Holinshed note (No. 37).

[86] Entry 2 and the first line of entry 4 are from Book 35 and apparently belong with the Raleigh note at the top of the page (No. 67). The other Thuanus citations on this page, from Book 71, obviously belong to the later group.

[87] Book 35. Not in later Thuanus hand.

[88] Book 29. With or later than the Camden note (No. 44).

[89] Book 63. Crowded between entry from Holinshed (No. 37) and Sir Thomas Smith (No. 39).

[90] The note regarding Charles Martel's parliament is given without reference but it is evidently from Thuanus cited in the next note on this page.

[91] Book 36. Not in later Thuanus hand. Probably contemporaneous with the Malmesbury entry at top of page (No. 35).

[92] The first entry is from Book 57. It is apparently earlier than the notes from Comines and Book 71 of Thuanus above and below it (Nos. 52, 54).

[93] Book 57. Not in later Thuanus hand. Later than Holinshed and Girard, Book I, which are written with the same heavy pen.

[94] The last part of this note (from Book 52) was apparently made with the same pen as the entry from Book 57 on page 186.

[95] Books 21 and 57. Simultaneous with first Sarpi entry (No. 39) but later than note from Sleidanus (No. 46).

France [96] (53, 61, 109,[97] 110, 112, 182, 183, 185, 186, 191).

54. Comines, Memoires [98] (53, 67, 110, 185, 220).

55. Gilles, Histoire des Eglises Vaudoises [99] (53).

### Fourth Group (later than Group III)

The note from Sinibaldus begins a new page, "Divortium," page 112, having been already filled with entries from Groups II and III. The note from Cyprian is crowded before an entry from Gerard, Book 4 (No. 53).

56. Cyprian, De Singularitate Clericorum (110).

57. Sinibaldus (Joannes Benedictus), Geneanthropeia [100] (116).

### MISCELLANEOUS ENTRIES

### A (probably before 1644)

58. Hardyng, Chronicle [101] (242).

59. Historia Scoticorum (186 [102]).

60. Sesellius (Claude de Seysel), De Monarchia Franciae [103] (186,[104] 242 [105]).

---

[96] Milton's citations fit the Paris folio of 1576.

[97] The second Girard entry on page 109 and the first on page 186, both from Book I, were apparently set down with the Holinshed note at the top of page 106 at an earlier period than the group of Girard entries in the characteristic hand of Group III at the bottom of page 186, in the eighth entry on page 109 and elsewhere, all of which are from Books 3–6.

[98] The Galiot edition of 1552, fol., Paris, is the first one in which Comines' chronicle has the title "Memoires" and is the one referred to by Milton (see Commonplace Book, page 67).

[99] The first and only edition was published in Geneva, 1644. The complete title is "Histoire ecclesiastique des églises reformées, recuiellies en quelque vallées de Piedmont et circonvoisines autrefois appelées vaudoises."

[100] *Geneanthropeiae, sive de Hominis Generatione Decateuchon*, Romae, 1642, fol. This was the only edition published before 1652.

[101] Two editions, published in 1543, were the only ones available to Milton. The entry appears to be contemporaneous with those from Holinshed, Camden etc. on this page (Nos. 39, 44).

[102] Indefinite reference. Either Boethius or Buchanan is probably meant. Cf. scribal entry on page 189 (No. 107). The note is perhaps simultaneous with the Holinshed-Girard group on this page (Nos. 37, 65, 53).

[103] Translated from the French by Sleidanus in 1545. The original is entitled "La grand monarchie de France," 1519.

[104] Apparently contemporaneous with first Thuanus entry (Book 57) and with the Cuspinian note (See Nos. 52, 61). The Speed-Camden group (Nos. 38, 44) on this page is in a paler brown ink.

[105] Crowded before an entry from Speed (No. 38).

61. Cuspianus, De Caesaris atque Imperatoribus Romanis [106] (151, 181,[107] 186,[108] 190,[109] 193).

62. Purchas, Pilgrimes [110] (13,[111] 57 [112]).

63. Campion, History of Ireland [113] (74 [114]).

64. Spenser, A View of the State of Ireland [115] (188,[116] 242 [116]).

65. Bacon, A Discourse of Church Affairs [117] (184).

66. Raleigh, History of the World (114 [118]).

67. Chaucer,[119] Canterbury Tales: Merchant's (109 [120]) ; Wife of Bath's (150, 191) ; Physician's (111).

---

[106] Milton's references to the folio edition published at Frankfurt, 1601, "cum Wolphgangi Hungeri I. C. annotationibus."

[107] Probably contemporaneous with the Holinshed entries at the foot of the page (No. 37).

[108] Apparently written at the same time as the Sesellius entries on this page (No. 59).

[109] Earlier than the Justinian notes (No. 71).

[110] Milton's references fit the first edition, London, 1625.

[111] This entry apparently belongs with that from Jovius (No. 48).

[112] This entry perhaps belongs with the Holinshed note at top of page.

[113] Milton must have used both Campion and Spenser (No. 64) in "The History of Ireland, collected by three learned authors, viz. Meredith Hanmer . . . Edmund Campion and Edmund Spenser." Dublin, 1633. His references fit the separate pagination of the two authors in this publication.

[114] The notes apparently belong to a later stratum than those from Holinshed and Speed (Nos. 37, 38).

[115] For the edition see Campion (No. 63).

[116] Perhaps contemporaneous with the Group II authors on these pages. The two Spenser notes were apparently made at the same time.

[117] Milton must refer to the London reprint of 1641, which alone carries this title. The original is "Certain Considerations touching the Better Pacification of the Church of England," 1604. The quotation is used in *Areopagitica,* but Bacon's remark about licencing books had already been noted by Milton when he wrote *Animadversions* in 1641 (See P. W., I, p. 189), and the entry was doubtless made in that year. It is later than the Malmesbury-Stow citation at the top of the page (Nos. 35, 36), being in a different and browner ink. [See Ruth Mohl, *op. cit.,* p. 450, n. 4. *JSD.*]

[118] This entry is apparently later than those from Holinshed on page 109-110 and contemporary with those from Thuanus, Book 35, on page 114. It is probably later than the entries from Book 71 of Thuanus on page 114, which are written with a finer pen (See Nos. 37, 51, 52).

[119] All the Chaucer entries fit Speght's edition, London, 1598, and its duplicate of 1602. This fact determines the Chaucer canon so far as Milton is concerned. Milton had been familiar with Chaucer from his youth (Cf. *Il Penseroso,* 109 ff.). "The Plowman's Tale" is quoted in *Of Reformation* (1641). It is evident that the Commonplace Book entries were made together, presumably in the early 40's.

[120] Earlier than the entry from Leunclavius (No. 75), which is crowded before it.

68. Chaucer, Romaunt of the Rose (191).

69. Gower, Confessio Amantis [121] (243).

70. Selden, De Jure Naturali et Gentium juxta Disciplinam Hebraeorum [122] (110 [123]).

71. Justinian, Institutiones Juris Civilis [124] (113, 179, 182, 190).

72. Bodin, De Republica (112).

73. Peter Martyr (Pietro Martire of Vermigli), In Librum Judicum (185 [125]).

74. Caesar, Commentaries (109 [126]).

### B (probably after 1643)

75. Leunclavius, Jus Graeco-Romanum [127] (109,[128] 112,[129] 182).

76. Selden, Uxor Ebraica (109 [130]).

---

[121] Milton used Berthelette's edition, London, 1532. Gower is quoted in *Apology* (1641/2) (See P. W. I, p. 321).

[122] Only one edition published in Milton's life. London, 1640. Selden is quoted in the second edition of *Doctrine and Discipline* (1643/4) and in *Areopagitica* (1644).

[123] Apparently later than the Holinshed entry at top of page.

[124] The Justinian notes, on whatever page they occur, are uniform in appearance and are pretty clearly contemporaneous entries. The position of the title "De Servis" (113) suggests that the entries antedate the Raleigh note (No. 66) under "De Matrimonio" (114). They are later than the Savonarola entry (119) and the Cuspinian entry (190) (See Nos. 33, 61). The fact that Milton makes no citations on divorce, though he had evidently carefully studied the subject in the *Institutes* before writing *Tetrachordon* (1644/5) and once refers to Justinian in the first edition of *Doctrine and Discipline* (1643), also points to a date before 1643 for these entries.

[125] Apparently simultaneous with the Holinshed-Stow-Smith entries (Nos. 37, 36, 39) on this page. Peter Martyr is cited in *Tetrachordon* (1644/5), *Judgment of Martin Bucer* (1644) and *Tenure of Kings* (1649). The last citation (P. W. II, p. 472) is to the passage indicated in the Commonplace Book.

[126] Earlier than entry from Girard, Book I (No. 53).

[127] Milton's references fit the Frankfurt folio of 1576, the first edition and the only one available in Milton's time. The note on page 112 is elaborated and discussed in *Tetrachordon* (1644/5). The general subject is treated in *Doctrine and Discipline*, Book I, chap. viii, without use of this passage. I therefore infer the note to have been made in 1644.

[128] Crowded before Chaucer entry (No. 67).

[129] Earlier than Berni entry in Milton's hand (No. 81).

[130] The earliest possible date for this entry is fixed by the publication of Selden's work in 1646. Milton cites it as a divorce authority in *Defensio Secunda* (1655), and he employs the passage cited here in *Likliest Means* (1659).

77. Von Herberstein (Sigismund), Rerum Moscoviticarum Commentarii [131] (112).

78. Tassoni, Pensieri (189 [132]).

79. Boccalini, De' Ragguagli di Parnasso (189 [132]).

80. Thomasinus Paduanus, Vita Petrarchi (189 [132]).

81. Berni, Orlando Inamorato Rifatto (182 [133]).

C (date uncertain)

82. Schickhard, Jus Regium Hebraeorum (186 [134]).

83. Gildas, De Excidio Britanniae [135] (114,[136] 195 [137]).

84. Spelman, Concilia, Decreta etc. . . . in Re Ecclesiastica Orbis Britanniae [138] (?) (183).

85. Sidney, Arcadia [139] (16, 17, 187, 188).

86. Guillim (John), A Display of Heraldry [140] (191).

87. Ward (Robert), Animadversions of Warre, or a Military

---

[131] A marginal jotting without specific reference, "Baro. ab Herber. de Mosch.," opposite to and probably contemporaneous with the note from Thuanus, Book 72 (No. 52).

[132] These entries (Nos. 79–81) apparently constitute a simultaneous group, later than the Sarpi entry which begins the page (No. 49).

[133] A later addition to the note from Leunclavius (No. 76).

[134] The passage is worked up in Defensio (P. W. VI, p. 59). The entry is in a paler ink than the Holinshed-Girard citations (Nos. 37–53).

[135] Milton's references fit the edition of Gildas contained in Commelinus' "Rerum Brittanicarum, id est Angliae, Scotiae, Variorumque Insularum ac Regionum Scriptores," Heidelberg, 1587. This publication contains also the histories of Geoffrey of Monmouth, Ponticius Verunius, Bede, Guilelmus Novericensis, and an epitome of Froissart.

[136] Later than Raleigh note (No. 66).

[137] This entry begins a third page under the title "Rex," pages 181 and 182 having presumably already been filled and many of the intervening pages written on. The note is followed only by amanuensis entries on this page.

[138] The entry is as follows: "If the Pope be not greater than a councel, then is no king to be thought greater than the Parlament. See de Conciliis." I have no assurance that the reference is to Spelman. The first volume of the Concilia was published in 1639. Milton refers to Spelman in the History of Britain (P. W., III, p. 143).

[139] Milton's citations fit the edition of 1621, also the duplicates of 1623 and 1638. He had doubtless known and admired the "vain and amatorious poem" from his youth (Cf. Areopagitica, P. W., II, p. 417). The citations, which are from Books 2 and 4, evidently belong later than the Group II entries. We may perhaps trace a connection between the evidences in these notes of a careful and meditative rereading of the work and Milton's discovery of King Charles' plagiarism (P. W., I, p. 346).

[140] Milton's reference fits the second and third editions, London, 1632 and 1638.

Magazine of Rules and Instructions for the Managing of Warre [141] (18).

88. Theodoretus, Historia Ecclesiastica (53,[142] 243 [143]).

89. Basil, Homiliae [144]: In Psalmum I (57 [145]); In Hexameron VIII (55 [146]); In Principium Proverborum (185).

90. Chrysostom, In Genesim Homiliae (5,[147] 151).

91. Socrates Scholasticus, Historia Ecclesiastica (111 [148]).

92. Gregory of Nyssa, De Virginitate [149] (109).

93. Guicciardini, Historia D'Italia [150] (182, 190).

94. Tasso, Gerusalemme Liberata [151] (71).

95. Villani, Chroniche di Firenze (12).

96. Codinus (Curopalata), De Officiis Magnae Ecclesiae et Aulae Constantinopolitanae [152] (181).

97. Frontinus, Strategmata (19 [153]).

98. Rivetus (André Rivet), Praelectiones in Exodum,[154] Cap. XX (160).

---

[141] Folio, London, 1639. There was no other edition of this work. The entry is later than Lactantius (No. 31).

[142] This entry, made on the same line with one from Eusebius (No. 1), perhaps belongs before 1639, but see next note.

[143] Certainly later than 1639, being an addition to a note from Holinshed.

[144] Milton's references are to the two volume folio of the *Opera,* Paris, 1618.

[145] Later than entry from Bede (No. 34).

[146] Added at a later time to entry from Smith (No. 39). The passage is quoted in *Tenure of Kings and Magistrates* (1648/9) (P. W., II, p. 466).

[147] Chrysostom is not named in this citation. The passage used is in the twelfth homily. The entry may be contemporaneous with that from Lactantius at the top of the page (No. 32).

[148] The writing would appear to indicate for this note, added to a Dante entry (No. 12), a date after 1639, but it may belong to the Horton period.

[149] Milton's reference fits the Paris edition of 1639.

[150] Milton's references fit the quarto of 1636, "di nuovo riveduta et corretta per Francesco Sansovino."

[151] Milton had no doubt long since become acquainted with the *Gerusalemme.* See introductory note to *Mansus,* probably written in 1645.

[152] Codinus was first published by Francis Junius in 1588 and a Paris text had appeared in 1625. We know, however, from Milton's own statement (see below, p. 102), that he began to purchase as it was issued from the Paris press the great series of "Byzantinae Historiae Scriptores," in which Codinus was issued in 1648. This may account for a late return to Byzantine history in Milton's reading.

[153] Later than the Holinshed note at the top of this page.

[154] Milton's reference does not fit the reprint of this tract in the Rotterdam edition of Rivet's works, pp. 1651 ff. The separate editions (1632, 1637) are not accessible to me.

Authors Entered after Circa 1650 (in Hands of Amanuenses

### First Group (Amanuensis A)

The entries in this group are pretty obviously in one hand. Horwood suggests comparison of the writing with that of the sonnet to Vane in the Cambridge MS. (1652) and with the inscription dictated by Milton in the Album of Christopher Arnold in 1651 (Sotheby, xiii, p. 1), but I can feel no assurance regarding these identifications. There is, however, one piece of scribal writing in the Milton documents not known to Sotheby or Horwood, which is almost certainly the work of this amanuensis: viz., the Italian sonnet copied on page 28 of Milton's copy of the *Rime* of Giovanni della Casa, now in the possession of the New York Public Library. Mr. Paltsitz, Keeper of Manuscripts in the New York Library, who has been so kind as to compare the Commonplace Book entries with the writing in the della Casa volume, confirms my judgment as to the identity of the two hands. The fact that the Commonplace Book contains another entry from Berni (No. 81) written by Milton himself, suggests the possibility that the block of reading represented in Group I may have been done just before his blindness became complete. As I shall show in connection with Group II, the Machiavelli entries seem also to be associated with the early '50's.

99. Berni, Orlando Inamorato Rifatto (71, 187).
100. Boiardo, Orlando Inamorato (77, 187).

### Second Group (Amanuensis B)

The two entries on page 197 are certainly not, as Horwood supposed, in the hands of Daniel Skinner, who recopied the first part of the Christian Doctrine manuscript and handled Milton's papers after his death. Skinner's hand, as seen in Sotheby's facsimiles (plates xx–xxiii), is much more regular than this. It has, moreover, an obviously different formation of the letters "e," "R," "f," "t," etc. Indeed, the hands have only the most superficial resemblance, and later students of Milton would not have accepted Horwood's assertion without question had they taken the trouble to compare them. I should judge, though not without hesitation, that the writing is that of Edward Philips (see specimen in Sotheby, plate xxiv).

The entries obviously belong in point of time with those of Group III. See below for a discussion of the probable date.

101. Machiavelli, Discorsi sopra la Prima Deca di Tito Livio (197).

### Third Group ("Machiavelli scribes," several hands?)

I am unable to decide how many hands are represented in these entries. They are all the work of careful writers and have many similarities. The notes from Book i, chapters 58–9 on pages 185, 245, and 198, those from Book ii, chapters 10 and 12 on pages 148, 242, and 243, and those from the later chapters of Book ii and from Book iii on pages 242, 243 and 198 constitute three units, representing, it would appear, successive sets of simultaneous entries, perhaps by the same scribe. The notes from Book i, chapters 2–10 on pages 193, 195, and 246 are more probably the work of a different, earlier hand. If we assume the reading to have been done consecutively (and the notes show almost conclusively that it was) Amanuensis B must have come in for a brief period, probably for a single session, shortly after the work was begun, since his entries refer to Book i, chapter 10. The index entry to the page written by him, inserted with the other titles at the close of the Commonplace Book, is in the hand of one of the other Machiavelli scribes. We seem here to have come to very close quarters with Milton in his use of literary assistance. One wonders who were the four or five persons who could read to him in Italian and write notes in Italian and Latin—fluently, since the appearance of these entries and those of Amanuensis A, D, and F forbids us to suppose that the notes were dictated literatim.

The fact that no recognizable echo of any of these entries, some of them markedly anti-tyrannical in character, appears in *Tenure of Kings and Magistrates* (1648/9), whereas the *Discorsi* constitute an important source of *Ready and Easy Way* (1660), affords some evidence as to the date of the Machiavelli groups. The entry from Machiavelli on page 243, concerning money as the "nerves of war," is perhaps connected with line 8 of the Vane sonnet, "move by its two main nerves, iron and gold." The passage on "successio," page 195, seems to find an echo in *Ready and Easy Way* (30, 25).

    102. Machiavelli, Discorsi (148, 243, 198, 242, 185, 195, 243, 245, 246).

### Fourth Group (*Amanuensis C*)

This group of entries is the work of the scribe who wrote the second part of the Christian Doctrine manuscript (Sotheby, plates xx–xxiii), the Milton signature on a conveyance to Cyricak Skinner, dated May 7, 1660 (Sotheby, plate xxiii, iv), the last entries in Milton's family Bible (*Milton Facsimiles*, published by the British Museum, 1908), and the transcript of the sonnet, "Methought I saw my late espoused saint," in the Cambridge MS. Now the two Bible entries record events of the years 1652 and 1657, but they were evidently made together after the death of Milton's second wife in 1657. The sonnet was composed and presumably copied in 1658. We have, then, the definite indication of a period during which Milton was making use of the services of this scribe, *i. e.,* circa 1657–8. There is, as I have shown elsewhere (Studies in Philology, July, 1920, pp. 309 ff.), no reason to think the *Christian Doctrine* transcript much later. We may, therefore, assume that the Group IV entries belong also to this period. The entry from Rivet bears a rather striking resemblance to the satirical passage on "the masterpiece of a modern politician" in *Of Reformation* (1641) (P. W., i, p. 34), but the similarities may well be accidental. The Commonplace Book entry is unlikely to be as early as 1641. It is the last piece of writing on the page, spaced evenly with the preceding notes, one of which is from Thuanus (No. 52). Milton had, however, become acquainted with Rivet's biblical commentary before 1643 (see *Doctrine and Discipline,* chap. iv).

    103. Rivetus, Commentarii in Exodum (188).
    104. Augustine, De Civitate Dei (195).

## Fifth Group (Amanuensis D)

This is, as Horwood observes, undoubtedly the hand which made the extant transcript of the first book of *Paradise Lost* (Sotheby, plate xxv). The transcript is presumably a duplicate for record of the press transcript itself, written, perhaps, just before the work was presented to the licenser in 1667. The entry is later than the two entries from Machiavelli in the hand of Amanuensis B. A date after 1647 is established for the Nicetas entry by the publication of the first edition of that author. We know that Milton owned a copy of the work before 1658.[155] He had, of course, become familiar with the Purgatorio at least as early as the sonnet to Harry Lawes (1646).

105. Dante, Purgatorio (197).

106. Nicetas Acominatus, Imperii Graeci Historia [156] (249).

## Sixth Group (Amanuensis E)

This badly written and badly spelled entry is later than the note from Machiavelli on page 198. Milton very probably studied Buchanan as early as the period of the entries from the English chronicles. He uses him throughout the prose.

107. Buchanan, Rerum Scoticarum Historia [157] (198).

## Seventh Group (Amanuensis F).

Horwood is, I think, mistaken in supposing these notes to be the work of the Christian Doctrine Scribe (Amanuensis C). I find no writing similar to this in the Milton materials. The Costanzo entry on page 248 begins a second title "Tyrannus," and must

---

[155] Epistle XXI. Since Milton lists the items in the *Byzantinae Historiae Scriptores* which were not at that time in his library we can, by referring to Fabricius' account of the edition (*Bib. Graec.*, VII, pp. 520 ff.) definitely name some dozen folio volumes which he possessed. These include, besides Nicetas and Codinus (See No. 96), the histories of Theophylactus, Georgius Monachus, Nicephoras Patriarcha, Nicephoras Caesariensis, Cedrenus, Anna Comnena, Georgius Acropolita, Cantacuzenus, Laonicus, Duca, the *Excerpta de Legationibus,* and the *Notitia Dignitatum,* all of which had appeared before 1658.

[156] Milton's page references fit the Paris folio of 1647 (see note 155, above).

[157] Milton cites "Edit. Edinburg," i. e. that of 1582, but, as Horwood observes, the page reference should be 131 and not 403.

therefore be later than the Group III entries from Thuanus, etc., on page 185. Page 248 is the next to the last page of the volume.

108. Sigonius, De Imperio Occidentali (19, 181).

109. Costanzo (Angelo di), Historio del Regno di Napoli [158] (5, 248).

The results of my attempt to chronologize the Commonplace Book materials on the basis of manuscript evidence are now complete. In spite of the indefiniteness of some of the data, it is clear that there need no longer be uncertainty regarding the document as a whole. The assumption of Horwood that the majority of the entries were made before Milton's Italian journey (1638–9) is certainly erroneous. Less than a third of the total number of authors and a much smaller proportion of the material itself were entered before this time. It remains true, however, that the Commonplace Book in general belongs to the earlier part of Milton's career, and the document is the more interesting on this account. Beginning, presumably, about 1636, Milton made fairly free notations until 1639, returning to the work with increased attention in 1639/40 and noting observations from his reading with great fullness in the year or two immediately following. A majority of all the entries belong to the first three years of Milton's middle period (1640 ff.). After 1644 Milton made only occasional additions to the notes. It is clear, however, that he continued to attach importance to the volume and frequently consulted it. We may assume, perhaps, that the later group of entries in Milton's autograph belongs in the main to the very end of the period in which he still had the use of his eyes (before 1652), his failing sight again furnishing a reason for his wishing again to record a few notabilia to which he might later have difficulty in referring in the volumes themselves. The most extensive portion of the scribal entries was apparently dictated in the early fifties, and none of them are demonstrably later than the Restoration.

The inference from these facts would seem to be that Milton used the volume in the main for general intellectual preparation for later work, and this observation is borne out by the character

---

[158] Milton's references fit the pagination of the edition published at Aquila by Gioseppe Caccio, 1581, and the duplicate of this, ib., 1582.

of the entries themselves. They are in no sense, as we have seen, notes set down for immediate use in controversial or learned writing. Thus the citations from the Chronicles do not constitute the materials for the *History of Britain*,[159] nor could Milton at the time when he wrote them have definitely foreseen the occasion for their use in such works as the first and second *Defensio*, the *Tenure of Kings and Magistrates*, and the *Ready and Easy Way*. Similarly the earlier entries from the church historians and the fathers, though they are employed in the ecclesiastical tracts, were not the product of research engaged in during the course of this controversy. It is genuinely surprising that the special study which Milton must have undertaken in writing the prose works leaves so little trace in the Commonplace Book. The exception in the case of the divorce entries from Sarpi, Leunclavius, Thuanus, and the French histories (Nos. 49, 75, 52, 53, 54) is more apparent than real. These were not, strictly speaking, Milton's divorce authorities, and from the authors which he actually investigated after the first edition of *Doctrine and Discipline* (1643) in search of support for his theory—Beza, Bucer, etc.—there are no citations in the notes. The inference would seem to be that the reading from Commonplace Book authorities was done as part of a program of independent study and that the notes on divorce were entered, like those from the same writers under other heads, simply because of Milton's general and continued interest in the topic.

All this is highly suggestive as to Milton's method in the use of books, and it affords strong confirmation of the natural supposition that the Commonplace Book authors were in general thoroughly read as being worth while in themselves. The list, therefore, becomes of greater significance for the history of Milton's intellectual development than a more miscellaneous one would be, compiled from the references in his published works. It is

---

[159] Naturally there are many parallels between the notes from the English chronicles and the *History* (see Horwood's list). But in no case does Milton in the Commonplace Book raise questions of fact or of the credibility of his authorities, points which in making a comparative study of the sources for his history he must have been primarily concerned with. See Firth, *loc. cit.* and especially Harry Glicksman, "The Sources of Milton's History of Britain" (*Wisconsin Studies in Lang. and Lit.*, xi, pp. 104 ff.).

unnecessary to remark that this list, as representing those writers, independent of the classics and of Scripture, in which Milton was most deeply interested, is incomplete. Milton's habit of citation is comparatively sparing; the scope of subject matter appropriate to the plan of the Commonplace Book was limited; and we must remember, too, that he kept at least one other set of learned notes, an Index Theologicus, referred to several times in the Commonplace Book, corresponding to the Index Ethicus, Oeconomicus, and Politicus of that volume.

It remains to consider some of the wider applications of the data thus far given. Without attaching too high a degree of certainty to any particular conclusion set down in connection with the chronological analysis, it is possible in the light of it and by reference to the known facts of Milton's life, to give a fairly detailed account of one large division of his studies and to fill some important gaps in his inner biography. Mark Pattison, speaking of the Horton period (1632–1638), deplores the fact that Milton kept no diary of his reading. "Of these years," he remarks, "the biographer would gladly give a minute account." But the Horton years, if we attend to all the evidence regarding them, are anything but dark. The outstanding inference from the Commonplace Book is that Milton began, during the period of his retirement, a clearly conceived program of historical study, to be continued with characteristic fidelity and thoroughness well into the period of his middle life. The reasons for his doing so are clear enough. His time at the University must have been pretty well occupied with the regular academic exercises then in vogue and with independent studies mainly classical. We know that he was profoundly dissatisfied with the curriculum as an instrument of liberal education. In *The Reason of Church Government* he complains, in true humanistic fashion, that honest and ingenious natures, who came to the University "to store themselves with good and solid learning," were filled with nothing else but "the scragged and thorny lectures of a miserable sophistry." His own scheme of education, a humanistic substitute for the mediævalism and pedantry of the university method, is founded on the principle that languages are acquired as a means to the study of "the solid things in them," and that disputation must be subsequent to the acquisition of a competent command of all the fields of knowledge, particularly of the tradition of those peoples who have been "most industrious after wisdom." To Milton, surveying his own accomplishment at the close of his Cambridge career, and contemplating the lofty ideals which he had always held up for his own attainment, the defects in his equipment would have been obvious, and his reason for wishing to continue the life of a student under his own guidance at Horton must have been primarily a resolve to make them good by a more exclusive attention to the "solid things." It was the very essence of his purpose that his studies should be shaped to no immediate practical application. To say this is not to deny that one guiding motive of his life was to write a work which after times should not willingly let die. But he knew that such an end would be best served indirectly through the development of his faculties and by the broad contemplation of human life in the light of the records of the past. For such a purpose, as well as for the more general one of spiritual and intellectual leadership in which it was involved, the study of history and literature was all important. He spent his time, he tells us, in reading ("evolvendis") Greek and Latin writers.[160] This doubtless means that he reread those classics with which he had long since been familiar, but I suspect that he then made his first acquaintance with some of the later and more obscure authors. We know that he purchased and annotated at that time the works of Lycophron and Heraclitus the Mythographer, while the reference in *Il Penseroso* bears witness to his study of Hermes Trismegistus.[161] He doubtless also read more widely in English literature, he certainly pursued the study of mathematics and of music, and finally, at some time during the five-year period he undertook an ambitious course of historical reading, proceeding chronologically.

The earlier authors read under this systematic program are not recorded in the Commonplace Book. A statement in the *Apology for Smectymnuus* (1642), however, supplies a comprehensive de-

---

[160] Not "turning over the Greek and Latin classics," as sometimes quoted.
[161] Milton's autograph copy of Lycophron (see above, p. 79) bears the date 1634; the Heraclitus was purchased in 1637 (Sotheby, p. 125). The latter volume (Gesner's edition of 1544) contains also some material ascribed to Psellus. Hermes was included in Milton's ed. of Justin (See No. 26).

scription of the study and suggests one of the purposes which animated it: "Some years I had spent in the stories of those Greek and Roman exploits, wherein I found many things nobly done, and worthily spoken; when coming *in the method of time* to that age wherein the Church had obtained a Christian emperor, I so prepared myself, as being now about to read examples of wisdom and goodness among those who were foremost in the Church; but to the amazement of what I expected, Readers, I found it all quite contrary; excepting in some very few, nothing but ambition, corruption, contention, combustion: in so much that I could not but love the historian Socrates," etc. Milton had, then, begun with the history of classical antiquity, studying the chief authorities, we may suppose, exhaustively. For the rest, the Commonplace Book gives us the detail and confirms Milton's statement that the reading was done "in the method of time." He proceeded with the records of the early Church in the father of Church historians, Eusebius, in the works of his continuators, Socrates, Theodoret, Sozomen, and Evagrius, and in Sulpicius Severus, turning aside, whether in the midst of this part of his program or later, to study the writings of the Church Fathers themselves. The contemporary secular history of the Greek empire was represented by Procopius, and, in its later phases, down to the fall of Constantinople, by Cantacuzenus, Nicephoras, and Cedrenus. The history of the Western Empire through the Middle Ages was studied in the *Historia Miscella* and in the two works of Sigonius. For further confirmation of the systematic character of the program, with an indication of the direction it was subsequently to take, we may turn to the statement in Epistle VII to Diodati, dated September 23, 1637. I quote the Latin, which is sometimes mistranslated: "Graecorum res continua lectione deduximus usque quo illi Graeci esse desiti; Italorum in obscura re diu versati sumus sub Longobardis et Francis et Germanis, ad illud tempus quo illis ab Rudolpho Germaniae rege concessa libertas est; eunde quid quaeque civitas suo Marte gesserit seperatim legere praestabit. . . . Interim quod sine tua molestia fiat Justinianum mihi Venetorum historicum rogo." [162]

We have no means of knowing whether the intention of study-

---

[162] The period of Italian history here indicated is, as Horwood points out, that covered by Sigonius, *De Regno Italiae.*

ing the history of the Italian cities was fulfilled in the interval
between this letter and Milton's departure for Italy in 1638. The
notes from Guicciardini, Villani, and Angelo di Constanzo (Nos.
92, 93, 109) are much later. There is, however, evidence in the
entries from Ariosto and Dante (Nos. 16, 12, 13, 105) that Milton
was renewing and extending his acquaintance with Italian literature.

If we turn now from the authorities which Milton studied
during the Horton period to a consideration of the notes which he
made from them, we find much that is of value as an index to his
early interests and aims. It is not within the scope of this paper to
discuss the entries in detail. They deserve to be carefully studied
in their chronological relations, for they represent a phase of the
early Milton which is generally ignored and for which we have
little other specific data. It is evident that he maintained in pursuing the course of study which has been described, besides the
general object of self-cultivation, a desire to acquire the materials
for correct thinking on the large political and religious issues of
the age, for Milton contemplated no activity as a poet which did
not involve an intimate relation with the currents of life and
thought in which he lived. Looking back on this period from a
later time, he speaks of "many studious and contemplative years
altogether spent in the search for religious and civil knowledge,"
and he remarks still more specifically in the *Second Defense*
(1654) : "I had from my youth studied the distinctions between
civil and religious rights." The early entries in the Commonplace
Book bear out these statements.

A considerable number of them reflect the contemporary interest in questions of ecclesiastical custom and in the precedents and
authorities regarding them, with a marked predilection for evidence in support of the more liberal Reformation practice. The
Puritanism, or more properly the liberalism, of Milton was evidently of very early growth. A note on Constantine's giving the
clergy immunity from civil office (171) and one praising the
modesty of princes who refuse to meddle in matters of religion
(181) show his fundamental convictions regarding the relations
of church and state to have been already in process of formation.

Even more striking are the political entries, which contain the gist of Milton's whole republicanism. In the earliest stratum a broad interest is manifested in the relation of prince and subject, as in the note on page 181: "Ad subditos suos scribens Constantinus magnus nec alio nomine quam fratres appellat." In the later (Group II) the political materials are more obviously related to the issues of the day. Thus the title "Rex" is begun, with entries relative to the deification of the Roman emperors, and that of "Subditus," with two notes giving instances of Papal release of subjects from allegiance to a sovereign (183). The setting down of the title, "Census et Vectigal" (220) is evidently connected with interest in the illegal exactions of Charles. And finally one note is definitely republican: "Severus Sulpitius ait regium nomen semper liberis gentibus fere invisum" (182). Were it not for the unquestionable evidence of the manuscript we should have been inclined, I think, to ascribe this last citation rather to the period of the *Tenure of Kings and Magistrates* (1649) than to that of *Lycidas* (1637). It will be remembered that in all the pamphlets written before the condemnation of King Charles in 1648/9, Milton carefully avoids saying or implying anything against the royal prerogative, and that in the *Second Defense* he takes pains to point out that he had not done so. That this was not for want of meditations on the subject or of convictions regarding it, but from a sense of what public policy required from him, we now see.

Perhaps the most genuinely illuminating of all the notes are those on page 109 under the title "Matrimonium." In the discussions of Milton's ideas on marriage and of the relation of the divorce pamphlets to his personal experience, this material has never been given proper weight. The entries begin by citing precedent for marriage of the clergy and patristic approval of the honorableness of the married state. This, of course, is simply reformed opinion, and the entries may reflect the popular nervousness regarding the Romish tendencies of Laud, who in a speech before the King in 1632 had dropped remarks in disparagement of a married clergy, but there follows (Group II) an entry from Justin to the effect that the Jews allowed polygamy "propter varia mysteria sub ea latentia," which shows Milton to have been already interested in the more radical Protestant thought regarding freedom in marriage. There are, to be sure, no divorce entries in this period, but sixteenth-century polygamists (for example, Ochino) were also divorcers, and Milton's later opinion is but the logical outcome of his whole early trend of mind.[163]

These and other more miscellaneous evidences from the Commonplace Book of the degree to which Milton had matured and formed his thought by meditative reading long before he found himself actually surrounded by the influences which determined his career, are an invaluable assistance to us in arriving at a complete conception of the significance of the Horton period. Biographers have been too much inclined to make the tone of the "long vacation" depend on the data afforded by the poems alone. The Commonplace Book should warn us that the "lost Paradise" of the Horton period bears far more resemblance to Milton's later years than we are accustomed to suppose. It was an era of industrious preparation, no less for the services rendered to the Commonwealth than for the composition of *Paradise Lost*. Indeed, the two preparations, in his own thought of his career, were one. Far from being in the dark regarding this epoch, we have perhaps the most explicit account that any poet before the era of biographia literaria has ever given of his student years:—the classified statement of literary and aesthetic enthusiasms in *L'Allegro* and *Il Penseroso,* the declaration of moral principle in *Comus,* the avowal of high ambition in *Lycidas,* and finally the record of humanistic thought and study in the Commonplace Book and in the annotated texts. The one gap is in our knowledge of the religious and theological movement of Milton's mind, and this

---

[163] A statement of the recently discovered early anonymous biographer confirms the conclusion that Milton's ideas on divorce were formulated under the influence of his early reading before his marriage with Mary Powell: "And therefore thought upon a Divorce, that hee might be free to marry another; concerning which hee also was in treaty. The lawfulness and expedience of this, duly regulat in order to all those purposes, for which marriage was at first instituted: had upon full consideration and reading good Authors bin formerly his Opinion." "The Earliest Life of Milton," ed. E. S. Parsons, *Colorado College Studies,* x, p. 12.

would probably have been filled had not the Index Theologicus unfortunately been lost.

For the remaining years the evidence of the Commonplace Book is less necessary and less valuable, but the chronology of the document is still of use in correcting false impressions. On his return to England in 1639, Milton did not, as is well known, plunge at once into the controversy of the time. He took up a way of life in London similar to that which he had followed at Horton, with the additional duty of instructing his nephews. "As soon as I was able," he writes, "I hired a spacious house in the city for myself and my books, where I again with rapture renewed my literary pursuits" (ad intermissa studia beatulus me recepi). The "interrupted studies" of the Horton period were evidently continued systematically and "in the method of time," though it is difficult to analyze this part of the program so precisely. The presence of the Lactantius notes in Group I is significant as indicating a first reading of or more probably a return to the one among the Church Fathers whose ways of thought Milton found, I think, most congenial, and to whose philosophy he was most deeply indebted.[164] He records a disagreement, however, with Lactantius' condemnation of dramatic spectacles (241), and at the conclusion of his note makes a significant statement regarding the value of tragedy: "quid enim in tota philosophia aut gravius aut sanctius aut sublimius tragoedia recte constituta quid utilius ad humanae vitae casus et conversatitiones uno intuitu spectandos." The idea and phraseology here are repeated in the preface to *Samson Agonistes.*[165] The entry from Savonarola suggests that Milton had now entered seriously on the study of the era of the Reformation. One of the chief sources of his knowledge was Sleidanus, but before 1644 he had evidently gone carefully through

---

[164] The quotations in the Commonplace Book are strikingly in accord with Milton's doctrine of disciplined freedom as seen in the prose works. The passage on the use of temptation in strengthening character might well serve as text for much of the argument of the *Areopagitica,* and there is a passage in chapter 15 of the sixth book of the *Institutes* (not cited in Milton's notes) to which he seems to be indebted for some of his phraseology.

[165] "Tragedy, as it was anciently composed, hath been ever held the gravest, moralist, and most profitable of all other forms."

Sarpi, and, of course, had read to some extent the reformers themselves, though, except for Peter Martyr, their names are conspicuously absent from the Commonplace Book.[166] The larger occupation of the period immediately following his return from Italy in 1639 was, however, English and Scottish history, to which he now turned, so far as we know, for the first time,[167] except that he had long been acquainted with the legendary material in Geoffrey. The first step was to work through Bede, Malmesbury, Holinshed, Speed, and Stowe, for the older period. The notes from the four last-named authorities are intermingled in the Commonplace Book, and we have confirmatory evidence in the Cambridge MS. that they constitute a reading unit.[168] The two sets of notes were doubtless made at the same time, and they illustrate respectively Milton's intellectual and imaginative interest in the materials. But the study of English history for scholarly purposes extended beyond these simple narratives to Malmesbury and Bede of the older authorities, and to Camden, DuChesne and others among the moderns. The wide scope of the study is illustrated by the inclusion of citations from the writers on English political theory and law—Sir Thomas Smith, Lambard, and, probably also at this time, Spelman. The fruits of his comprehensive research were ultimately to be embodied in the *History of Britain,* but there is no reason for supposing the reading to have been done with this intention. The fact more probably is that the purpose of writing an English history grew out of the study, as the opening sentences of Milton's work suggest. When in 1646 he gave himself to this work he found it necessary to devote primary attention to a number of sources unrepresented in the Common-

[166] The Index Theologicus would doubtless have contained them. Milton gives the impression in the Dedication to the *Christian Doctrine* of having studied exhaustively the systems of the Reformation divines.

[167] Firth's assumption that Milton's studies in English history date from the Horton period is based on a misconception of the chronology of the Commonplace Book (Milton as a Historian, pp. 227–8).

[168] Bede is also once referred to in the list of British Tragedies, along with Geoffrey, both being recollected and referred to when the story of the slaughter of the monks of Bangor was met with in Holinshed (p. 104). The citations from the Scotch Chronicles (i. e. Holinshed's version of Boethius, to which Milton's page references apply) appear separate from and later than the others in the Cambridge MS.

place Book or quoted at second hand only—Nennius, the Anglo-Saxon Chronicle, Henry of Huntington, Matthew Paris, Matthew of Westminster, Simeon of Durham, Bracton, and others.[169] On the other hand, Milton's historical sense and his philosophic point of view as shown in the incidental judgments of men and events had been in process of formation since the beginning of his systematic study in the Horton period.

No less inadequate is the idea that Milton was in this reading primarily searching for poetic materials. The jottings of literary subjects from the Chroniclers are simply incidental gleanings, made with little definite expectation of using any particular one of them. What he really aimed at was the enrichment and maturing of his mind through study, with a view both to the fulfillment of his ambition to write a poem "not to be raised from the heat of youth or the vapors of wine," and to the playing of a part in public events if occasion should require. Viewed in the light of this purpose, the Commonplace Book is quite as important as a revelation of the process of preparation for *Paradise Lost* as is the Cambridge MS. It is a partial record of the "industrious and select reading," which, "with steady observation and insight into all seemly and generous arts and affairs," he held to be a prime requirement. The historical material probably surprised him by its richness, and it is not strange that we hear no more of the Arthurian epic after the time when Milton had become deeply interested in the non-legendary part of English story.

It is difficult to tell just how long these English studies continued. Very probably the course of Milton's program was interrupted or modified by his deliberate entry into the ecclesiastical controversy in the summer of 1641. "I determined," he writes in the *Second Defense,* "to relinquish the other pursuits in which I was engaged and to transfer the whole force of my talents and

---

[169] For an account of the sources of the *History* see the articles of Firth and Glicksman already alluded to. Milton is much influenced by Holinshed, as was natural. Firth shows that he follows him rather than Speed and Stowe in passages in which they are at variance. In the Commonplace Book the Speed and Stowe citations are generally used in a subsidiary way. Milton was well aware of the secondary character of all three chronicles, and his references in the *History* are wholly to the older and more reliable sources.

industry to this one important object." It is noteworthy that the authors who were of the greatest assistance to him were not those which he was then reading, but those which he had already worked through before the Italian journey. He doubtless turned to them again, but there is no evidence that he continued to set down observations based on them in the Commonplace Book. The following passage from *The Reason of Church Government* (1641) helps to elucidate the situation, and its full bearing becomes clear in the light of the material here presented: "If I hunted after praise by the ostentation of wit and learning I should not write thus out of my own season, when I have neither yet completed to my mind the full circle of my private studies, although I complain not of any insufficiency to the matter in hand," his confidence on the latter point being, of course, grounded on the consciousness of having covered with thoroughness in the Horton period the origins and early history of the Church.

The character of the notes made from this first stratum of reading in English history is a sufficient indication of the detached attitude of mind which Milton held toward it. Besides continuing the earlier topics of miscellaneous interest and beginning others, Milton expands the items of political philosophy in great detail, with a manifestly increasing application of his reading to the general state of public affairs, though not to the immediate ecclesiastical issue. New pages are begun with the significant titles "Tyrannus" (248), "Rex Angliae" (186), "Rapina seu Extorsio Publica" (221), the last containing entries pointedly contemporary in significance. A body of particularly careful notes tracing English constitutional precedent for the subjection of the king to law is set down on page 179. Clearly Milton was well prepared in thought, long before he could definitely have foreseen them, for the coming events of English history and for the rôle he was to play from 1648 to 1655 as a defender of the Revolution. The notes relative to the philosophy of marriage are also continued, and an item from Bacon, probably made before 1641, on the unwisdom of prohibiting books, shows very clearly that the sources of Milton's defense of the freedom of the press (1644) lie deep in his early reading and tends to minimize the merely personal and occasional element in the work.[170] In general, these entries afford abundant evidence that Milton had developed by 1641 a remarkably coherent body of ideas, involving fixed views on a wide variety of topics—and that he had already acquired a firm grasp on the substance of works which were yet unwritten.

From 1641 Milton was much engaged in controversy and his study must have been shaped to the various issues with which he had to deal. We have in the *Areopagitica* (1644) a striking statement of the thoroughness of his ideals of research. Yet he evidently refused to allow himself to be altogether warped out of his course. In the *Apology for Smectymnuus* (1642) speaking of the Councils of the Church, Milton says that he has looked into them all but read them only here and there, and adds "If I want anything yet I shall reply that which in the defense of Muraena was answered by Cicero to Sulpitius the lawyer, If ye provoke me, (for at no hand else will I undertake such a frivolous labour) I will undertake in three months to be an expert councilist." Happily the Remonstrant desisted and spared Milton the frivolous labor of the councils. In considering the question of Milton's intellectual occupations during the Commonwealth we must remember that much of the materials of the prose tracts came from authors with whom he was already familiar or whom he was then reading on more general grounds of interest, also that the tracts appear to have been written very rapidly, with considerable periods of leisure intervening. Thus five of the ecclesiastical pamphlets were composed in the single year 1641, and *The Tenure of Kings and Magistrates* (1648/9) could have occupied Milton but a few weeks at most,[171] the materials, as we have seen, being

---

[170] The degree to which Milton's convictions on this subject antedate the composition of *Areopagitica* and the order of Parliament which occasioned it has been too little regarded by the editors of the tract. Beside the Bacon passage on page 184 of the Commonplace Book Milton has set down on page 53 certain ideas from the Church historians which lie at the very center of his argument (See Socrates, No. 1, Eusebius, No. 3 and Theodoretus, No. 88). The anecdote concerning Dionysius contained in Eusebius (No. 1) is worked up in *Areopagitica,* P. W., II, p. 409. But we do not have to rely on the Commonplace Book alone for evidences of Milton's early interest employed in his defense. See the passage in *Of Reformation* (1641), P. W., I, p. 29.

[171] He states in the *Second Defense* that he was led to write it because of the Presbyterian clamor which arose after the trial of Charles and before the

already at hand as a result of the political studies recorded in the Commonplace Book since 1639 and before. As a matter of fact, even in some of the years of greatest productivity, we seem to see Milton continuing his independent study. The study of French history and political philosophy in De Thou, Girard, Comines and perhaps Sesellius (Nos. 52, 53, 54, 60) an evident continuation of the original project, appears to coincide with the period in which Milton was most busily occupied with the later divorce tracts.

There is, moreover, the miscellaneous reading—from Gower, Sidney, Chaucer, and Machiavelli's *Art of War*—which cannot be exactly dated, but some of which was certainly done amid the barbarous and distracting noise of public dispute. Perhaps we have attached too much importance to Milton's impatient complaint of the disturbing influences which surrounded him. The Commonplace Book would seem to show that he continued to pursue with freedom the path of liberal study and meditation which led to *Paradise Lost*. His use of Von Herberstein and other authorities on Russia (Jovius, Thuanus, and Purchas) is particularly interesting as indicating the broad scope which his plan of study continued to exhibit. The entries, too, are suggestive of a mind not altogether bent to the pressing issues of the time. Thus in the notes included in Group III we have beside the political observations and the exempla of "divorce at will," a number of entries of purely liberal and academic character: one on the foundation by Englishmen of the universities of Paris and Padua (53), and one on the need of fostering humane culture "in medio etiam bellorum aestu" (53). There are also two notes from Girard on the history of music, continuing a topic begun in the Horton period. The continuity of Milton's interests remains unbroken, though there is a progressive widening of the scope, especially of his political reflection.

A very valuable addition to the evidence of this sort is afforded by the later Italian entries, which I would gladly date with more precision. Milton's return to this field took place certainly before

---

execution. The trial took place the last of January and Milton's pamphlet was out in February.

1652. Possibly the entries represent a more or less continuous occupation throughout his public life with the literature to which he owed so much of literary inspiration. The notes in the Commonplace Book are certainly later than the period of the ecclesiastical and divorce tracts (1641–5), however, and I believe them to belong to the years 1650–52. Among the authors read are, besides the histories of the Italian cities, the satirical writings of Tassoni and Boccalini, Tasso, and the rifaciamento of Boiardo, probably also Petrarch, since Milton quotes a life of him, and, if we suppose the amanuensis entries to belong to the same period, Giovanni della Casa, and the *Orlando Innamorato* itself. The notes deal with such detached matters as the occasional permissibility of falsehood (71) and the study of law (not a liberal art, "ma mestiere, ed arte veramente mechanica, nel mondo introdutta per affligere il genere humano" (189)).

The dictated material on the Commonplace Book, aside from the evidence it affords of Milton's later occupation with the Italians, adds little to our knowledge of his mind.[172] The study of Machiavelli's *Discorsi* connects with Milton's interest in politics and served his turn in *Ready and Easy Way* (1660), though the entries reflect rather the kind of speculation which had already received practical application in *Tenure of Kings and Magistrates* (1648–9). The Dante entry in the *Paradise Lost* hand is from the *Purgatorio*, whereas those made in the Horton period were from the *Inferno* and the *Paradiso*. The two last named books alone are referred to in *Reason of Church Government* (1641), although the authority of Dante on the separation of Church and State is more clearly stated in the passage here copied out from the *Purgatorio*. Can it be that a discriminating Puritanism made Milton pass over the second part of Dante's epic in his first reading? In reality the human atmosphere of Purgatory is far more congenial with Milton's thought than that of either Hell or Para-

---

[172] The isolated reference to St. Augustine's *De Civitati Dei* (No. 104), which was probably set down circa 1658, is interesting in view of the very remarkable agreement of the interpretation of the fall of man set forth in this work with Milton's treatment of the theme in *Paradise Lost*. For an excellent discussion of Milton's special esteem for, and indebtedness to St. Augustine see Denis Saurat, *La Pensée de Milton*, pp. 264–271.

dise, and it is interesting to find him rereading the second book of the *Comedia,* perhaps in the very period when he was undertaking the actual composition of *Paradise Lost* (1658). His appreciation had already been recorded in the exquisite close of the sonnet to Harry Lawes.

This entry, with that from Nicetas Acominatus under the heading "De Re Nautica," are in all probability the last set down by Milton in the volume which he had maintained so carefully and for so many years. They conclude a list of reading, varied and yet coherent, which corresponds in a striking way, for the modern period, with the program of humane culture through the classics which Milton outlines for younger students in the tractate on Education (1644), having for its generous object the same that is described in the famous definition—the more complete fitting of this man "to perform justly, skillfully, and magnanimously all the offices both public and private of peace and war." The total effect of the Commonplace Book, read with an eye to the chronological order of the entries is to deepen the impression of the essentially humanistic character and attitude of Milton in all his periods. There is a breadth in his interests and a philosophic detachment in his point of view which lifts him well above his age. Practically all the great Renaissance subjects of speculation—all seemly and generous arts and sciences, except, indeed, the art of love—are represented in the titles under which he collected observations: man's moral nature, justice and the law, suicide, temperance, the poetic art, education, usury, patriotism, the state, the sovereign, the family, the principles of rule, nobility, sports and pastimes, military affairs and character; and the selection of materials is made in the spirit of a time when learning had not yet begun to degenerate into pedantry. Far less than one would expect, moreover, are the entries set down in the spirit of the seventeenth century controversialist. Those which concern the burning issues of the time or have a bearing on Milton's special doctrines are intimately associated with those which do not. They are, like the rest, primarily materials for the formation or confirmation of opinion on the large principles in which they are involved. Thus the items on divorce grow out of the general consideration of marriage, and the exempla of revolution form a part of the study of the state and sovereign.

All this tells heavily against the conception of Milton, in the period of the prose works, as a rabid controversialist, swayed almost wholly by personal bias and party passion. Despite the opinion of Raleigh that Milton's classification of his writings in the *Second Defense* (1652) was an afterthought, an attempt to make them seem in his own mind and that of others more objective and impersonal than they really were, I think it represents the substantial truth. He tells us that he wrote his pamphlets on divorce, education, and the freedom of the press as the result of a deliberate plan to further the cause of liberty according to a systematic classification of its parts. Everything that we know of him is in accord with the method and consideration implied in this statement, and the Commonplace Book, by showing his early concern with all these subjects, tends to corroborate it. Much has been said of the fierce personalities in which Milton allowed himself to indulge in his prose writings, and their tone has been taken as a trustworthy indication of the degree to which the iron of the struggle was entering his soul. But I am inclined to take him at his word when he disclaims love of contention (P. W., I, p. 142) and avows absence of personal anger (*ib.*, p. 256), though I remember that he has in the *Christian Doctrine* described the sin of wrath as one to which even the saints are liable. His own violence is that righteous indignation which is commanded by the word of God. A note in the Commonplace Book (176), later echoed in the *Apology for Smectymnuus* (1641/2), to the effect that Luther did not abstain in a righteous cause from using "words not civil at other times to be spoken," shows Milton justifying in his own mind the deliberate adoption of the worst controversial habits of the times, and doing so, moreover, before he had himself written anything to incur severe reprobation on this ground.

The discussion thus far has borne chiefly on the relations of the Commonplace Book to the Milton of scholarship and thought, and the illustrations of his application of the materials collected from his reading have been drawn primarily from the prose. I have, however, tried also to suggest that the process here represented was of a wider scope and advanced him steadily toward the ultimate goal of his life work. If a study of the Commonplace Book is illuminating in regard to the prose of Milton, it is still more so in its bearing on his poetry. The entries illustrate in a remarkable way the degree to which his studies, even in what might seem unprofitable fields, were made to contribute depth and richness to his mind, and, when thoroughly assimilated in his consciousness and touched with his emotion, furnished him with the materials of his poetic art. It is not to Andreini or Vondel that we must look for the sources of what is most characteristic and vital in *Paradise Lost,* but to the meditative reading of Milton in the records of human experience wherever they had been authentically set down—Scripture first, and then the classics, but also in the historians, philosophers, and poets of later times. To Milton almost no material was incapable of receiving the stamp of art. He has even embodied in a line from *Samson Agonistes* the technical phrase which gives the title to Selden's learned volume:

> Against the law of nature, law of nations.

We must not, of course, expect to find the passages referred to in the Commonplace Book appearing in recognizably explicit form in the poetry as they often do in the prose, though an exception is to be noted in the case of a citation from Ariosto, made in the Horton period and used over twenty years later in a famous passage in *Paradise Lost.*[173] In general, the material has undergone such transformation that the parallels are indefinite and suggestive only. Yet it is not too much to say that almost the entire body of convictions and ideas implied or stated in the Commonplace Book underlies and even in one form or another finds a place in the poetical works. A few illustrations must here suffice.

Under the heading "De Curositate" on page 55, in the earliest stratum of Milton's Horton entries, occurs a note on the vanity of

---

[173] "Eleemosynae post mortem datae in iis rebus perditis, et vanis numerat Ariostus quas ad circulum Lunae volare fingit sine ullo dantium fructu. L'elemosina è, dice, che si lassa alcun, che fatta sia dopo la morte." Cant. 34. Cf. *Paradise Lost,* III, 444 ff. Milton's "Not in the neighboring morn, as some have dreamed" is a specific allusion to Ariosto.

speculation about the unknowable: "Quaestiones profundas de deo quas humana ratio difficilius interpretetur, aut, assequatur, aut non cogitandas, aut silentio premandas ne in vulgas edantur, deturque hinc materies schismatum in Ecclesia, sapientissime monet Constantius in epist: ad Alexandrum, et Arium. Euseb." etc. It is followed by a parallel observation, made after 1640, from Basil and by another from Sleidanus. This is the position adopted by Raphael in his reply to Adam's more abstruse inquiries (*Paradise Lost*, VII, 109 ff.).[174] The idea lies at the heart of Milton's whole intellectual attitude and the note in the Commonplace Book is the first explicit evidence of its formulation. Again in the Horton period and from the same set of authors the correlative idea (by no means contradictory in Milton's thought) of freedom of knowledge and inquiry is affirmed in a note citing authority for the use of profane authors by Christians (53). The specific argument here given is put into the mouth of Satan in *Paradise Regained:*

> The Gentiles also know, and write, and teach. . . .
> Without their learning how wilt thou with them,
> Or they with thee hold conversation meet?
> How wilt thou reason with them, how refute
> Their Idolisms, Traditions, Paradoxes?
> Error by his own arms is best evinc't.

Nor is its force altogether denied by Christ:

> Think not but that I know these things, or think
> I know them not.

The entry from Tertullian on Gluttony (13), with the suggestion that this was an aspect of the sin of Eve, and the citations on drunkenness (17) and lust, connect with *Comus*, with *Samson Agonistes* and especially with *Paradise Lost*, in the account of Eve's greedy ingorging of the apple and in the portrayal of the subsequent behavior of the pair. They exhibit as a first result of their sin something like the "dry intoxication of the mind" regarding which Milton quotes an observation of Thuanus (No. 52,

---

[174] The passage is more directly related to one in Lactantius, Inst. II, O, not quoted in the Commonplace Book. See Leach, *loc. cit.*, pp. 307–8.

p. 17). Similarly the notes on true nobility (191), including citation of the memorable utterances of Dante and Chaucer, point to some of the literary sources of Milton's convictions on this topic, illustrating the lines from *Comus,*

> Shepherd, I take thy word
> And trust thy honest offer'd courtesy,
> Which oft is sooner found in lowly sheds
> With smoky rafters, than in tapestry halls
> And courts of princes, where it first was named
> And yet is most pretended.

and, more directly, those from *Samson,*

> For him I reckon not in high estate
> Whom long descent of birth
> Or the sphere of fortune raises.

The effects of the early reflections of Milton on government and leadership are too pervasive in his later poetry to permit of full discussion here. A study of the Commonplace Book serves to throw into high relief the importance of these elements in the intellectual fabric of *Paradise Lost* and *Paradise Regained.* Thus Milton's historical reading and his philosophical meditation on the part played by moral character in the conduct of public affairs underlies his treatment of the political career of Satan, and the fruits of his elaborate study of statecraft are to be seen throughout both poems, most clearly perhaps in the grasp with which in *Paradise Regained* he handles the military and political situation in the Roman world. Several times Milton has copied out from his authors striking statements of the true ideal of kingship, as a burden rather than a delight and an opportunity for service rather than for spoil. So on page 182: "officium et definitio imperatoris egregia est. Jus Graeco Romanum . . . ex lib. de jure qui est Basil. Constant. Leonis ubi ait τέλος τῷ βασιλεῖ τὸ ἐνεργετεῖν, κὰι ἡνίκα τῆς ἐνεργεσίας ἐξατονήσῃ δοκεῖ κιβηλεύειν τὸν βασιλικὸν χαρακτῆρα. vide etiam Orlando Inamora. del Berni cant. 7. stanz. 2 un re se vuole il suo debito fare, non e re veramente ma fattore del popolo etc." And in the hand of the Christian Doctrine scribe on page 195: "Si in principatu politico aliqua est servitus, magis proprie servus est qui praeest, quam qui subest: August. de Civit. Dei. lib. 19 cap. 14." This theme is finely elaborated in Christ's rejection of the kingdoms of the earth in *Paradise Regained*. The first lines of my quotation are touched with Shakespearean recollections but the last three are manifestly a distillation of the sentences set down in the Commonplace Book:

> What if with like aversion I reject
> Riches and realms; yet not for that a crown
> Golden in shew, is but a wreath of thorns,
> Brings dangers, troubles, cares and sleepless nights
> To him who wears the regal diadem,
> When on his shoulders each man's burden lies;
> For therein stands the office of a king,
> His honour, vertue, merit and chief praise,
> That for the public all this weight he bears.

In a passage which follows in the same speech Milton seems to be adapting and elaborating one of the scribal entries from Machiavelli's *Discorsi:* "Laudatissimos omnium inter mortales, eos esse quo vera Religione hominum mentes imbuunt, immo is etiam laudatiores qui humanis legibus Regna et Respub: quamvis egregie fundarunt." (197)

> But to guide nations in the way of truth
> By saving doctrine, and from error lead
> To know, and knowing, worship God aright,
> Is yet more kingly: this attracts the soul
> Governs the inner man, the nobler part,
> That other o'er the body only reigns.

Words of Machiavelli in the mouth of Christ! Nothing could be more characteristic of the way in which Milton has laid under contribution in his poetry the wisdom of a lifetime spent in the pursuit of truth, even to her strangest and most alien haunts.

As affording, therefore, an insight into the real and abiding intellectual temper of Milton and as a revelation of the preparatory intellectual processes which culminated in his greatest work, the Commonplace Book is an invaluable Miltonic document. It shows him in his quiet hours, philosophical and humane, though anything but indifferent, "turning over the whole book of knowledge," "reading all manner of tractates and hearing all manner of reasons," "scouting even into the regions of sin and falsity," but rejoicing in nothing so much as to find and record for memory and use, the examples of virtue and embodied truth. More, perhaps, than any of his formal writings, this accidentally preserved record of Milton's private studies serves to bridge the gap between his poetry and his prose and to show the essential oneness of his culture according to the best ideals of the Renaissance.

### INDEX TO AUTHORS CITED IN MILTON'S COMMONPLACE BOOK [175]

*(The numbers refer to the designated position of the individual works in the preceding list)*

Ariosto, *Orlando,* 16
Aristotle, *Ethics,* 40
Ascham, *Toxophilus,* 47
Augustine, *De Civitate,* 104
Bacon, *Discourse,* 65
Basil, *Homiliae,* 89
Bede, *Historia,* 34
Berni, *Orlando,* 81, 89
Boccaccio, *Vita di Dante,* 15
Boccalini, *Ragguagli,* 79
Bodin, *De Republica,* 72
Boiardo, *Orlando,* 100
Buchanan, *Historia,* 59 (?), 107
Caesar, *Commentaries,* 74
Camden, *Annales,* 44
Campion, *History,* 63

Cantacuzenus, *Historia,* 11
Cedrenus, *Compendium,* 28
Chaucer, *Canterbury Tales,* 67; *Romaunt of the Rose,* 68
Chrysostom, *Homiliae,* 90
Clement, *Paedagogus,* 18; *Stromata,* 17
Codinus, *De Officiis,* 96
Comines, *Memoires,* 54
Costanzo, *Historia,* 109
Curopalata (See Codinus)
Cuspinianus, *De Caesaris,* 61
Cyprian, *De Disciplina,* 19; *De Singularitate,* 56; *De Spectaculis,* 21; *Epistolae,* 20

---

[175] The following entries in the Commonplace Book are set down without specific reference to the author from which they were derived: p. 12, Martino quarto. vide de bonis Eccles. (Villani?); p. 14, in fabulis nostris etc. (i. e. Geoffrey of Monmouth, II, 6, quoted from memory); p. 73, Anlafe's souldier etc. (Malmesbury, see No. 35, note 46); p. 75, Read K. Kanute's act by the seaside (The anecdote is ascribed to Henry of Huntingdon in the *History of Britain,* but Milton is probably here citing it from one of the later chronicles); p. 109, Conjugal affection etc.; p. 110, Carolus Martellus etc., Ferdinandus etc. (These notes apparently go with the citations to Girard); p. 177, the form of a state etc.; p. 182, clergy commonly corrupters etc. (Holinshed?); p. 183, Parlament by three estates etc. (Girard?).

# 3

## The Pastoral Elegy and Milton's *Lycidas*[1]

### i

To most modern readers the pastoral setting of Milton's *Lycidas* is far from being an element of beauty. It is doubtful whether anyone, approaching *Lycidas* for the first time, fails to experience a feeling of strangeness, which must be overcome before the poem can be fully appreciated; and not infrequently the pastoral imagery continues to be felt as a defect, attracting attention to its own absurdities and thereby seriously interfering with the reader's enjoyment of the piece itself. The reason for this attitude lies in the fact that we have to-day all but forgotten the pastoral tradition and quite lost sympathy with the pastoral mood. The mass of writing to which this artificial yet strangely persistent literary fashion gave rise seems unendurably barren and insipid; to return and traverse the waste, with its dreary repetitions of conventional sentiments and tawdry imagery, is a veritable penance. Yet this, if we are to judge fairly of *Lycidas,* or if we are to remove the hindrances to our full enjoyment of it as poetry, is what in a measure we must do. For in Milton's eyes the pastoral element in *Lycidas* was neither alien nor artificial. Familiar as he was with poetry of this kind in English, Latin, Italian, and Greek, Milton recognized the pastoral as one of the natural modes of literary expression, sanctioned by classic practice, and recommended by not inconsiderable advantages of its own. The setting of *Lycidas* was to him not merely an ornament, but an essential

---

[1] Reprinted by permission from *PMLA,* XXV, 1910.

element in the artistic composition of the poem. It tended to idealize and dignify the expression of his sorrow, and to exalt this tribute to the memory of his friend, by ranging it with a long and not inglorious line of elegiac utterances, from Theocritus and Virgil to Edmund Spenser.

To consider this tradition with reference to *Lycidas* is the object of the present essay. I do not propose to write a history of the pastoral elegy, but simply to indicate the origin of those elements of the elegiac tradition which appear in *Lycidas,* and to show in detail Milton's indebtedness to each of the greater examples of the type. Many of the borrowings are noted in the various editions of Milton's works; [2] some of the identifications are new. The material has never, so far as I know, been collected and used for the present purpose.

## ii

The trifling and artificial spirit of the pastoral would seem at first thought to render the form utterly inappropriate for serious laments; according to the accepted view the pastoral was in its very origin a sort of toy, a literature of make-believe. The poetry which grew up in the happy school of Greek bards who masqueraded as countrymen on the "pleasant sward" of Cos, and whiled away the hours learning to be poets by imitating the song contests of the Sicilian shepherds, could hardly have been anything but pretty and artificial.[3] We might have supposed that it would be as transitory as the conditions which gave it birth. That this *jeu d'esprit* became a permanent literary form and a mode of expression for serious as well as lighter themes, was due to the superior

---

[2] See especially the annotations to *Lycidas* in David Masson's *The Poetical Works of John Milton,* London, 1894, Vol. III; and in the Pitt Press edition of Milton's Minor Poems, ed. A. W. Verity, Cambridge, 1891. Cf. also W. P. Mustard's article in Vol. XXX of the *American Journal of Philology:* "Later Echoes of the Greek Bucolic Poets," to which I have made frequent reference in the earlier part of this essay.

[3] For an account of the origin of the Alexandrian pastoral see the extensive work of Ph. E. Legrand, *Étude sur Théocrite,* Paris, 1898; R. J. Cholmondeley, *The Idyls of Theocritus,* Intro.; A. Lang, *Theocritus, Bion and Moschus,* London, 1906, Intro. The seventh idyl of Theocritus gives a lighthearted account of an incident in the daily life of these poets and incidentally illustrates the beginning of the personal and artificial pastoral.

genius of Theocritus, whose dramatic imagination, aided by his knowledge of the sober realities of Sicilian shepherd life, carried him beyond the imitation of mere externals and led him really to identify himself with the characters which he portrayed. All the charm of rustic manners, all the fresh beauties of Sicilian scenery were preserved in the idyls of Theocritus; but these served only as a setting for human passions.

That the change in point of view, the shift of attention from the machinery of the pastoral to its essence, did not come to Theocritus all at once, may be inferred from the idyls themselves.[4] In the Polyphemus idyls, for example, where the monster Cyclops is represented in the grotesque rôle of a sentimental lover, we seem to see the poet barely touching the serious note. The sixth idyl gets little farther than burlesque; in the eleventh,[5] on the other hand, the author makes us feel not only the absurdity of Polyphemus in love, but also, by flashes, the pathos of it:

"Come forth, Galatea," he cries, "and forget as thou comest, even as I that sit here have forgotten, the homeward way. . . . There is no one that wrongs me but that mother of mine, and her do I blame. Never, nay, never once has she spoken a kind word for me to thee, and that though day by day she sees me wasting. I will tell her that my head and both my feet are throbbing, that she may also suffer somewhat, since I too am suffering. O Cyclops, Cyclops, whither are thy wits wandering? Ah that thou wouldst go, and weave thy wicker-work and gather broken boughs to carry to thy lambs; in faith, if thou didst this, far wiser wouldst thou be."

The author is still trifling, but his imagination has carried him into the situation; he seems to be holding two points of view, that of the Cyclops, and that of the unsympathetic world which is laughing at him. In another lover's lament (Idyl III) extravagant sentimentality takes the place of incongruity as an element of humor. The song is addressed to cruel Amaryllis by her disappointed lover, who, when he finds himself rejected in spite of

---

[4] The chronology of Theocritus is carefully worked out by Ph. E. Legrand, *op. cit.;* his results are summarized by Cholmondeley, *op. cit.,* Intro. I am much indebted in the following criticism and throughout this essay to Professor E. K. Rand of Harvard University.

[5] *Bucolici Græci,* Wilamowitz-Moellendorff, Oxford, 1905, p. 22. The quotations from Theocritus, Bion, and Moschus are taken from Andrew Lang's excellent translation.

presents, prayers, and harmless threats, gives way to despair. "My head aches, but thou carest not. I will sing no more, but dead will I lie where I fall, and here may the wolves devour me." In this passage the contemplation of death as the result of the thwarting of the shepherd's passion brings us a step nearer to the elegy. The spirit of the piece is, to be sure, not too serious; this lover's "complaint" is the very stuff of which the later sentimental or burlesque pastoral was made. Still there are serious and even tragic possibilities in the theme; characters and passions originally designed as burlesques may spring into life under the creative touch of genius, and refuse to remain within the narrow bounds of parody.

It is in the first and second idyls that Theocritus becomes fully possessed by his theme. Here the spirit of banter and make-believe is cast aside for a serious artistic purpose. The subject of the poems is still disappointed love, but the laments are no longer mere lovers' rhetoric. They claim and receive our sympathy. The second idyl is not pastoral and does not concern us here, except as it serves to show the trend of Theocritus's poetic and dramatic genius. It is the monologue of a ruined and deserted girl, who is trying the forlorn hope of magic to bring back her faithless lover. She tells the story of her passion with poignant pathos, murmuring an incantation to the moon the while, and directing a servant in the magic rites. In Virgil's imitation of this poem (Eclogue VIII) the incantations prove successful; in Theocritus no lover comes, and the ending is consistent with the hopeless tone of the whole piece. "But do thou farewell, and turn thy steeds to Ocean, Lady, and my pain I will bear, even as till now I have endured it." Virgil is primarily interested in the magic machinery and in the sonorous poetry; Theocritus, in the truth of the character and the tragic pathos of the situation.

The greatest of the idyls and by far the most important for the present discussion is the first. For not only is it in many respects the archetype of the pastoral elegy, but it bears a direct and particularly significant relation to *Lycidas*. The poem opens with a pretty scene in which Thyrsis, the sweet singer of the vale, is urged by a goatherd to make pleasant the noontide hour by singing the "Affliction of Daphnis." A wondrous ivy bowl, and the privilege of thrice milking a goat that is mother of twins, shall be his reward. Thyrsis consents and begins the beautiful lament. The theme is how Daphnis, the ideal hero of pastoral song, was subdued by a new love, after his marriage to the fairest of the nymphs, and chose rather to die than to yield. The singer first rebukes the nymphs for failing to save their Daphnis, and tells of the universal lament of nature for his loss; he then describes the visits of Hermes, Priapus, and Cypris to the afflicted shepherd, the first two with words of consolation, the last with a cruel taunt. To her alone does Daphnis reply, reproaching her and bidding her begone to boast of her success; he bids farewell to his native woods and rivers; bequeaths his pipe to his successor, and dies lamenting his own sad fate. The shepherd-singer concludes and claims the gifts, which the goatherd gladly grants, with praise for his companion's song.

The extent to which this poem moulded the tradition of the pastoral elegy will be clear from our discussion of the later examples of the form. That Milton was familiar with it at first hand and consciously adopted it as one of the classical models for *Lycidas* seems practically certain, notwithstanding the wide divergence of the two poems in setting, spirit, and subject matter. For the general plan of making various beings come one after another to add their part to the lament, Milton had a precedent also in the tenth eclogue of Virgil.[6] It is impossible to say that he was influenced more by the one poet than by the other. It is noteworthy, however, that in the *Epitaphium Damonis*, where Milton uses the same motive, he is clearly following Theocritus I. The poem is twice explicitly referred to,[7] and the name of the mourner in both laments is Thyrsis. In the *Epitaphium* the shepherds and nymphs come, not to mourn for the dead as in *Lycidas*, but, in their mistaken way, to bring comfort to the mourner;[8] the contrast

---

[6] See below, p. 139.

[7] See below, p. 136.

[8] Tityrus, Alphesibœus, Ægon, and Amyntas bid Thyrsis enjoy the delights of nature; Mopsus asks what flirt is plaguing him; the nymphs reproach his cloudy brow and bid him not reject the joys of youth and love. There are detailed resemblances to Theocritus I.

between the affliction of the shepherd and the shallow consolations of his friends serves, as with Theocritus and Virgil, to heighten the effect.

A more detailed borrowing is to be found in the passage in *Lycidas* beginning "Where were ye, Nymphs." The lament of Thyrsis opens thus:

> "Begin, ye Muses dear, begin the pastoral song.
> Thyrsis of Etna am I, and this is the voice of Thyrsis. Where, ah! where were ye when Daphnis was languishing; ye nymphs where were ye? By Peneus beautiful or by the dells of Pindus? for surely ye dwelt not by the great stream of the river Anapus, nor on the watchtower of Etna, nor by the sacred water of Acis.
> Begin, ye muses dear, begin the pastoral song."

The familiar lines from *Lycidas* are substantially the same, but they bear the touch of a mightier hand:

> "Where were ye, Nymphs, when the remorseless deep
> Closed o'er the head of your loved Lycidas?
> For neither were ye playing on the steep
> Where your old bards, the famous Druids, lie,
> Nor on the shaggy top of Mona high,
> Nor yet where Deva spreads her wisard stream."

For the use of this motive too Milton had the double precedent of Theocritus and Virgil; [9] that the lines are directly reminiscent of the Greek rather than the Latin poet is clear from the fact, pointed out long ago by Keightley,[10] that whereas Milton, like Theocritus, mentions places near the region where his shepherd met his fate, Virgil declares that the nymphs were absent, not from Arcady where the scene of his Eclogue is laid, but from their accustomed haunts in Sicily.

At the close of the lament in Theocritus I there is a passage

---

[9] Eclogue x, vv. 9 ff. The lines are as follows:
> "Quæ nemora aut qui vos saltus habuere, puellæ
> Naides, indigno cum Gallus amore peribat?
> Nam neque Parnasi vobis iuga, nam neque Pindi
> Ulla moram fecere, neque Aonie Aganippe."

The motive appears again and again in the pastoral elegy of the Renaissance; see Mustard, *op. cit.*, for references.

[10] *The Poems of John Milton, with Notes*, London, 1859. Annotations to *Lycidas*, Vol. II.

which bears a still more essential relation to *Lycidas* and has, so far as I know, never been pointed out:

"Nay, spun was all the thread that the fates assigned," the shepherd sings, "and Daphnis went down the stream. The whirling wave closed over (literally 'the eddy washed away')[11] the man whom the muses loved, the man not hated of the nymphs."[12]

In view of the circumstances of the death of Edward King, these lines are particularly interesting. That Milton noticed their special applicability to his own subject is clear from the passage already quoted:

"Where were ye, Nymphs, when the remorseless deep
        Closed o'er the head of your loved Lycidas?"

May it not be that these lines from Theocritus first suggested to Milton the idea of giving his elegy on the death of his friend a pastoral form? It is quite possible that this passage occurred to Milton when he first learned that King was drowned, thus drawing his attention to Theocritus I and to the pastoral elegy in general as an instrument for the expression of idealized grief. The external circumstances of Daphnis's death would at least lead Milton in a manner to identify his own dead shepherd with this legendary hero of pastoral song, and to regard Theocritus's exquisite lament as the prototype of his own elegy.[13]

The influence of Theocritus on *Lycidas* is by no means limited to the Daphnis idyl. The elegiac pastoral tradition is only a part of the pastoral tradition in general, and the whole body of the poetry of Theocritus, as the ultimate source of this general tradition, must be regarded as contributory to the pastoral elegy. Theocritus was the great store-house of pastoral material; he was plundered again and again, and his plunderers were plundered in their turn, until the incidents, expressions, and motives used by him became common property among pastoral writers. Of this material a due proportion appears in *Lycidas*, whether borrowed di-

---

[11] Εκλυσε δίνα etc. vv. 140 ff.
[12] Lang, p. 10.
[13] I shall have occasion to note a probable connection between *Lycidas* and two other elegies, the subjects of which met their death by drowning. See below, pp. 149 and 153 ff.

rectly from Theocritus or descended from him through many hands.[14]

Of the later bucolic writers of the Alexandrine age, but two are known to us by name: Moschus and the somewhat younger Bion,[15] both of whom flourished in the latter half of the third century B.C. Bion's most famous idyl, the *Lament for Adonis*, ('Αδώνιδος ἐπιτάφιος) ,[16] is, strictly speaking, not a pastoral at all; Adonis was a hunter, not a shepherd.[17] The poem is associated with the pastoral, however, because of its form and because it is the work of a pastoral poet. Its erotic tone serves also to ally it with pastoral poetry. It is not surprising, therefore, that we find the poem influencing the pastoral elegy. The sober and classic genius of Milton seems to have rejected this decadent elegy; for neither *Lycidas* nor the *Epitaphium Damonis* shows any direct trace of its influence. Other pastoral writers, however, have made liberal use of the poem, and it must rank as one of the great classical models of the pastoral elegy.[18] The poem, moreover, derives a special importance in the development of the tradition from its connection with the *Lament for Bion* (Βίωνος ἐπιτάφιος) .

The latter piece,[19] which is commonly attributed to Moschus but probably belongs to a somewhat younger Italian contemporary, is of the greatest significance in the history of the pastoral elegy. It marks, as we shall see, the full development of the pastoral lament as an independent type, and, notwithstanding its sentimentality and absurd exaggeration of the pathetic fallacy, it was adopted as a model by numerous later writers.[20] The originals of

---

[14] The passages in Milton which are directly and certainly traceable to other idyls of Theocritus are very few. Cf., however, Id. VII, 35 ( Ξυνὰ γὰρ ὁδός, ξυνὰ δὲ καὶ ἀώς ) with *Lyc.*, 25–7. (The reference is from Mustard, *op. cit.*, p. 235.) Verses 16–7 of Id. I (not a part of the lament) are repeated in *Ep. Dam.*, 51–2; and the description of the cup in Id. I is echoed in *Ep. Dam.*, 181 ff.

[15] *Bucolici Græci*, App.; Lang, *op. cit.*

[16] *Bucolici Græci*, pp. 122 ff.

[17] Virgil, presumably because of this poem, assumes that he tended sheep: "Et formosus ovis ad flumina pavit Adonis" (Ec. x, v. 18).

[18] Cf. Mustard, *op. cit.*, pp. 275 ff., for an extensive account of the influence of this poem in the Renaissance and later. Shelley's *Adonais* is formally modelled on the *Lament for Adonis*.

[19] *Bucolici Græci*, pp. 91 ff.

[20] Mustard, *op. cit.*, pp. 279 ff.

the *Lament for Bion* were clearly Bion's own *Lament for Adonis* and Theocritus's first idyl; but the poem differs conspicuously from its predecessors in being a lament for the death of an actual person conceived as a shepherd. Adopting the lyric form of the *Lament for Adonis* and the pastoral setting and many of the motives of Theocritus I, the writer has substituted for the legendary character, whether shepherd or hunter, the person of his own friend. Bion was a writer of pastorals; therefore for poetical purposes Bion was a shepherd. By thus applying the imagery of the pastoral to a real person, the author of the *Lament* had transformed what was previously a *genre* of erotic verse into the more serviceable type of the personal elegy in pastoral form.[21]

The pastoral fiction, once employed in lamenting a pastoral poet, was easily extended to poets who did not touch on pastoral themes, and then to men who were not poets at all. The time was soon to come when as unpastoral a figure as Julius Cæsar could be dubbed Daphnis and made the subject of a shepherd's lament. Poor poet as he was, the author of the *Lament for Bion* has the credit of having established a permanent literary form.

The influence of the *Lament for Bion* extended farther than merely to establish the use of pastoral imagery in elegies on the death of real persons; many of the particular motives and ideas which characterize the later tradition may be traced to this first example of the form. The favorite application of the pastoral treatment continued to be to poets. Thus in later times Sir Philip Sidney, John Keats, Arthur Hugh Clough and Matthew Arnold,[22] have been mourned in pastoral song. Even when the person lamented is not primarily a poet, the writer is prone to adopt the old convention and refer to him as one of the sweet singers of the vale. Edward King was not a poet; but Milton did not forget that he wrote verse:

---

[21] The love motive is not wholly abandoned; we are told, for example, that the art of kissing has died with Bion. The psychological process of transferring to Bion the poet the attributes of a shepherd hero, may be observed in the following lines: "Not of wars, not of tears, but of Pan would he sing, and with herdsmen would he chant, *and so singing he tended the herds*."

[22] *Corydon, An Elegy, In Memory of Matthew Arnold and Oxford,* by Reginald Fanshawe, London, 1906.

"Who would not sing for Lycidas? He knew
Himself to sing and build the lofty rhyme."

This character of the shepherd as a poet gives rise to another
common motive: namely, the fiction that the writer of the elegy is
himself the poetical successor of the dead shepherd. In the first
idyl of Theocritus Thyrsis, who sings the lament, was, as Daphnis
had been before him, the most famous of the rustic poets. The
writer of the *Lament for Bion* professes to be heir to his master's
song.[23] This sense of personal relation as a poet to the subject of
his song justifies the writer in allowing himself digressions concerning his own poetic achievements and aspirations. In *Lycidas*
this tendency appears in the passage about fame, beginning:

"Alas! what boots it with incessant care
To tend the homely slighted shepherd's trade,
And strictly meditate the thankless Muse."

In the *Epitaphium Damonis* the digression is still more personal
and explicit.

Closely connected with the supposed superiority of the shepherd as a rustic poet, is the fiction that he is the particular darling
of all the creatures of the vale, and that they all lament his death.
The first suggestion of this motive was undoubtedly found in
Theocritus. Not only were the boys and maidens stricken with
grief at the loss of Daphnis, but jackals, lions, bulls, and calves
bewailed his death. In the *Lament for Bion* everything worth
mentioning in nature adds after its fashion to the universal moan.
Indeed, the first third of the poem is wholly given over to the
agonies of created things. In *Lycidas* we have the motive employed
in a passage which may be a direct echo of the *Lament for
Bion:* [24]

"Thee, Shepherd, thee the woods and desert caves,
With wild thyme and the gadding vine o'ergrown,
And all their echoes mourn.

---

[23] "To others didst thou leave thy wealth, to me thy minstrelsy" (1. 97);
Lang, p. 201.
[24] Cf. Bion, vv. 1 ff. and vv. 27–32. "Thy sudden doom, O Bion, Apollo
himself lamented, . . . and Echo in the rocks laments that thou art silent."

The willows, and the hazel copses green,
Shall now no more be seen
Fanning their joyous leaves to thy soft lays."

From this conventional use of the "pathetic fallacy" Milton, it will be observed, gets a very different effect from that of his Greek originals. For he does not dwell on the fiction that the natural objects express grief; he is taken up with the beauty of the things themselves. It is the description that we remember, not the conceit.

That Milton regarded the *Lament for Bion,* together with the first idyl of Theocritus, as a great classical original of the pastoral elegy is clear from the invocation in the *Epitaphium Damonis:*

"Himerides Nymphæ (nam vos et Daphnin et Hylan,
Et plorata diu meministis fata Bionis)
Dicite Sicelicum Thamesina per oppida carmen." [25]

Traces of direct imitation, on the other hand, are very slight. In addition to the lines quoted above, the flower passage in *Lycidas* has been cited as echoing the opening lines in the *Lament.*[26] The resemblance is a shade closer than to the similar passages in Virgil.[27]

With the *Lament for Bion,* the pastoral elegiac tradition in Greek, at least so far as we can trace it, comes to an end. The pastoral form was on its way toward complete decadence; it seemed on the point of total dissolution when it was revived in a new spirit by Virgil.

---

[25] The second allusion is to Theocritus XIII, an epyllion on the story of Hylas and Heracles. Strictly speaking the poem is neither a pastoral nor an elegy.

[26] Mustard, *op. cit.,* pp. 281–2.

[27] Moody in the Cambridge edition of Milton's poems (p. 321) remarks that the *Epitaphium Damonis* is formally an imitation of the *Lament for Bion.* Doubtless Milton had the Greek poem in mind when he wrote his Latin elegy; the similarity of name, as well as the lines quoted above, indicate this. But there is not a single passage in Milton's poem which shows unmistakably the influence of the *Lament for Bion,* while there are many which may be directly traced to Theocritus and Virgil. The two poems are also unlike in form; for Milton has the customary narrative setting as in Theocritus I, whereas the *Lament* does not purport to be sung by a shepherd at all.

## iii

The ampler strain in which Virgil bids the Muses sing his prophecy of the approaching millenium [28] is the keynote of a change in the style and spirit of the pastoral which is of the greatest importance in the history of the pastoral elegy. The tone of the Virgilian eclogue is determined not by the lightness and delicate urbanity of Theocritus, nor by the decadent beauty of his successors, but by the essentially dignified and noble genius of Virgil himself. With all his literary indebtedness to the Alexandrians, Virgil was thoroughly Roman; he was by nature an epic poet, and even in the bucolics he strikes the epic note. Corresponding to this change in expression, and intimately related to it, there came with Virgil a change in the nature of the tradition. The Roman poet, unlike his master, had never known a shepherd life like that which Theocritus describes; the peculiar conditions of simplicity and happiness which had existed in Sicily two centuries before could hardly have been found among the peasants of northern Italy at the close of the civil wars. Hence if Virgil was to write pastorals at all, he must either change the setting so as to bring it into accord with the rural life he knew, or he must accept the pastoral setting of his master as a literary convention. But the fiction of a shepherd contest was the very essence of the pastoral as a literary form. Accordingly, Virgil took the latter course, thereby completing the process of which we have seen the beginning in the *Lament for Bion*. From Virgil's time forth, conventionality in setting, adherence to an established literary tradition, is a marked characteristic of the pastoral.

That Virgil should have been willing to accept his pastoral setting ready made is partly explained by the fact that he was not particularly interested in this setting for its own sake. His purpose was first of all stylistic. There is in Virgil no such insight into character and dramatic situation as in the first and second idyls of

---

[28] Ec. IV, vv. 1 ff. "Sicilides Musæ, paulo maiora canamus!" etc.

Theocritus; there is no such variety of pastoral ideas and images. In compensation, the Roman poet has taken infinite pains to secure artistic finish. Each eclogue is a carefully constructed whole, usually beginning with something corresponding to an invocation and progressing to a definite artistic close. The verse is polished almost to a point of over-refinement. But style and form are not by any means Virgil's only interest in the eclogues. The methods of personal reference suggested by the practice of Theocritus and the author of the *Lament for Bion* are extensively employed by Virgil and turned to panegyric purposes. The pastoral was, with Virgil, to a large degree personal and allegorical; indeed, if we take the realistic idyls of Theocritus as the type, the eclogues can hardly be considered as pastorals at all.

This change in the spirit and intention of the pastoral in Virgil's hands was, as I have already remarked, of the greatest importance in the history of the pastoral form. It is not only that Virgil reinstated the pastoral and exemplified it in a language which was to be the literary medium for centuries; he also transformed it into an easy and serviceable instrument for a variety of literary purposes. It was no longer necessary to know anything about country life in order to write good pastorals; it was only necessary to know the pastoral formulas,—to be able to manipulate the pastoral machinery. Moreover, the pastoral was henceforth to be a garment that would fit all figures. It was a thin and graceful disguise for personal allusion, and especially for panegyric.

What, then, was Virgil's influence on the pastoral elegy? The form already had, as we have seen, a certain grace and pathos to recommend it; it suffered, at least in its later examples, from pettiness, from exaggeration, from erotic sentimentality. In Virgil's hands it was ennobled and made an instrument really worthy of the highest themes. True it is that there were few who could follow Virgil in raising the pastoral by exalted expression; but for those who could, Virgil had shown the way. Of all his successors in the higher pastoral vein, none had more clearly the spirit of the master than John Milton. He echoes the Roman's very lines in bidding his muse rise to the dignity of a loftier theme:

"Begin then, Sisters of the sacred well,
  That from beneath the seat of Jove doth spring;
  Begin, and somewhat loudly sweep the string." [29]

If Virgil had never written his eclogues, Milton might yet have
sung of the death of King in an epic strain; for such expression
was as native to Milton's genius as to Virgil's own; but it is not so
likely that he would have chosen the pastoral as the form in which
to cast his lament. With this elevation of the tone of the pastoral
elegy there comes also an enlargement of its scope. The character
of the subjects treated by Virgil, which are in many cases serious
and far beyond the narrow range of strictly pastoral interests,
brought the pastoral nearer to the elegy proper, in which we
naturally expect an element of contemplation and didacticism. It
also established a precedent for the introduction into the pastoral
elegy of a great variety of miscellaneous material, a practice of
which the invective against the clergy in *Lycidas* is a striking
example.

Two of the eclogues of Virgil, the fifth and tenth, are deserving
of especial consideration. Eclogue x is a love lament in imitation
of Theocritus i; but here the shepherd is no mythical Daphnis
but the flesh and blood poet, Cornelius Gallus, whose disap-
pointment in love is presumably an actual fact. The poem is
conventional in imagery, but sincere in feeling and elevated in
tone. It begins with an invocation of Arethusa.[30] There follows a
passage lamenting the absence of the nymphs from their accustomed haunts; then comes the inevitable lament for nature,
"Illum etiam lauri, etiam flevere myricæ." [31] The shepherds,
Apollo and Pan, come to offer their consolation. At length, as in
Theocritus i, Gallus himself bewails his misfortune, struggles for
a time against fate, then yields. The poem concludes with eight
lines in the regular style of the Virgilian close.

In general outline this poem resembles *Lycidas* much more

---

[29] Cf. above, n. 28.
[30] Cf. *Lycidas,* 1. 85, "O Fountain *Arethuse* and thou honour'd flood."
[31] I have used the Clarendon Press text of Virgil, rec. F. A. Hirtzel,
Oxford, 1900.

closely than any other of the poems of Virgil or Theocritus. In both we have an invocation at the beginning but no mention of the shepherd singer until the end; in both the motive of a procession of mourners is employed; both poems close with eight lines, very similar in spirit, referring to the end of day and the departure of the shepherd.[32] In addition to these general resemblances there are a few detailed borrowings.[33]

"Pauca meo Gallo. . . .
Carmina sunt dicenda: neget quis carmina Gallo" (vv. 2–3).

"Who would not sing for Lycidas?"

"Venit et agresti capitis Silvanus honore" (v. 24).

"Next Camus, reverend sire, went footing slow,
His mantle hairy, and his bonnet sedge"

"Sic tibi, cum fluctus subterlabere Sicanos,
Doris amara suam non intermisceat undam" (vv. 4–5).

"So may some gentle muse" etc.

Virgil's fifth eclogue marks a step in advance in the development of pastoral elegy; for here we have for the first time a lament for a great man who was not a poet and who appears, not in his own person, but disguised under a pastoral name. The Daphnis of the fifth eclogue is in all likelihood Julius Cæsar.[34] Reference is apparently made to his reputed descent from Venus, to his introduction into Rome of the Bacchic rites, and lastly to his apotheosis. The setting is the familiar dialogue of Theocritus I. Two shepherds, Menalcas and Mopsus, meet and sing together the death of Daphnis. Mopsus tells of the sorrows of nature for the shepherd's fate: the nymphs wept; lions, mountains, and forests are said to have uttered groans. Pales and Apollo have left the fields;

---

[32] The general resemblance between these two concluding passages, and several of the parallels quoted below, were first suggested to me by Professor Rand.

[33] There are several echoes of Eclogue x in the *Epitaphium Damonis;* cf. Ec. x, vv. 55–68 with *Ep. Dam.* vv. 35–43; also v. 42 with v. 71, v. 8 with v. 73, v. 63 with v. 160.

[34] The identification goes back to the time of Servius. See Connington's edition of Virgil, I, pp. 59 ff.

darnel and oats grow instead of barley, thistles instead of violets. Scatter flowers over Daphnis's grave and build his tomb. Then Menalcas concludes, addressing Daphnis as a god:

> "Candidus insuetum miratur limen Olympi
> Sub pedibusque videt nubes et sidera Daphnis."

The note of joy, thus introduced by Virgil with reference to the deification of the first Cæsar, is henceforth seldom or never absent from the pastoral elegy. In general, the resemblance between this passage and the end of *Lycidas* is not specific. Christianity has lent a new coloring to the consolation in the later poem. With the last three lines, however, where Lycidas is invoked as the "genius of the shore," the case is different. The conception contained in them is more pagan than Christian, and it is hard to believe that they would have appeared in *Lycidas* had not the idea held an important place in this eclogue of Virgil. The uncommon usage of the word "good" as the equivalent of "propitious" seems to rest on the word "bonus" in the Virgilian passage under discussion.[35]

The influence of the bucolics on *Lycidas* is by no means confined to the fifth and tenth eclogues. No edition of *Lycidas* has ever given anything like an exhaustive list of the passages in Virgil which Milton either borrowed or imitated. One can never feel sure that one has got them all; for they extend to the merest minutiæ, such as the borrowing of a single word. The beautiful passage in *Lycidas* beginning "Bring the rathe primrose" bears only a general resemblance to the similar flower groupings in the bucolics;[36] Milton is far more imaginative in his description than Virgil. The Roman poet speaks of "pallid violets," "waxen prunes," and "quinces with their tender bloom"; the English, of "cowslips wan that hang the pensive head." The reference to myrtles and laurels at the beginning of *Lycidas*, however, is

---

[35] "Sis bonus O felixque tuis!" (v. 65). Cf. also v. 61; "amat bonus otia Daphnis." I owe this point also to Professor Rand. The passages in *Lycidas* and Eclogue v should be compared with the similar one in the *Epitaphium Damonis*. See below, p. 159. The line "Æthera purus habet, pluvium pede reppulit arcum" and the expressions "Dexter ades, placidusque fave" serve to connect the latter with the Virgilian original.

[36] Cf. Ec. IV, 19 ff.; Ec. v, 35–40; *Æneid* VI, 883–4; cf. also above, p. 136.

clearly reminiscent of a line in Eclogue II.[37] In Eclogue III there is a touch of satire which reminds us of *Lycidas*.[38] The moving of natural objects to the song of a shepherd is twice mentioned in Virgil; [39] so, too, Milton's "smooth sliding Mincius, crowned with vocal reeds" is an echo of Virgil's "hic viridis tenera prætexit harundine ripas Mincius." [40] The phrase "Touched my trembling ears," used of the admonition of Phœbus, is borrowed from Eclogue VI. The beginning of the passage on fame, "Were it not better done as others use,/To sport with Amaryllis in the shade," is evidently modelled on Virgil II, 14–5: "Nonne fuit satius tristis Amaryllidis iras Atque superba pati fastidia." [41]

In trying to appraise the relative influence of Theocritus (including the *Lament for Bion*) and Virgil on Milton's pastoral style, it is necessary to take into account the fact that the Greek muse, as the first inspirer of pastoral verse, was naturally regarded as the more original and the more authentic. In *Lycidas* both the Greek and Roman pastoralists are invoked together:

> "O fountain Arethuse and thou honored flood,
> Smooth sliding Mincius crowned with vocal reeds."

But *Lycidas* is called a "Doric lay," and after the church digression, Milton bids the "Sicilian Muse" return. So, too, in the *Epitaphium* it is the "Himerides Nymphæ" who are invoked. On the other hand, as we have seen, the direct reminiscences of Theocritus in *Lycidas* are few, while those of Virgil are many. The latter passages, too, have been more completely assimilated; the Virgilian phrases are part and parcel of the style. It seems probable, therefore, that though Milton honored the Sicilian as his

---

[37] "Et vos, O lauri, carpam, et te, proxima myrte" (II, 54). "Yet once more, O ye laurels, and once more, Ye myrtles brown" (l. 1 ff.).

[38]     "Non tu in triviis, indocte, solebas
Stridenti miserum stipula disperdere carmen?" (vv. 26–7).
"Grate on your scrannel pipes of wretched straw" (l. 124).

[39] Ec. VI, vv. 27–28 (directly imitated in *Lycidas*, ll. 33–35); and Ec. VIII, v. 4.

[40] Ec. VII, vv. 12 13.

[41] Two further parallels might be given: Ec. I, 2, "musam meditaris"; cf. *Lycidas*, l. 66, "strictly meditate the thankless muse." Ec I, 84, "Maioresque cadunt altis de montibus umbræ"; cf. *Lycidas*, l. 190, "And now the sun had stretched out all the hills."

original and consciously incorporated some of his motives, he turned to Virgil with greater familiarity. It was the Virgilian rather than the Theocritean phrase which sprang first to his mind when he would express himself in pastoral terms. We may, perhaps, refer the gentler and sweeter passages in *Lycidas* to the flexible and sunny Greek of the author of Daphnis; we must certainly attribute the "higher strain," which is most characteristic of the poem, to the influence of him who could sing in pastoral verse—

> "uti magnum per inane coacta
> Semina terrarumque animæque marisque fuissent
> Et liquidi simul ignis."

It is perhaps significant that Milton, in changing from the harsh tones of invective to strains of pathos and beauty, invokes the presence of the Greek pastoral alone:

> "Return, Alpheus; the dread voice is past
> That shrunk thy streams; return, Sicilian Muse."

## iv

The paramount importance of the classical examples of the pastoral elegy, not only as establishing the type for future ages, but also as furnishing Milton with his most important models, has led me to dwell on the subject at considerable length. But these poems are not alone sufficient to account for the form of *Lycidas*, nor are they the only elegies to which Milton is indebted for motives, phrases, and minute turns of style. The pastoral elegy was greatly enlarged in scope by the freer treatment of the Middle Ages and Renaissance; it was to a certain degree changed in essence by its contact with Christianity. It remains, therefore, to examine the chief later modifications of the elegiac tradition, and to consider in particular those poems with which Milton seems to show familiarity.

The later Roman pastoral writers, Calpurnius and Nemesian,[42]

---

[42] *The Eclogues of Calpurnius Siculus, and M. Aurelius Nemesianus,* C. H. Keene, London, 1887.

had but little influence on the pastoral tradition. Their eclogues reveal the tendency inherent in the pastoral as interpreted by Virgil, to become more and more personal and allegorical. The pastoral writers are no longer content to suggest a personal application of the eclogue as a whole; but, following what they believe to have been the practice of their master, they attempt to give a meaning to each detail, to make each character in the dialogue represent a definite person. The pastorals of Calpurnius contain no elegy; Nemesian I, entitled "Epiphunus Melibœi," is a lament after the style of Virgil v, but containing possible reminiscences of Theocritus. The aged Melibœus is probably a real person, but there is no evidence for his identification. It is interesting to observe that the pastoral consolation does not appear in this elegy. Melibœus is said to be worthy of the councils of the gods, but not to have been made one of their number. In the ordinary pagan eclogue such a passage could find no place. Its occurrence in the fifth eclogue of Virgil was due to a special fact connected with the subject of the lament. With the introduction of Christianity into the elegy, the consolation became essential.

The slender stream of pastoral writing which connects the classical eclogues with the bucolic poetry of the Renaissance need detain us but a moment. The renewed tradition owes little if anything to the Middle Ages, but derives its source directly from the classical originals as interpreted by the allegorical method which had been applied to the works of Virgil almost from the start. The pastoral poetry of the Carolingian Renaissance has, however, an interest of its own, and one elegy belonging to this period deserves consideration here as illustrating the trend of the form in Christian hands, and as anticipating, if it did not suggest, certain important later developments. The poem is a lament for Adalhard, Abbot of old and new Corbeil, and was written by Paschasius Radbertus.[43] Two maidens, Galatea and Fillis, who prove to be personifications of the two monasteries, mourn for their abbot in alternate strains; as usual in the Carolingian eclogue, the writer is interested rather in the content than in the

---

[43] *Monumenta Germaniæ Historica: Poetæ Latini*, Vol. III, rec. Traube. pp. 45 ff. I owe my acquaintance with this poem to Professor Rand.

form. The pastoral idea had in it little to attract the writers of the circle of Charles, but fortified as they were with the allegorical interpretation of Virgil, they saw in the eclogue a convenient form for the expression of a wide variety of non-pastoral ideas. The pastoral setting tends constantly to fall away from the skeleton of the dialogue. Radbertus, in the poem under discussion, has not gone so far as to desert entirely the Virgilian model, but he has dealt freely with the form, and by introducing into this poem several new features has taken a further step in the progressive widening of the scope of the pastoral elegy. Chief among these features are the following: (1) extended praise of the subject of the lament; (2) abundant references to his life and work; (3) an invective against death (vv. 60 ff.) ; (4) a description of the joys of Paradise. The allusions in the poem to the immortality of the deceased were pretty clearly suggested by Virgil v, but they contain a note of joy and rapture which is new to the pastoral elegy and reminds us forcibly of *Lycidas*. Of particular importance in the history of the pastoral elegy is the confusion, or rather the direct combination of the classical pastoral imagery with the Christian figure of the pastor and his flock, which inevitably took place when the pastoral came to be treated by religious writers. In a Latin eclogue of the fourth century by Severus Sanctus, Christ is introduced as averting a plague from the cattle of a shepherd who worshiped him. In the poem just discussed, the identification of the two kinds of "pastor" and the two kinds of "flock" is clearly made. The connection thus established between the classical pastoral and the Christian religion served greatly to extend the utility and scope of the pastoral form. It opened the way, in the eclogue, for the treatment of matters ecclesiastical, and rendered the pastoral elegy as appropriate to the death of a member of the clergy as it was to that of a poet. The significance of these remarks will be clear when we recall the ecclesiastical satire in *Lycidas* and remember that Edward King had intended to enter the church.

It is not to an obscure elegy of the Carolingian Renaissance, however, that we must trace the direct impulse toward the introduction into the pastoral of ecclesiastical material, which was so strong in later times, but to the first users of the form in modern times, Boccaccio [44] and Petrarch. [45] Adopting the allegorical practices of the Middle Ages and following closely in the supposed footsteps of Virgil, these poets used the pastoral solely as a means of expressing their political, religious, and moral ideas. In Eclogues VI and VII of Petrarch an elaborate allegorical satire against the corruptions of the church is introduced. In Eclogue VI Pamphilus, Saint Peter in pastoral guise, rebukes Mitio, Clement V, who was leading a corrupt life at Avignon, for the ill-keeping of his flocks; in Eclogue VII Epy or France conspires with Mitio, whom she has corrupted. In the introduction of ecclesiastical satire into the pastoral, Petrarch led the way for Mantuan and Marot, who were followed in turn by Spenser. It is the latter poet to whom we naturally look as the predecessor in this respect of Milton. Yet the presence of Saint Peter in the satires of both Milton and Petrarch suggests a connection between the two works, [46] and it is quite possible that Milton had read the Latin eclogues.

The freedom with which Petrarch and Boccaccio treated the pastoral form in general is observable in their handling of the pastoral elegy, in so far as they entered that field at all. In the two or three poems of Petrarch's which can be called elegies, [47] the formal lament is subordinate to an elaborate allegorical setting. The classical motives appear, but not in great abundance. Boccac-

---

[44] *Carmina Illustrium Poetarum Italorum,* Florence, 1719, Vol. II, pp. 257 ff.

[45] Francisci Petrarchæ, *Poemata Minora,* Milan, 1829. Vol. I.

[46] The temper of the invective is much the same: Pamphilus in Petrarch's poem addresses Mitio thus:

> "Furcifer, hic, Mitio? nec te durissima sontem
> Sorbet adhuc tellus? Iam iam mirabile nullum est,
> Si nemus et messes atque omnia versa retrorsum
> Spem lusere meam. Cui proh! Custodia culti
> Credita ruris erat? Cui grex pascendus in herba?
> Intempestivis perierunt mortibus agni." etc.

[47] Eclogues II, X, XI. The first of these, an allegory on the death of Robert of Naples (Argus), is generally suggestive of Virgil V. The consolation at the close is untouched by Christian coloring. Eclogue X is not strictly speaking a pastoral elegy, since it contains no formal lament; it is rather the story of the shepherd's loss with incidental expression of his sorrow. The subject of the poet's grief is a cherished laurel (*i. e.,* Petrarch's Laura). His friend bids him solace himself, since the tree has been transplanted to the Elysian fields! Eclogue XI is a kind of debate between heavenly and earthly consolation. It concludes with two contrasting laments for the dead Galatea.

cio's interesting fourteenth eclogue, though it is rather a vision than a lament, is allied to the pastoral elegy by the elaborate description which Olympia, the spirit of Boccaccio's dead daughter, gives of Paradise and her happiness there. I am unable to find traces in any of these poems of direct influence on Milton's *Lycidas*.

The practice of making the eclogue a vehicle for didacticism and personal allegory, thus inaugurated by Petrarch and Boccaccio, characterizes in a varying degree the work of their successors in the pastoral literature of the Renaissance. The typical representative of this didactic tradition is Giovanni Battista, called Mantuan, whose ten eclogues, connected in a kind of series, and entitled *Adulescentia*,[48] were in the sixteenth century regarded not only as an ideal example of pastoral composition, but as a goodly moral work, more worthy of being put into the hands of boys than the eclogues of Virgil. They furnished the models for a host of later didactic dialogues, including the crude English pastorals of Barclay, and, in a degree, the *Shepheards Calender* of Spenser. The influence of this conception of the eclogue on the pastoral elegy was to open the way still further for the introduction of alien materials, personal, philosophic, and didactic. The long personal digressions in the *Epitaphium Damonis* and *Lycidas*, while they are hardly to be paralleled in any preceding elegy, are easily explicable when we consider that the pastoral ecologue had been used again and again since Petrarch as a means of expressing in a modest disguise the personal aspirations of its author.[49]

But while poets like Mantuan were handling the classical eclogue in what may be called the Mediæval spirit, the Renaissance had seized upon the pastoral for purposes of its own. Elaborating

---

[48] *Carmina Illustrium Poetarum Italorum*, vi, pp. 184 ff.

[49] Numerous examples of the Latin elegy may be found in the *Carmina Illustrium Poetarum Italorum*. I have examined the following: Ludovici Alamanni *Melampus*, i, 450; Petri Angeli Bargæi *Varchius*, i, 211; Balthasaris Castilionii *Alcon*, iii, 259; Maphæi Barberini *Julus*, ii, 60; Petri Bembi *Leucippi et Alconis Tumulus*, ii, 123; Nicolai Parthenii *Thyrsis*, v, 309, *Dorylas*, v, 321 (both of these poems are marine elegies, modelled on Sannazaro's *Phyllis*); M. Hieronymi Vidæ *Daphnis*, xi, 4; Actii Synceri Sannazarii *Phyllis*, viii, 365. Other elegies may be found in the collection of Latin bucolic verse entitled, "En habes Lector Bucolicorum Autores xxxviii," etc., Basel, Johannes Oporinus, 1546. I have not had access to this work.

the original pastoral motive of simplicity into the fully developed conception of the golden age, the pastoral writers of the Renaissance soon found a wider field for their activity. The new wine of Arcadianism could by no means be contained in the old bottles of the classical eclogue form; and the pastoral idea invaded the realms of the drama and the prose romance. These developments were, to be sure, reserved for the vernacular; but the renewed interest in the pastoral setting for its own sake had its influence, too, on the more conservative Latin eclogue, bringing about a more consistent employment of the pastoral machinery and a closer adherence to the original form. Especially important was the effect of the rediscovery of Theocritus, whose idyls, unlike the bucolics of Virgil, furnished models in which the interest was purely pastoral. It was no longer felt as essential, though it was still common, to conceal an elaborate idea beneath the "cortex" of the eclogue.[50]

From this renewed tendency to seek classical models, the pastoral elegy was not entirely exempt; the laments of the later humanistic writers are generally characterized by excessive conventionality and the absence of real grief. The *Lament for Bion* furnished an abundance of new motives, which were repeated *ad nauseam*. The interest of the pastoral poet was apt to be fully as much in the spectacle of the woeful shepherd and in the propriety of his pastoral language as in the substance of his lament. Nevertheless, the form remained of necessity personal, and might at any time in the hands of an individual poet be expanded to include new elements growing out of special circumstances connected with the subject of the elegy or his personal relation to the writer.

Among the few Latin elegies which are, like the *Epitaphium Damonis* and *Lycidas,* the expression of personal feeling, restrained through artistic combination with the conventional elements of the form, is Castiglione's *Alcon.* The poem is especially interesting for the present discussion because of its emphasis in

---

[50] For a general account of the pastoral literature of the Renaissance, especially Italian and English, see W. W. Greg's extensive work, *Pastoral Poetry and Pastoral Drama,* Oxford, 1906.

pastoral terms of the friendship existing between the dead shepherd and the singer of the lament. "We lived together from tender years," the shepherd sings; "we bore together heat and cold, nights and days; we fed our kine together. These flocks of mine were thine also." The resemblance between these lines and the passage in *Lycidas* beginning, "For we were nursed upon the self-same hill," is less striking when we consider how narrow the range of pastoral equivalents for friendship must necessarily be. The possibility of a connection between the poems is strengthened, however, by still another resemblance. Castiglione's shepherd regrets the fact that he was absent when Alcon died; and says he will build an empty tomb, "nostri solatia luctus." So the singer in *Lycidas*, "to interpose a little ease," fancies that he is decking the tomb of Lycidas. There follows in *Alcon* a flower passage like that in *Lycidas*.

The only other Latin elegy of the Renaissance which has, so far as I know, been suggested as having furnished material for *Lycidas*, is Sannazaro's first piscatory eclogue, a lament for the drowned shepherdess Phyllis, put into the mouth of a shepherd named Lycidas. Unlike the majority of the Renaissance elegies this poem is, apparently, pure fiction. It was characteristic of Sannazaro, who wrote the most famous of all the pastoral romances, and made his Latin eclogues an interesting innovation on the old tradition by shifting the scene from the plains of Arcady to the shores of the Bay of Naples, to be interested even when writing an elegy in the pastoral fiction for its own sake. We must look, then, in the poem, not so much for personal feeling as for a beautiful and appropriate handling of the old material. What must have attracted Milton to this poem, if he did indeed know it, is its felicity of style, and the circumstance that the lament is for one who had met death by drowning. The closest parallel to *Lycidas* is to be found in the passage in the Latin work in which the shepherd hails the departed spirit wherever it may be and bids it look towards its former home:

"At tu, sive altum felix colis æthera, seu iam
Elysios inter manes cœtusque verendos

Lethæos, sequeris per stagna liquentia pisces;
Seu legis æternos formosa pollice flores,

. . . . . . . . . . .

Aspice nos, mitisque veni. Tu numen aquarum
Semper eris; semper lætum piscantibus omen."[51]

In *Lycidas,* it will be remembered, the shepherd after speculating
where the body of his friend may be,

> "Whether beyond the stormy Hebrides," etc.,

bids his spirit "look homeward." Later he invokes Lycidas not
merely as a protecting spirit, as in Virgil's fifth eclogue, but
specifically as the "genius of the shore," and that in words almost
identical with those used by Sannazaro:

> "Henceforth thou art the Genius of the shore,
> In thy large recompense, and shalt be good
> To all that wander in that perilous flood."

The lines in Lycidas following that quoted above,

> "Where thou perhaps, under the whelming tide,
> Visit'st the bottom of the monstrous world,"

may perhaps have been suggested by an earlier passage in Sannazaro's poem, in which the shepherd declares that he will wander
through and over the sea, amidst its monsters.[52] It is interesting to
note, too, that Sannazaro as well as Milton mentions the name of
the not very familiar nymph, Panope.[53] These resemblances are
too striking to be the result of accident.[54] Sannazaro's eclogues
were among the best known of the Latin pastorals of the Renais-

---

[51] Vv. 91 ff. The passage is imitated in the close of the pastoral lament by
Nicholaus Parthenius, *loc. cit.* After declaring that Thyrsis is following the
happy fishes in Elysium, "felicior ipse," Mopsus addresses him as a god:
"O Corydon, Deus ille, altarum et numen aquarum;
Sis felix faustusque tuis."
[52] Vv. 72–75.
[53] She is mentioned twice by Virgil: *Æneid* v, 240 and 825.
[54] Nevertheless Milton's debt to Sannazaro is comparatively slight. Such a
sweeping statement as the following from the *Dictionary of National Biography* (*Sub* King, Edward) wholly disregards the existence of a conventional
elegiac type: "Milton probably modelled his poem after an Italian (*sic*)
eclogue entitled, 'Phyllis,' in which Phyllis' death is bemoaned by a shepherd
named Lycidas."

sance, and it is natural that Milton should have read them.[55]

From the new vernacular developments of the pastoral, the pastoral elegy in the stricter sense remained apart. Lovers' laments exist in the Arcadian literature of the Renaissance in abundance; laments for the death of imaginary shepherds may occasionally be found; but the renewed interest in the pastoral idea for its own sake, which is predominant in the romances of Sannazaro, Montemayor, and Sidney, excluded the lament for a real person. Such belong to the didactic and classical tradition of the eclogue, and when serious elegies came to be written in the vernacular they adhered more closely to the original forms. Even in the case of the fictitious elegy, the influence of the classical conventions remained strong. Eclogue xi, in Sannazaro's *Arcadia,* for example, is an almost slavish imitation of the *Lament for Bion,* with the addition of the inevitable consolation. Eclogue v [56] in the same work is, to be sure, composed in an elaborate lyric stanza rather than in the *terza rima,* which was the common measure for the didactic eclogue in Italian; but even in this poem there is hardly a motive which is not derived from the *Lament for Bion* or from the fifth eclogue of Virgil.

Of the vernacular elegies which preceded *Lycidas,* other than those in English, very little need be said. In general they conform to the type established by the Latin works and depend in large measure on the classics for their pastoral and elegiac motives. The process of transplanting and naturalizing the elegy was not, however, entirely without its effect. Conformably to the spirit and genius of the Renaissance, and to its freer conception of the pastoral, the elegies of the vernacular are somewhat richer in coloring, somewhat more prone to the use of fanciful ornament, than are the classical representatives of the form. The adoption of rhyme and in some cases of a less regular measure made possible a

---

[55] The influence of Sannazaro may be traced in England in Phineas Fletcher's *Piscatorie Eglogues,* which were published only four years before *Lycidas.*

[56] "Ergasto sovra la sepultura"; cf. also Ronsard, Ec. vi, "Sur le mort de Marguerite de France," *Œuvres complètes* . . . par M. Prosper Blanchemain, Paris, 1860, t. iv, p. 22; and Spenser's November eclogue in the *Shepheards Calender.*

more effective handling of the music of the dirge with its changing keys. The tendency of the didactic Latin pastoral to make the rustic setting merely perfunctory, as in the case of Mantuan, was somewhat checked; the vernacular elegies have rather more of the pastoral atmosphere and of the original grace of the pastoral imagery. On the other hand, the vernacular elegy was even freer than the Latin in its admission of personal references and digression. Ronsard's elegy on the death of Henry II,[57] though sung by a fictitious shepherd in the course of an elaborate pastoral contest, contains references to Henry's deeds under the slightest veil of pastoral imagery:

> "La sera ton Janot, qui chantera tes faits,
> Tes guerres, tes combats, tes ennemis desfaits,
> Et tout ce que ta main d'invincible puissance
> Osa pour redresser la houlette de France."

Deserving of particular mention among the French elegies, as the original of Spenser's November eclogue, is Marot's lament for Louise de Savoy.[58] The poem resembles *Lycidas* in having no one of the great classical elegies as its particular model, but employing motives from them all and handling these motives with unusual freedom. Notwithstanding the fact that Marot takes care in general to preserve the genuine pastoral mood, the poem is filled with personal allusions. We are told, for example, how "Bergère Loyse" used to lecture her shepherdesses (the maids of honor?) on the sin of indolence; and how they would straightway betake themselves, one to her needle, another to planting her garden, another to feeding doves. After a description of the happy state of the blessed spirit, which may have influenced Milton through Spenser, we have a flower passage, interesting as showing how this classical motive was inevitably elaborated and colored in the vernacular. One stanza may be quoted.

> "Passeveloux de pourpre colorez,
> Lavande franche, œilletz de coleur vive,
> Aubepins blanc, aubepins azurez,
> Et toutes fleurs de grand beauté nayfve."

---

[57] Ronsard, *op. cit.*, p. 22.
[58] *Œuvres Complètes de* Clément Marot, par B. Saint-Marc. Paris, 1879, I, pp. 485 ff.

The influence of the Renaissance pastoral in Italian and French may in a general way be traced in *Lycidas;* but it is improbable that Milton owes a special debt to any one of the Continental writers. He must of course have read the great dramas of Tasso and Guarini and the romance of Sannazaro; [59] he probably knew

> "Where other groves and other streams along,
> In nectar pure his oozy locks he laves."

A similar passage occurs in the eclogue of Ronsard, already mentioned:

> "Tu vois autres forêts, tu vois autres rivages,
> Autres plus hauts rochers, autres plus verds bocages,
> Autres prez plus herbues," etc.

many of the elegies. It is not surprising, however, if few of the latter impressed themselves upon his memory. Samuel Johnson, in his criticism of *Lycidas,* remarks that Milton owed the peculiar metrical structure of his poem to the Italians. This seems entirely probable. The irregular introduction of short lines and the use of an irregular rhyme scheme are characteristic of the choruses of the *Aminta* and the *Pastor Fido,* and they occur but rarely, if at all, in English poetry before *Lycidas.* But what Milton owes to the specifically Renaissance developments of the pastoral he derived not so much from the Italian and French direct as through the pastoral tradition of his native land.[60]

## V

First among the English pastorals in importance, and practically first in time, stands the *Shepheards Calender* of Spenser, published anonymously in 1579. The earlier attempts of Barclay and Googe were by that time forgotten, and Spenser regarded himself

---

[59] Eclogue v in Sannazaro's *Arcadia* contains a passage which Milton may have had in mind when he wrote the concluding lines of *Lycidas:*
> "Altri monti, altri piani,
> Altri boschi e rivi
> Vedi nel cielo, e piu novelli fiori."

Cf. *Lycidas,* ll. 174–5:

[60] The vernacular works of Luigi Alemanni, Antonio Fereira, Jean-Antoine Baïf contain pastoral elegies. Others may be found in the pastoral collection of G. Ferrario, *Poesie Pastorali e Rusticali,* Milan, 1808.

as a pioneer, setting out deliberately, as "E. K." tells us, "to furnish our tongue with this kind wherein it faulteth." From the publication of this work the stream of pastoral writing in English flows on without interruption until the date of the publication of *Lycidas*. Spenser's poem exhibited a striking divergence from the familiar pastoral tradition, and improvement on it. First of all, it combined in an unusual way the two main tendencies of the Renaissance pastoral, that represented by the Latin eclogue and that represented by the various classes of pastoral writing in the vernacular. Spenser drew without discrimination from the works of Mantuan, Sannazaro (both in his Latin eclogues and in his Italian romance), from the French eclogues of Marot, and from the classics.[61] He added, moreover, to the didactic elements of the eclogue and to the pretty sentiment of the Arcadian pastoral, a freshness of interest in rustic life and a lyric quality which are peculiarly Elizabethan and English. The eclogues of Spenser have little of the epic sweep of Virgil; they have rather the qualities of gentleness, grace, and rustic charm which are characteristic of Theocritus and are more congenial to the true pastoral.

The most important of Spenser's innovations in the pastoral was his introduction of artistic unity into a series of eclogues. Three of the eclogues[62] deal with progressive stages in Colin's love, and the moods of the poems change with the changing year. Now the story thus narrated is melancholy, even tragic, and the prevailing tone of the series, notwithstanding the fact that single eclogues are light-hearted or even humorous, is one of gloom. The poems in which Colin gives expression to his grief and despair are particularly mournful; they produce essentially the same effect as the first and second idyls of Theocritus, and are thus closely allied with the pastoral elegy. The series contains, moreover, one formal elegy, a lament "for some maiden of great blood, whom he, the author, calleth Dido." The poem, which is modelled closely on Marot's lament for Louise de Savoy, forms a striking contrast in spirit and style with *Lycidas*. The dominant characteristics of the

---

[61] See O. Reissert, *Spenser und die frühere Bukolik, Anglia* IX, p. 205.

[62] January, June, December; Colin's hard case is also discussed by Hobbinol in the April eclogue.

earlier poet's pastoral style were such as tended to emphasize the very qualities which pastoralism lends to the elegy, a grace and charm which relieve the sad theme and make grief more tolerable by surrounding it with images of beauty. The elaborate lyric stanza in which the poem is written gives an effect far different from the irregular versification of *Lycidas,* which is hardly lyric at all. The fact that Spenser adopts the form of his eclogue with little modification from Marot minimizes the personal element in the elegy.

Less conventional and richer in personal allusion but equally in contrast with *Lycidas* in tone, is Spenser's *Astrophel,* one of the numerous pastoral elegies on the death of Sir Philip Sidney. The prevailing note of gentleness is struck in the opening stanza of lament:—

> "A gentle shepherd borne in Arcady,
> Of gentlest race that ever shepherd bore,
> About the grassie bancks of Hæmony
> Did keep his sheep, his little stock and store.
> Full carefully he kept them day and night,
> In fairest fields; and Astrophel he hight."

The spirit of the closing lines of *Lycidas* has, to be sure, much in common with the above-quoted passage; but in general the later poem strikes a higher note than any heard in Spenser's pastorals. For a parallel in the pastoral to the loftiness of Milton's style we must go not to the *Shepheards Calender* nor to any English poem, but to the eclogues of Virgil.

Yet Spenser too had his share in supplying the pastoral material of *Lycidas.* Three poems in the *Shepheards Calender,* the May, July, and September eclogues, contain ecclesiastical satire; and one passage in the first of these bears a marked resemblance to the invective in *Lycidas.*[63] That Milton found in Spenser the best and

---

[63] May, ll. 38 ff.:—

> "Those faytours little regarden their charge,
> While they, letting their sheepe runne at large,
> Passen their time, that should be sparely spent,
> In lustihede and wanton merryment.
>
> . . . . . . . . . . . . .
>
> But they been hyred for little pay
> Of other, that caren as little as they
> What falleth the flocke, so they han the fleece

nearest precedent for the introduction of such material into the elegy can hardly be doubted. He may also have found there a precedent for bringing in allusions to his own poetic aspirations. The October eclogue sets forth "the perfect patern of a poet, which, finding no maintenance of his state and studies, complaineth of the contempt of poetry, and the causes thereof." Cuddie, the disheartened bard, laments thus to his friend Piers:

> "The dapper ditties that I wont devise,
>   To feede youthes fancie, and the flocking fry,
>   Delighten much: what I the bett forthy?
>   They han the pleasure, I a sclender prise:
>   I beate the bush, the byrdes to them do flye:
>   What good thereof to Cuddie can arise?"

And Piers replies:

> "Cuddie, the prayse is better than the price,
>   The glory eke much greater than the gain." [64]

The familiar passage in *Lycidas* about fame is prompted by the same feeling of the uselessness of poetic endeavor, and it contains a very similar turn of thought:

> "'But not the praise,'
> Phœbus replied, and touched my trembling ears."

The consolation in *Lycidas* resembles the close of the November eclogue to a marked degree; the parallels are, to be sure, little closer than in some of the other Christian elegies; but it is natural to refer the passage particularly to Spenser, from whom, aside from the classics, Milton would have been most likely to derive his conception. It seems probable also that the flower passage in *Lycidas* owes something to the lines in the April Eclogue, beginning—

> "Bring hether the pincke and purple cullambine,
>   With gelliflowers;

---

> . . . . . . . . . . . .
> I muse what account both these will make
> . . . . . . . . . . . .
> When great Pan account of shepeherdes shall aske."
> Cf. *Lycidas,* ll. 113 ff.
> [64] October, ll. 13 ff.

> Bring coronations, and sops in wine,
> Worne of paramoures." [65]

For Milton, like Spenser, adds to the conventional enumeration a considerable amount of fanciful description:—

> "Bring the rathe primrose that forsaken dies,
> The tufted crowe-toe, and pale jessamine,
> The white pink, and the pansy freaked with jet," etc.

The above-mentioned general parallels, together with a few detailed reminiscenses,[66] are, I believe, sufficient to place Spenser among Milton's direct sources for the pastoral tradition, second only in importance to Virgil.

The vast and multifarious pastoral literature which was written in England between the publication of the *Shepheards Calender* in 1579 and that of *Lycidas* in 1638, did little or nothing to modify the types established by the classics and by the Arcadian and didactic traditions of the Renaissance. In the eclogues and lyrics, the influence of Spenser continued strong, imparting to the English pastoral a healthier and more genuinely rustic tone than that of the sentimental Italian models which were dominant in the drama and romance.[67] Throughout this literature there was the usual proportion of pastoral elegies on the death of real individuals. A great impulse to this kind of composition was given by the death of Sir Philip Sidney in 1586, an inevitable subject for the pastoral lament. Most important of the tributes to Sidney was the series entitled *Astrophel*,[68] containing the Spenserian elegy already

---

[65] Ll. 136 ff.

[66] Cf. November, ll. 37–8:
> "For dead is Dido, dead alas! and drent,
> Dido, the greate shephearde his daughter sheene"
and *Lycidas,* ll. 9–10:
> "For Lycidas is dead, dead ere his prime,
> Young Lycidas, and hath not left his peer."
For a similar repetition see *Astrophel,* ll. 6–8. The phrase "scorn of homely shepheard's quill" (June, l. 67), seems to be echoed in Milton's "homely slighted shepheard's trade" (*Lycidas,* l. 65).

[67] For an account of the formal eclogue in English from the time of Spenser to the middle of the seventeenth century, see H. E. Cory, *The Golden Age of the Spenserian Pastoral, PMLA,* xxv, 2. Cf. also Greg. *op. cit.,* and Oskar Sommer, *Erster Versuch über die englische Hirtendichtung.* Marburg, 1888.

[68] First published in 1595; most of the poems must have been written shortly after 1586. The series is reprinted in the Cambridge Edition of Spenser, Boston, 1908, pp. 699 ff.

referred to, the *Doleful Lay of Clorinda*, written probably by the Countess of Pembroke, two poems by Lodowick Bryskett, and three non-pastoral laments. The volume contained also a long elegy by Spenser, the *Daphnaïda*, which, though pastoral in imagery and tone, has little relation to the formal elegy, being modelled on Chaucer's *Book of the Duchess*. Among the later elegies, William Browne's poem on the death of Mr. Thomas Manwood, the fourth eclogue in the collection entitled *The Shepheard's Pipe*, published in 1614, is frequently referred to as the source or inspiration of *Lycidas*. It is doubtful, however, if a single undoubted borrowing on Milton's part can be established. The poem, like a dozen others, belongs to the general type of *Lycidas;* it differs from the latter elegy, however, in having the narrative introduction, and in being without digressions. The passages which have been quoted in evidence of a connection between the two poems are of little weight in view of the extreme conventionality of the form.[69]

It is not likely that Milton was much impressed by any of the English elegies beside those of Spenser. Adhering in general to the established tradition, and offering little that was individual in thought or expression, they would, while carrying on the didactic and elegiac tradition to the very date of *Lycidas* and making the eclogue a contemporary type of literature,[70] simply range themselves in his mind with the three or four great examples of the form. Pastoral poetry had a remarkable faculty of holding to the

---

[69] W. W. Greg, *op. cit.*, p. 117, remarks that the only resemblance between the two elegies is the fact that the subjects of both were drowned; but Browne's poem contains no allusion to the circumstances of Manwood's death. One of the upholders of a connection between the two poems is Katrina Windscheid, *Die englische Hirtendichtung von 1579–1625*, Halle, 1895. The following is a fair specimen of the parallel passages cited by her in proof:

> "Milton: 'But O the heavy change now thou art gone.'
> Browne: 'But he is gone; then inward turn your light.
> Behold him there; here never shall you more.' "

The most striking resemblance is the closing stanza; but both poets are merely following the conventional Virgilian close.

[70] *The Shepherd's Oracle* by Francis Quarles, written a few years before *Lycidas* but not published till 1646, contains an abundance of religious satire.

commonplace. It was easy to write pleasingly in the pastoral style; to write in that style a poem that was really great, demanded a genius which could triumph over the restrictions imposed upon it by the fact that it must accept much of its poetry ready made. In all the long history of the pastoral before *Lycidas* there are three or four great names. For later writers their works sum up the pastoral tradition. It is to them that the poet will look for direct inspiration. Theocritus, Virgil, and his own Spenser,—with these Milton felt a kinship of genius; from them, when he chose to write at all in the most conventional of literary forms, he drew both the conventions themselves and the secret of finding his way beyond them into the realms of lofty and original poetry.

Yet *Lycidas* is to a remarkable degree the result of growth; "it gathers within its compass," says Greg, "as it were, whole centuries of pastoral tradition." The vast assimilative power of Milton had here its greatest opportunity; for the merit of a pastoral consisted not so much in its originality as in its faithful reproduction of the type. In one important respect Milton does indeed depart from, or rather greatly extend, the traditional practice: in no previous poem of the kind had the author introduced so many allusions to his own poetic career. The opening passage in *Lycidas*, the digression on fame, and the concluding line, are purely personal; in the *Epitaphium Damonis*, fifteen lines are devoted to a description of Milton's Italian journey and over twenty-five to an account of his poetic projects.[71] The introduction of ecclesiastical satire is also new to the pastoral lament. The other characteristics of *Lycidas* were without exception predetermined by the literary tradition of the pastoral elegy, and even for these Milton had, as we have seen, ample precedent in the pastoral at large.

---

[71] Vv. 125 ff. and 155 ff. The account in the *Epitaphium* of the former association of the two shepherds is very similar to that in *Lycidas* (ll. 22 ff.). The consolations have some specific resemblances apparently not due to their common original. There is also in the *Epitaphium* one pretty clear reminiscence of the phrasing of *Lycidas*:

> *Ep.* v. 28: "Indeplorato non comminuere sepulchro."
> *Lyc* v. 12: "He must not float upon his watery bier unwept."

In both poems Milton refers to the digression on his own aspirations as being in a higher strain. *Ep.* 160; *Lyc.* 87.

What, then, shall we say of *Lycidas* as a work of art? Is it the less a perfect whole because it is composite? Does the fact that it is conventional make it any the less original in the highest sense? If we know *Lycidas* well and read it in a fitting mood, we find ourselves forgetting that its pastoral imagery is inherently absurd. The conventions which at first seem so incongruous with the subject, gradually become a matter of course. And when once we have ceased to regard these conventions as anything more than symbols, we find them no longer detracting from the beauty of the poem, but forming an essential element of its classic charm. For the supreme beauty of *Lycidas* lies partly in the very fact of its conventionality. Its grief is not of the kind that cries aloud; it soothes and rests us like calm music. For a moment, indeed, we are aroused by an outburst of terrible indignation, but the dread voice is soon past and we sink back again into the tranquil enjoyment which comes from the contemplation of pure beauty, unmarred by any newness of idea, unclouded by overmastering emotion.

# 4

## Milton and the Return to Humanism[1]

It is now some two centuries and a half since John Milton gave forth his greatest poem to an alien world, consoling himself in the isolation of his evil days with the thought that, whatever its immediate reception might prove to be, *Paradise Lost* was a work of lofty thinking and uncompromising art which would always find "fit audience though few" and which "after times" would not willingly let die. Time has amply justified his faith. Through all revolutions of taste and thought, despite much "barbarous noise" of controversy and "detraction rude," the chorus of praise has risen in ever increasing volume. It would seem paradoxical to say that Milton has received less than his due measure of that lasting fame which was for him, though in his sterner thought he held it vanity, an object of intense desire. Yet, looking back upon the history of Milton's triumph over the judgment of mankind, one is tempted to affirm that he has fared but ill even at the hands of his most devoted friends. The mass of critical appreciation seems in large measure to have missed its mark, to have been, on the whole, perversely directed to aspects of his work which he himself would have deemed of secondary importance. It is not strange that it has been so. For the appeal of Milton, as of all the great forces in the literature of the past, has been conditioned by the moral and intellectual outlook of successive generations of readers, and in so far as the atmosphere of the later age has differed, vitally, from that in which Milton lived, criticism has inevitably suffered limi-

---

[1] Reprinted by permission from *Studies in Philology,* xvi, 1919.

tations. It has suffered, also, from the character of polemic which
so much of it has assumed. The ardent defense of Milton against
one charge after another leveled against him by enemies of his art
or thought has led of necessity to partial views. And as the dust of
controversy has subsided the discussions which have grown out of
it have come to seem unsatisfactory and incomplete. For the present generation even the "standard" interpretations and estimates
of the Victorian era savor too much of the special bias of the time.
Meanwhile the signs multiply of an important departure in Milton investigation and criticism. The number of studies which
have dealt anew with the themes of *Paradise Lost* and *Paradise
Regained,* have re-examined Milton's relations with Spenser
and the Elizabethans, have overhauled his doctrines in both his
poetry and his prose, have subjected to analysis his political as
well as his moral and religious philosophy, are evidence that the
effects of an altered viewpoint, which is itself the fruit of a new
age of experience, are beginning to be felt.[2] These studies are in
the main scholarly rather than controversial in character. They
aim at interpretation rather than defense. Out of them we are
about to write a new chapter in Milton criticism which, without
altogether invalidating the old, will testify to the enduring vitality
of the supreme works of human genius not for their art alone, and
will reaffirm the principle that poetry is a higher and more philosophical thing than prose. It is perhaps an appropriate moment to
pass in brief review the Miltonism of the past in its chief phases,
with the aim of defining more clearly the special character of the
new approach. Materials for such a review are already at hand in
recent monographs and articles devoted to the history of Milton's
reputation.[3] Discussion naturally centers in *Paradise Lost,* for in

---

[2] A few of the more significant contributions are: E. N. S. Thompson,
*Essays on Milton;* Alden Sampson, *Studies in Milton;* A. H. Gilbert, "The
Temptation Motive in *Paradise Regained"* (*Journal of English and Ger-
manic Philology,* 1916) ; Edwin Greenlaw, "A Better Teacher than Aquinas"
(*Studies in Philology,* 1917) ; H. W. Peck, "The Theme of *Paradise Lost"*
(*Publications of the Modern Language Association,* 1914) ; John Erskine,
"The Theme of Death in *Paradise Lost"* (*Ibid.,* 1917) ; and "Was Paradise
Well Lost?" (*Ibid.,* 1918) ; and R. L. Ramsey, "Morality Themes in Milton's
Poetry" (*Studies in Philology,* 1918) .
[3] R. D. Havens, "Seventeenth Century Notices of Milton," and "Early
Reputation of *Paradise Lost"* (*Englische Studien,* 1909, 40: pp. 175 ff.) ; John

that poem, by common consent, the influences which shaped Milton's art and thought met in the most perfect balance, and it is by *Paradise Lost* that his position in English literature is determined.

By a strange fatality the audience for which *Paradise Lost* was ideally intended had at the moment of its publication already ceased to exist. Conceived and partly executed in a time when the forces of the Renaissance had not altogether lost their potency and when a synthesis of the two great movements of the age was still possible, the poem was not actually given to the world until years of conflict had made an irremediable breach in the soul of man. Puritanism, indeed, outlived the Restoration, but it was a Puritanism narrowed and hardened into opposition to poetry, a Puritanism committed solely to conduct and no longer capable of being blended with art and thought. Its literary forms are the sermon and the tract and the didactic allegory. Such a Puritanism had existed in the earlier period, but until the civil wars it had existed simply as a check upon and a protest against the more extreme secular tendencies of the Renaissance. Milton's true kinship is not with Bunyan or Baxter, nor yet altogether with Cromwell and the heroes of the battle for religious and political liberty, but with those men of the older day, whose spiritual aspirations were united with the human passion for truth and beauty and who trusted the imagination as an important medium for the attainment of their ideals. Of the Elizabethans Spenser might have read *Paradise Lost* with a comprehending soul. So too in their degree might Taylor, the Fletchers, Herbert, Donne. Even in Milton's own day there were perhaps a few whose outlook was sufficiently akin to his—men like Marvel or the gentle and humane Colonel Hutchinson, or the musician Lawes, or Lawrence "of virtuous father virtuous son." But Puritans like this were rare and becoming rarer. In the Restoration period Milton stood alone, as unintelligible in his point of view to the author of *Pilgrim's Progress* as he was to Dryden and the literary wits of the court of Charles II. The point is often overlooked by those who, focusing their view on his Puritanism, conceive of him as a poet for the Puritans. Orthodox theology in the eighteenth century did

W. Good, *Studies in the Milton Tradition* (University of Illinois *Studies in Language and Literature*, 1915).

indeed derive some support from *Paradise Lost,* but no one surely will claim that Milton came to his own as a champion of the dying cause of Calvinism.

In the end it was, paradoxically enough, the wits and not the Puritans who first seriously undertook the criticism of *Paradise Lost,* and in their appreciations and discussions we may discover the initial phase of the perverted emphasis which has dominated Miltonic interpretation to our own day. Their efforts were directed primarily to an examination of Milton's poetic art in the light of the principles of poetry set forth by Aristotle and reinterpreted by the theorists of the neo-classic school. The process had already begun during the Restoration period when Dryden, taking a narrow view, finds in the "unprosperous event," the disproportion between the divine and human personages, and other technical shortcomings, a violation of epic principles. But the condemnation of Milton on these grounds could not satisfy the better sense of the critics themselves. Possessed of a more genuine responsiveness to sincere and lofty poetry than we sometimes give them credit for, they recognized the genius of Milton as they did of Shakespeare and desired to justify him on some valid and accepted critical basis. It was in this spirit that Addison in the next generation wrote the famous critique in the *Spectator,* vindicating Milton's epic art by a sympathetic analysis of *Paradise Lost* according to the method of Aristotle, with comparison of Homer and Virgil. Other critics fell back on the standard conclusion that Milton, like Shakespeare, was a great irregular genius, rising superior to rule. Dennis founded the poet's claims on the higher inspiration due to his Christian theme, and finally Warburton defined *Paradise Lost* as a new species of epic poem, deserving a place independent of but equal to the epic forms invented by Homer and Virgil.[4]

---

[4] "Milton produced a third species of poetry; for just as Virgil rivalled Homer, so Milton emulated both. He found Homer possessed of the province of Morality, Virgil of Politics, and nothing was left for him but that of Religion. This he seized as aspiring to share with them in the Government of the Poetic world; and by means of the superior dignity of his subject, got to the head of that Triumvirate which took so many ages in forming. These are the species of the Epic poem; for its largest province is human action, which can be considered but in a moral, a political or a religious view; and these the

It is unnecessary in this place to pronounce on the respective merits of these viewpoints. We have only to note that the discussion centered in questions of literary art. With the great controversy over Milton's blank verse which raged throughout the period it is the same. For the eighteenth century critic the major point at issue regarding Milton was the basis of æsthetic theory on which his fame must rest.

Now we must recognize that the attitude assumed in these discussions was perfectly valid as far as it went, and later critics along this line have had little to do but to choose and amplify one or the other method of approach as their critical creed or temperament inclines them to the classical or romantic estimate of æsthetic values. Milton himself invited consideration of his works from this angle, in his frequent claims of artistic relationship with the ancients, in his defense of blank verse against the "modern bondage of rhyme," and in his obvious consciousness of the formulated theories of epic and dramatic poetry which the Renaissance inherited from antiquity. Progress, therefore, was real enough in the critical treatment of *Paradise Lost* in the eighteenth century, but if it constituted in the end a pretty complete vindication of Milton's art, it contributed little to a fuller comprehension of his substance, led to no real interpretation of his greatest work, and furnishes no evidence as to whether this work was actually read in the spirit and from the point of view from which it was written.

Meanwhile, however, other notes were struck in eighteenth century Milton appreciation which concern themselves rather with substance and spirit than with form. A consideration of these developments will bring us forcibly to the conclusion that the dominant spiritual outlook of the period resulted in the playing up in Milton's work of values which were not the essential values and rendered the age incapable of seeing *Paradise Lost* in its true light.

In so far as the currents of eighteenth century thought set

three great creators of them: for each of these poems was struck out at a heat, and came to perfection from its first Essay. Here then the grand scene is closed, and all further improvement of the Epic is at an end." Quoted by Good, *op. cit.*, p. 160.

toward rationalism Milton, with his faith in the supernatural governance of the world and his recognition of the authority of the divine imperative within the soul, could waken little real sympathy. To the philosophers of the scientific dispensation the moral and theological system which had held sway in Milton's mind and with which he would have believed the poem bound to stand or fall, was dead. No longer valuing him for his ideas they were obliged, if they regarded him at all, to fall back upon his art. But the immense popularity of Milton in the eighteenth century and the high esteem in which *Paradise Lost* was held, were not primarily based on an æsthetic appreciation. Writers like Addison did not create the fame of Milton; they found him already in the field, holding his place against all comers. Their service was, by exploring the grounds of admiration, at once to increase its volume and to determine its direction. The *Spectator* papers, with their popular adaptation of the critical technique of the day, tended to justify the public in their instinctive choice. But already in Addison's critique much space is devoted to other aspects of the poet's work. In his running commentary on the separate books, as well as incidentally in the course of the formal analysis to which the earlier papers in the series are devoted, Addison emphasizes deeper values in the poem, the recognition of which came ultimately to make Milton seem like the prophet of a new era.

The turn of the century had seen an important change in the position of Milton in relation to the dominant thought and feeling of the age. During the Restoration the reaction against Puritan "enthusiasm," the cynical scorn of virtue, the repression of emotion in all its forms had resulted in a general lack of sympathy with the substance of Milton's poetry, while the unpopularity of the poet's politics served also to throw his merits into collapse. The political revolution of 1688 and the revolution in moral sentiment which attended it called his work again into esteem. Religion and virtue being no longer unfashionable, a religious poem commending virtue might be read with approval by a gentleman. The poetical tributes, with their emphasis on the poet's pure morality and on the divinely inspired character of his imagination fall in with the traditional admiration of the "sublimity" of his subject and the majesty of his style. There is, too, an increasing tendency to stress the emotional and human elements in *Paradise Lost,* in so far as these fall within the perceptions of its readers of those days. In a social age, as Good points out, the social features of the epic came in for particular attention, the more so because Milton had portrayed society in its elements and in an idealized form. It would appear from Steele that *Paradise Lost* in this aspect had already been introduced on terms of familiarity into the drawing-room life of the time. He represents a party of women remarking that Milton had said "some of the tenderest things ever heard" in the love speeches of Adam and Eve, and on another occasion he speaks of a fan on which was painted "our first parents asleep in each others arms." Steele himself never tires of quoting passages and commending "beauties" of *Paradise Lost,* selecting almost invariably scenes and speeches from the domestic life of the first lovers. And Addison, with a somewhat wider range, does the same. Much is said in the Critique of the "justice" and "beauty" of Milton's "sentiments." He is claimed to have "filled a great part of his Poem with that kind of writing the French critics call the Tender and which is in a particular manner engaging to all sorts of readers." In his discussion of the character and relations of Adam and Eve Addison writes almost entirely from this standpoint. The representation is said to be "wonderfully contrived to influence the Reader with Pity and Compassion." The characters are drawn "with such sentiments as do not only interest the Reader in their afflictions, but raise in him the most melting passions of Humanity and Commiseration." Detailed illustrations follow, particular emphasis being placed on the reconcilement of the sinning pair.

These passages should be read in the light of those other *Spectator* essays which comment on the domestic virtues, sentimentalize over conjugal affection, and look with indulgent commiseration on the weaknesses of man and woman which so often make their common pathway through the world a vale of tears.

We recognize at once that the emotional expansion of the era had opened new gateways of Miltonic appreciation, and we do not wonder at the degree to which he became an ally of the forward movements of the age. If, however, we consider for a moment the philosophical postulates which were behind the sentimental attitude we shall see why it was impossible for anyone deeply touched by the new creed to grasp the central reality of Milton's view of life. The cardinal fact is that the doctrine of original sin, with all its implications, had given way to the theory of the natural goodness of the human heart. The evil of the world is evil of circumstances only, and as such it is apparent rather than real, an inevitable part of the perfect system of the universe formed by divine intelligence. The logical consequence of such a view is the weakening of conviction regarding human responsibility, and with it the disappearance of all ideas of the tragedy of character. We see the operation of this principle in the eighteenth century drama of pity, in which the greatest crimes are condoned and attention distracted from the momentous consequences of moral choice to the misfortunes of those persons who because of wrong education or the overwhelming pressure of temptation pursue the wretched path which leadeth to the gallows. The effect of this attitude is apparent everywhere in eighteenth century comment on *Paradise Lost*. We feel it, for example, in Addison when he speaks of "the miserable aspects of eternal infelicity," and it gives ludicrous results in Bentley's cheerful alteration of the last two lines of Milton's epic from

> They hand in hand with wandering steps and slow,
> Through Eden took their solitary way.

to

> Then hand in hand with social steps their way
> Through Eden took, with Heavenly comfort cheered.

We may note also a final fruit of the softening of Milton's grim realities in Burns's humorous commiseration of Satan in the *Address to the Deil:*

> But, fare you weel, Auld Nickie-ben!
> O, wad ye take a thought an' men!
> Ye aiblins might—I dinna ken—

168

Still hae a stake:
I'm wae to think upo' yon den,
Ev'n for your sake!

Obviously it would be impossible for the eighteenth century man
of feeling to enter into the heroic consciousness of John Milton;
for him the Puritan poet's central theme of the operation of
divine justice through which Paradise was lost to man as the
consequence of his own sin and restored to him again by the
exercise of the righteous will, could mean nothing. We find in the
characteristic eighteenth century rhapsodies on Milton a steadfast
avoidance of this issue. A perusal of the long list of poetic tributes
quoted by Good will show that Milton lovers throughout the
period praise everything about the poet but the strength and
fidelity of his handling of the fundamental problem which he set
out to treat.

An intensification and a deepening of eighteenth century feeling for Milton was brought about by the rise of emotional religion. Men like Wesley found an important source of inspiration
in *Paradise Lost,* while to Cowper Milton, congenial both in his
art and in his religious thought, became an ever present companion in the daily meditations of the heart. The religious use of
Milton, which caused *Paradise Lost* as a devotional work to retain
even to the present day a place coördinate with *Pilgrim's Progress*
and second only to the Bible, hardly produces a critical interpretation, but it does involve a shift of attention to the spiritual and
meditative aspects of the poem. Thus the loves of Adam and Eve
received less attention than their pure devotions in Eden and their
ultimate reconciliation to the will of God. A closer sympathy with
Milton's deeper interests results, but it must be admitted that in
so far as the new religion partakes of the unchecked emotionalism
of the sentimental movement it is foreign to Milton's balanced
and temperate philosophy of life. The stern yet hopeful outlook of
the poet's creed had given way to a morbid melancholy. The idea
of man's struggle toward moral freedom, the sober consciousness
of difficulties and dangers which might yet be overcome by the
exercise of the firm and enlightened will was lost in the subjec-
tivism of the Methodist revival, with its insistence on sudden

conversion (an idea quite alien to Milton's thought) and its tendency to emphasize salvation by grace rather than by character.

The true measure of the eighteenth century reading of *Paradise Lost* is clearly given by a consideration of the various forms of the Miltonic influence in the literature of the period. Natural admiration for the poet's genius, the spell exercised by his exalted utterance, the fact that with all his irregularities he yet afforded the one great English model of epic poetry on classical lines, combined to make him a major force in eighteenth century poetry. In one aspect the Miltonism of the age is to be interpreted as a phase of classicism. The doctrine of imitation was extended to include the use of older English authors and Milton became a favorite model of style and form. As a pattern of the epic *Paradise Lost* completely dominated the eighteenth century. Thus the *Rape of the Lock*, despite its professed adherence to ancient models, owes perhaps more to Milton than it does to Homer or Virgil. With the serious epics of Blackmore it is the same. In style Milton is the father of eighteenth century blank verse, and here the influence joins with the currents which set toward the romantic movement. The deeper effects of the study of Milton are to be seen in Thomson and Cowper, who found in him the serious feeling, the reverent attitude, the sincerity and warmth of poetic utterance which they missed in the writings of the school of Pope. It is impossible to discuss this subject at any length. The point is that the influence of Milton was felt first of all in matters of style and form by poets who were utterly removed from him in spirit; and that even where it counted for the deepening of poetic sensibility it produced no re-embodiment of his philosophy of life, no attempt to carry further his imaginative presentation of the problem of evil, no echo, in short, of the humanistic attitude which he inherited from the Renaissance both on its intellectual and moral side. Alienated in interest and aim from the whole period the poet finds neither in its intellectual elite nor in its deeper emotional and religious natures more than a partial comprehension.

From the eighteenth century view of Milton to the nineteenth the transition is direct but strongly marked. The close of the century saw, on the one hand, an increased emphasis on the spiritual values in *Paradise Lost,* and, on the other, a tendency to make the poet a champion of radicalism in politics, religion, and art. Details of the romantic application need not be given here.[5] We may, however, note its most significant phases, and again raise the question whether it affords a view sufficiently in accord with Milton's purposes to be acceptable as a basis for critical interpretation.

The beginnings of a more liberally conceived justification of Milton's art we have already noted. The new romantic criticism revolted sharply against neo-classic standards and prided itself upon having rescued Milton, with Shakespeare, from the Procrustean bed of eighteenth century formalism. Setting a supreme value on the imagination as opposed to form or thought the romantic writers saw in Milton the English poet who above all others

> rode sublime
> Upon the seraph wings of ecstacy,

and they made, more emphatically than the eighteenth century appreciators had made, Milton's imaginative sublimity the true criterion of his greatness. They expatiate on the grandeur of his characters, his images, his verse, illuminating the Miltonic quality with a rich abundance of qualifying phrase. A typical essay is that of Hazlitt, whose treatment of Satan, for instance, considered as a piece of purely descriptive appreciation, can hardly be surpassed:

> The poet has not in all this given us a mere shadowy outline; the strength is equal to the magnitude of the conception. The Achilles of Homer is not more distinct; The Titans were not more vast; Prometheus chained to his rock was not a more terrific example of suffering and of crime. Wherever the figure of Satan is introduced, whether he walks or flies, "rising aloft incumbent on the dusky air," it is illustrated with the most striking and appropriate images: so that we see it always before us, gigantic, irregular, portentous, uneasy and disturbed —but dazzling in its faded splendor, the clouded ruins of a god.

Such a passage suggests the changed relationship of the new age to the poetry of Milton, on the æsthetic side. But the true secret

---

[5] A discussion of the romantic use of Milton in the eighteenth century is to be found in Good, *op. cit.,* pp. 208 ff.

of the Miltonic "revival" of the late eighteenth and early nineteenth centuries lies not solely, not primarily, in a revised estimate
of his poetic quality, but in a new interpretation of the moral and
spiritual content of his work—a new reading of his "message" to
the generations of mankind. It is here that the Romanticists give
us a new Milton constituted in their own image and worshipped
as they believed, at last in spirit and in truth. This new Milton is
first of all a seer, a mystic. His imagination is not so much a
quality of literary excellence as it is an instrument wherewith the
spirit of man is enabled to pass "the flaming bounds of time and
space" and be at one with supersensuous and divine reality. Such
he was to Blake, who, notwithstanding his abhorrence of Milton's
fundamental creed, had impregnated himself with *Paradise Lost*
as he had with Scripture and had fed his own distorted imagination with the poet's creations, unconscious of the impassable gulf
which yawned between himself and one whose most rapt imagination never led him for a moment to trespass beyond the bounds of
sanity. But more characteristically, perhaps, the romantic Milton
is an individual. Admiration for his art is lost in admiration for his
personality. His poetry becomes a sublime embodiment of will and
passion, an expression of the grandeur of soul which elevated him
above the pettiness of his human environment and made him stand
firm against the shock of circumstances. For Shelley and Byron he
is the type of the free personality, a hero in the warfare against the
tyranny of law. It is thus that Shelley apostrophizes him in *Adonais:*

> He died,—
> Who was the sire of an immortal strain,
> Blind, old, and lonely, when his country's pride,
> The priest, the slave, and the liberticide,
> Trampled and mocked with many a loathed rite
> Of lust and blood; he went, unterrified,
> Into the gulf of death; but his clear Sprite
> Yet reigns o'er earth; the third among the sons of light.

And Byron in the Dedication to *Don Juan:*

> If, fallen in evil days on evil tongues,
> Milton appealed to the Avenger, Time,
> If Time, the Avenger, execrates his wrongs,

And makes the word "Miltonic" mean "sublime,"
He deign'd not to belie his soul in songs,
Nor turn his very talent to a crime;
He did not loathe the Sire to laud the Son
But closed the tyrant-hater he begun.

The "sublimity" of Milton thus becomes a personal quality—sublimity of soul. His works are interpreted in the light of his career, and are read as the record of his life-struggle. This attitude marks an important advance over the sentimental or the purely literary approach of the eighteenth century; its limitation is to be sought in the essential contradiction between the Miltonic and the romantic ideal of character. For Byron, and, to a large extent, Shelley, make Milton what he assuredly was not, an individualist like themselves, averting their eyes from the fact that the controlling principle of his life was after all not rebellion but free obedience. The official morality of *Paradise Lost* is discountenanced; Milton's insistent condemnation of Satan as the inversion of all good is ignored. The poet becomes a witness in spite of himself to the absolute value of "the will not to be changed by time or place" and a chief assailant of the moral and theological system of which he had innocently supposed himself to be a chief defender. Thus *Paradise Lost* is made the text of works and the source of sentiments the purport of which its author would not even have comprehended. From such discipleship as that of the creator of Cain and Manfred the great Puritan would surely have prayed to be delivered. The "fit audience though few" would not have included Byron, and the fame arising from his praise would have sounded something worse distorted than the vain plaudits of the "herd confused" who extol things vulgar and admire they know not what. The poet has himself pronounced the fitting condemnation:

Licence they mean when they cry liberty;
For who loves that, must first be wise and good.

With Shelley the case stands somewhat differently. Inspired to resistance, not by mere passion and expansive egoism, but by a clearly discerned ideal of good, he saw Milton engaged, like him-

173

self, in a heroic conflict with the principle of evil in its earthly manifestations of tyranny and injustice. But for Shelley the principle of evil is incarnate in tradition and comes dangerously near to being identical with law itself. Hence in *Prometheus Unbound,* which more than any other of his works was written under the inspiration of *Paradise Lost,* the typical utterance of the enchained Titan has a Satanic ring. His protest is against government itself, and not solely against government which is tyrannical and corrupt; and, what is more serious, he is an uncompromising enemy of historical Christianity, particularly on its Hebraic side. With such an attitude Milton could have had nothing in common. Had Shelley been less inclined to look in the works of poets he admired as in a mirror, finding there solely an image of himself, he might have remembered that his hero's ideal of government was embodied in the regime of Oliver Cromwell and that his personal religion and morality were squarely founded on the Hebrew Scriptures. Evidence of Shelley's complete inversion of the Miltonic viewpoint is to be found in the following judgment on the morality of *Paradise Lost:* "Milton's Devil, as a moral being, is as far superior to his God as one who perseveres in some purpose which he has conceived to be excellent in spite of adversity and torture, is to one who in the cold security of undoubted triumph, inflicts the most horrible revenge upon his enemy, not from any mistaken notion of inducing him to repent of a perseverance in enmity, but with the alleged design of exasperating him to deserve new torments." In other words Satan and God stand in exactly the relation of Prometheus and Jupiter, and it is in Satan that Shelley finds the true embodiment of Milton's personality and of his moral ideal.

Wordsworth takes a saner view of Milton's personality. He has little to say of his rebellion, much of his stern righteousness and uncompromising idealism. To him the "sublimity" of Milton is a sublimity of character and spiritual insight, not one of passion and will. He invokes the poet's influence against the selfishness and base materialism of the times, crying, as every age has done and will do:

# MILTON AND THE RETURN TO HUMANISM

Milton, thou should'st be living at this hour.

In the noble ode in which he formally renounces the authority of impulse in favor of that of the moral law he catches the very phrase with which he addresses his new divinity from Milton's lips:

> Stern *daughter of the voice of God,*
> O Duty, if that name thou love.

All this brings Wordsworth very close to the spirit of Milton; it should be noted, however, that his appreciation of Milton is chiefly biographical, and gives no interpretation of *Paradise Lost,* though it points the way to one. Wordsworth shares in the tendency of his age to read Milton's works subjectively, as a personal record, ignoring the objective values which the formal eighteenth century criticism, whatever its limitations, is to be commended for having sought. Characteristically he derives his chief inspiration, not from the epics or dramas, but from the sonnets, the most personal of Milton's works.

As regards interpretation it was the emphasis given by men like Shelley and Byron rather than that of Wordsworth that was destined to survive. Though, to be sure, the excesses of Satan worship did not outlive the Byronic philosophy of life of which they were an essential part, it is not too much to say that later nineteenth century criticism has been largely dominated by the romantic point of view. For most critics Satan has remained the real, if not the technical hero of *Paradise Lost.* The earlier books of the poem have been admired at the expense of the whole, as by Macaulay, who remarked that Milton's reputation would have stood higher if he had written only the first four. The personality of the poet has been sought everywhere in his works and even his most objective utterances have been treated as expressions of his private point of view. That these values exist in *Paradise Lost* no one will for a moment deny. Considered as a whole the romantic appreciation of Milton is more vital, surely, than the Augustan and has justly enough discountenanced it. It has led, however, to the neglect of values not less vital, has distracted attention from important aspects of the poet's genius, and, above all, has stood in the way of a full acceptance of *Paradise Lost* as an embodiment of human truth, a poetic application, in Arnold's phrase, of moral ideas to life.

The fundamental difficulty in the nineteenth century approach to Milton is, after all, identical with that of the eighteenth. It lies in the fact that in either age his way of thought—not his theology only, but his general attitude and outlook—was felt to be obsolete. In the eighteenth century it encountered the general scepticism and materialism of the intellectual classes or the enervated amiability of sentimentalism; in the nineteenth it was supplanted by a new idealism, which, having just escaped the shackles of orthodoxy, reacted against the irrationality of Milton's hard and coherent system of theology and, even more violently, against the materialistic terms to which he reduces supersensuous reality. He is unfavorably contrasted in this respect with Dante, whose Heaven of light, and love, and pure spirit is set against Milton's battlemented and bejewelled city of God, which, despite its splendors, is, as Milton has taken pains to make it, analogous at all points to earth. The same indictment is drawn against the naive materialism of Milton's entire narrative, which is held to do violence even to his own best thought. When, for example, Satan affirms that "the mind is its own place" and when Gabriel holds up to Adam's contemplation "a paradise within thee happier far" Milton has seemed to be transcending the limitations of Puritanism and to be speaking the language of modern idealism, but these utterances are felt to be in contradiction with the basic assumptions of the poem. The idea of a Heaven and Hell of spirit has seemed to accord but ill with the tragedy of the fall, with the facts of Satan's revolt, and with the constitution of a material Hell. To insist on such doctrines would be "to shatter the fabric of the poem." They must not, therefore, be insisted on. From the standpoint of idealism the substance of *Paradise Lost* must be condemned and the whole poem be regarded as an absurd but glorious fiction, based on an obsolete tradition which Milton naively accepted and which he exalted by virtue of his poetic power.

This, essentially, is the view taken by Sir Walter Raleigh, whose work on Milton must rank as the most brilliant treatment of the poet's art in the history of nineteenth century criticism. The study is, indeed, too broad and rich to be confined within a formula, but despite the freshness and sympathy of its treatment and the fullness with which it voices the accumulated wisdom regarding Milton of preceding generations of critics, it is yet limited in scope by preconceptions which its author holds in common with writers like DeQuincy, Masson and Pattison, not to mention others of a still earlier school. In his discussion of the scheme of *Paradise Lost* Raleigh is chiefly concerned with noting the insuperable difficulties imposed not merely upon our belief but on our imagination by the necessity Milton was under of giving "physical, geometric embodiment to a far-reaching scheme of abstract speculation and thought—parts of it very reluctant to such treatment." This undoubtedly is sound, but it assumes that the abstract speculation, namely the theology, and not the human reality which coexists with it and takes its significance partly but only partly from it, constitutes the true substance and content of the poem. For Raleigh *Paradise Lost* is neither more nor less than "an imposing monument to dead ideas." When he comes to deal with the characters of the poem Raleigh's failure to rate the moral insight of Milton at its true value leads him to judgments to which it is impossible for the present writer to subscribe. By exalting the grandeur of Satan Milton is said to have "stultified the professed moral of the poem and emptied it of all spiritual content, led by a profound poetic instinct to preserve epic truth at all costs." In his treatment of Adam and Eve he is felt to be dealing essentially with unrealities. Raleigh, though he does not go to such lengths of ridicule as Taine, sees Adam as little better than a stupid and wooden projection of the more forbidding elements of Milton's Puritan personality. To Eve he allows a certain degree of humanity, but he makes her chiefly the vehicle of a Miltonic diatribe against woman. The concluding judgment is stated quite flatly. "While Milton deals with abstract thought or moral truth his handling is tight, pedantic, and disagreeably hard. But when he comes to describe his epic personages, and his embodied visions, all is power, and vagueness, and grandeur. His imagination, escaped from the narrow prison of his thought, rises like a vapor, and, taking shape before his eyes, proclaims itself his master."

Now all that Raleigh or any critic claims for the grandeur of Milton's imagination is undeniably true, but it is to be doubted if the poet himself would have valued an immortality of fame accorded to him only on such terms. The theme of his epic was to him no poetic fiction, and a judgment of his work based on this assumption would have outraged his deepest convictions. For him at least the fall was true, and the conviction of its truth is a condition of the entire sincerity of his treatment. The subject was dignified in his mind, not by its grandeur, but by its superior validity as an explanation of human experience. For it he had discarded the Arthurian material; into it he had thrown his heart. That readers for whom it was no longer in some sense true could by any means enter into a full understanding of his work he would never have believed.

For most modern readers the nineteenth century estimate, as embodied in Raleigh's *Milton,* is the final estimate. The poem is read, if read at all, for its art, its eloquence, its elevation. The events which it recounts and Milton's interpretation of those events are felt to belong to an order of belief which can possess, at best, but a curious historic interest. The poem remains, in Raleigh's phrase, "a monument to dead ideas." It is, of course, of little avail to attempt to restore *Paradise Lost* to its original authority by asking such readers to suspend their disbelief and adopt the convictions which underlie it simply because, without them, it is impossible to regard the work with Milton's eyes. If Milton's thought is really dead it is impossible to galvanize it into life. But it is to mistake the real drift of the newer Miltonic study to assume that it proposes any such factitious rehabilitation of *Paradise Lost.* It proposes rather, as I read it, a reinterpretation and a revaluation of the poem in terms neither of sentimentalism nor of romanticism nor of Victorian idealism but of humanism, and it seeks as a first step toward such revaluation to see Milton's philosophy as a whole by exploring his prose as well as his poetry, to set him in his right relation, not to Puritanism alone, but to the entire Renaissance, and so to realize, through a richer understanding, the significance of his work as poetic criticism of life.

For such a reinterpretation of Milton the way is paved by the fact that the Calvinistic theology is no longer a subject of controversy. It has become possible at last to approach him dispassionately, with due sympathy for whatever we may recover permanently true and valid from the religious thought of the age. Indeed the virtues of the orthodox way of thinking are quite as apparent to us now as its defects. Thus Chesterton maintains intelligibly enough the validity of the doctrine of original sin. Certainly our reaction against the facile optimism of Victorian religious liberalism, which banished Satan to the limbo of illusion and discovered the joyous fact that all roads lead to Heaven though it were through Hell, has tended to restore to us in a marked degree the moral atmosphere in which Milton lived. Finally the tendency to find sanity and truth in the ideas of the Renaissance has infused new zeal into an Elizabethan scholarship not always so divorced from its human objectives as the critics of our Germanized research would have us believe, with the result that there has been constructed a sounder basis for Miltonic criticism than that afforded by the biographical history of Masson.

The outstanding effect of the study of Milton's philosophy as embodied in his poetry and prose, and of the endeavor to relate him more closely to his English predecessors has been to minimize the importance of his theology in the narrower sense, and to exalt in its place, not merely his art and eloquence and imagination, but those elements of insight and reflection which he holds in common with Spenser, Hooker, Shakespeare, and Bacon—men in whose work the northern and southern currents of the age are fused in that richer and profounder creative humanism which is the special contribution of the English Renaissance. The essential character of that humanism is its assertion of the spiritual dignity of man, its recognition of the degree to which his higher destinies are in his own hands, its repudiation of the claim of his lower nature to control his higher or of any force or agency external to his own mind and will to achieve for him salvation. This humanism is sharply and irreconcilably at odds with mediæval thought.

It discards, first of all, the ascetic principle and releases for enjoyment and use all the agencies of self-realizing perfection. It proposes, moreover (and this is its essential character) to achieve its goal through the study not of God but of man and it trusts the human reason as well as intuition and revealed truth as the instrument of its knowledge. It turns, therefore, to Scripture for the best record of man's nature in its relation to the God of righteousness and love, then to the *litterae humaniores* of antiquity, where it finds a wider revelation of man as an individual and a citizen, this latter source constituting no denial but a completion of the data afforded by the former.

Now Milton, throughout his life, was a humanist in both his method and his aim. Though inheriting certain mediæval tendencies in thought and art, the bent of his mind, as R. L. Ramsay has shown, carried him further and further away from them. He retains to be sure certain fundamental postulates and assurances in common with mediæval Christianity. He is convinced of God, of the fact of evil, of the inevitableness of retribution, and of the hope of Heaven. These postulates are the postulates not of Puritanism alone but of the total humanism of the Renaissance. They are absolutely vital to Milton's thought. The intellectual scaffolding with which they are supported and which, because the subject demanded it, is given in *Paradise Lost,* though not in *Paradise Regained* or *Samson,* is not thus vital. The real "system" which Milton erects is not a theology but an interpretation of experience, based on the bed rock of human freedom, and formulated under the guiding influence of the Bible, the ancients, and the thinkers and poets of the preceding generation.

To embody such ideas as were really living in Milton's consciousness in imaginative form was in no sense a work of violence. His imagination, instead of "proclaiming itself his master," in the way in which it proclaimed itself, for example, Blake's master, because he surrendered himself wholly to it, is for Milton the powerful instrument wherewith, following methods analogous, in some ways to those of Spenser, in others to those of Shakespeare, he gives to his philosophy of life a local habitation and a name. Nor is he greatly hampered by the literalness of his acceptance of the data afforded by the Biblical tradition. For if the events connected with the fall of man were to him literal facts they were also symbols, and it is upon the rock of their symbolic or universal rather than of their literal and particular truth that his faith was based. In his treatise on Christian Doctrine Milton boldly avows the principle of Biblical interpretation which controls his treatment of the subject matter of *Paradise Lost*. The expressions of Scripture are indeed to be accepted in their literal sense, but they are to be interpreted by the individual judgment and in accord with the superior revelation of the Inner Light, which in the language of the poet's art means nothing less than the inspired imagination. In *Paradise Lost* Milton affirms that the account of the battle in Heaven is merely a way of representing spiritual truth to the human understanding. Obviously his belief is anything but naive. And as to the actual experience of Adam and Eve, not to mention the desperate plot of evil men in Hell to overthrow the reign of righteousness and law, they are richer in human truth than anything in English imaginative literature outside of Shakespeare, and Milton has been able to give them wide and permanent significance by virtue of a lifetime spent in the study of man's nature in its relation to the moral and spiritual forces by which his destiny is shaped.

In this view, therefore, Milton is no mere poetic voice speaking irrationalities, nor yet simply a transcendent imagination, but a poet of humanity, and *Paradise Lost* is primarily the epic of man's moral struggle, the record of his first defeat and the promise of his ultimate victory. Its necessary counterpart is *Paradise Regained,* in which that promise is fulfilled by the spiritual triumph of the human Christ.

Such is the emphasis toward which the Miltonic scholarship of the present day inevitably leads us. This scholarship is, in general, an outcome of the return to humanism, and contemporary humanists, whatever their special creed, should rejoice in the result. For Milton freed from the perversities of pseudo-classicism, sentimentalism, and romanticism, viewed without controversial rancor, and brought into line with his great predecessors of the Renaissance, is surely an ally. The true Milton is subject to no

181

one of the counts in the fierce indictment which Babbitt, and
More, and Sherman are directing against the literature of our own
day and of our romantic past. Deeply sympathetic with the aspirations of men toward freedom of life he yet esteems freedom only as
the essential condition for the functioning and self-development
of the "inner check." Outward freedom and inward control or
freedom with discipline is the authentic humanistic formula
which Milton applies in all the domains of education, politics,
morality, religion, and art. Champion of liberty though he is he
yet knows that

> orders and degrees
> Jar not with liberty but well consent.

The Platonic subordination of the lower faculties of man to the
higher is the central doctrine of his philosophy of life. Yet he
avoids the danger of asceticism inherent in Plato's thought, con-
demning the Utopian politics of the *Republic* and repeatedly
vindicating the free use of all the instrumentalities of man's self-
realization. In the intellectual sphere, filled as he is with the zeal
of knowledge and willing to toil unendingly in the search for the
scattered members, even to the smallest, of the sacred body of
truth, he yet affirms that

> Knowledge is as food and needs no less
> Her temperance over appetite,

and he permits the angel to warn Adam to

> Think only what concerns thee and thy being.

a sentence which, well pondered, might serve as a text for the
whole humanistic indictment of the scientific preoccupations of
today. In religion he does not rest with "vague intuitions of the
infinite," though he is not without them, but soberly worships the
God of righteousness whose dwelling is the heart of man. Finally,
in art he knows what he wants and knows how to attain it.
Creative and original, untrammelled in his effort to realize to the
full his imaginative conception and untouched or nearly so by the
formalism of the neo-classic creed, he is yet obediently loyal to the
laws of a disciplined taste and he is wisely regardful of the an-

cients, those "models as yet unequalled of any" in excellence of literary form.

These profound convictions put Milton clearly on the side of contemporary humanism, a humanism which, however "new," is not without its essential community with the old. Such in future appreciation he will more and more be felt to be. We have insisted too long on the supposed austerity of his temper and on the narrowness of his Puritan thought; we have misinterpreted the character of the change in viewpoint of his later years and have failed to perceive that instead of passing farther from the Renaissance he had moved nearer to its central truths. Finally, adopting Arnold's hard and fast distinction of Hebraism and Hellenism, we have assumed too readily that the Reformation and the Renaissance are in Milton contradictory and irreconcilable motives, omitting to credit him with a conscious and consistent endeavor to harmonize them, which at least challenges attention. This, indeed, is Milton's peculiar contribution to the cause and philosophy of humanism, and there is a special significance in the fact that his is the final word of the whole era. Not earlier perhaps, was even an attempt at such a conscious synthesis possible, and without the aid of poetry it could hardly even so have been accomplished. Due allowance being made for an antiquated manner of expression, Milton has given as goodly and comprehensive a formula for the aim and method of education as is to be found in the literature of the Renaissance or as any humanist could wish:

The end then of learning is to repair the ruins of our first parents by regaining to know God aright, and out of that knowledge to love him, to imitate him, to be like him, as we may the nearest by possessing our souls of true virtue, which being united to the heavenly grace of faith, makes up the highest perfection. But because our understanding cannot in this body found itself but on sensible things, nor arrive so clearly to the knowledge of God and things invisible, as by conning over the visible and inferior creature, the same method is necessarily to be followed in all discreet teaching. And seeing every nation affords not experience and tradition enough for all kinds of learning, therefore we are chiefly taught the languages of those people who have at any time been most industrious after wisdom. . . . I call therefore a complete and generous education, that which fits a man to perform justly, skilfully and magnanimously all the offices, both private and public, of peace and war.

Complementary to this is his description of the poet's function:

These abilities, wheresoever they may be found, are the gift of God,
rarely bestowed, but yet to some (though most abuse) in every nation;
and are of power, beside the office of a pulpit, to inbreed and cherish
in a great people the seeds of virtue and public civility, to allay the
perturbations of the mind, and set the affections in right tune; to
celebrate in glorious and lofty hymns the throne and equipage of
God's almightiness, and what he works, and what he suffers to be
wrought with his providence in his church; to sing the victorious
agonies of martyrs and saints, the deeds and triumphs of just and pious
nations, doing valiantly through faith against the enemies of Christ; to
deplore the general relapse of kingdoms and states from justice and
God's true worship. Lastly, whatsoever in religion is holy and sublime,
in virtue amiable and grave, whatsoever hath passion or admiration in
all the changes of that which is called fortune from without, or the
wily subtleties and refluxes of man's thoughts from within; all these to
paint out and describe with a solid and treatable smoothness.

There is little need to quarrel with the didactic bias of Milton's
theory. It imposes no necessary limitation on the scope of his art,
but merely commits him to a high seriousness of purpose which is
in accord with the best traditions of the age. Its practical results
are *Paradise Lost, Paradise Regained,* and *Samson Agonistes,*
works in which the total Renaissance is summed up and revealed
as one, through a harmony of its great ideals of beauty, righteousness, and truth. Such a harmony, though made, no doubt, in
the special language of the times, is valid for all times. We shall
yet learn, it may be, to regard Milton as a more authentic spokesman than we had believed of three great centuries by no means
silent, and we shall know his as a powerful voice of guidance amid
the chaos of the present day.

# 5

## Milton and the Art of War [1]

No more interesting pages are to be found in Masson's *Life of Milton* than those in which the ever-curious and indefatigable biographer discusses the question of his hero's experience in arms. Were there good and valid reasons why Milton should have served in the Parliamentary army? Masson thinks that there were. Did he actually do so? Very properly but with evident reluctance he concludes that he did not. On the basis, however, of certain military details in *Paradise Lost* the biographer is assured that Milton must at some time in his life have acquired a practical knowledge of drill and manœuvres, and, from the evidence of a statement in the *Apology for Smectymnuus* he infers that he was actually under training with the London militia in 1642. The statement of Philips that there was in 1643 a project to make Milton an adjutant-general in Sir William Waller's army Masson dismisses as a myth. Finally, regarding the sonnet *On His Door when the Assault Was Intended to the City,* he apparently feels the possibility of drawing damaging inferences from it regarding the state of Milton's nerves and endeavors to forestall them by suggesting the conclusion that "the thing" was a jest or a semi-jest, written in mere whim, in answer to the banter of some of his neighbors.

Throughout this discussion Masson's aim is, as it should be, primarily biographical. The subject which he opens up is, however, of much wider scope, and Masson, in his preoccupation with

---

[1] Reprinted by permission from *Studies in Philology,* xviii, 1921.

questions of fact and with the desire to reveal a hidden episode of
Milton's life quite fails to do it justice. Certain important aspects
of the material he entirely overlooks, with the result that even his
biographical inferences rest on insecure foundations. It is the
purpose of this study to supplement these deficiencies by giving as
comprehensive an account as possible of Milton's relation to the
Art of War. This requires, first, a description of the poet's sources
of knowledge in the field of military science, and, second, a fuller
analysis of the military elements in his work. The biographical
questions raised by Masson are to some extent involved, and I
shall take occasion to suggest a revision of his conclusions, at least
in so far as they are affected by considerations of which he failed
to take account.

i

For an explanation of the attention devoted by Milton to the
acquisition of military knowledge it is necessary to go no further
than his famous and characteristic definition of a complete and
generous education as that which "fits a man to perform justly,
skillfully and magnanimously, all the duties both public and
private of peace and war." Framing his own scheme of instruction
in the spirit of this definition he inevitably assigned an important
place to military studies. Philips lists among the works read by
himself and his brother under Milton's tutelage Xenophon's *Institution of Cyrus* and *Anabasis*, Ælian's *Tactics* and the *Strategmata* of Frontinus and Polyænus, works which as we shall see were
regarded in Milton's time as text books and not as classics, and
Milton proposes for the ideal academy as outlined in the tractate
*Of Education* a thorough training in the art of war, both through
the study of these and similar authors and through actual exercises
in arms and drill. The description of this part of his program is so
important for the present study that it must be quoted at length:

About two hours before supper they [the students] are by a sudden
alarum or watchword, to be called out to their military motions, under
sky or covert, according to the season, as was the Roman wont; first on
foot, then, as their age permits, on horseback, to all the art of cavalry;

186

that, having in sport, but with much exactness and daily muster, served out the rudiments of their soldiership, in all the skill of embattling, marching, encamping, fortifying, besieging, and battering, with all the helps of ancient and modern strategems, tactics, and warlike maxims, they may as it were out of a long war come forth renowned and perfect commanders in the service of their country.

Now it is obvious that the presence of military study and discipline in Milton's system is not, as Masson implies, necessarily the result of some accidentally acquired personal experience, or even of the posture of public affairs at the time when the tractate *Of Education* was written. It is an essential part of Milton's attempt to carry out consistently in a definite educational program the humanistic ideal, so nobly formulated by the scholars, philosophers, and poets of the Renaissance, of a trained leadership, in which practical skill is integrated with and based on liberal culture. In this ideal, as it was developed under classical influence on the groundwork of mediæval chivalry, the military element had always held a predominant place. Milton consciously subordinates it, but he does not discard it. Comparing his academy with those of the ancients he proudly boasts that he has surpassed them in comprehensiveness of aim.

Herein it shall exceed them, and supply a defect as great as that which Plato noted in the commonwealth of Sparta, whereas that city trained up their youth most for war, and these in their academies and Lyceum all for the gown, this institution of breeding shall be equally good both for peace and war.

But if the military element was an integral part of Milton's ideal of a training for leadership it is not to be supposed that, while prescribing it for others, he would have failed to incorporate as much of it as was consistent with his particular bent and occupation in his own carefully elaborated plan for self-development. He had also special motives for continuing a study initiated under this general humanistic impulse beyond the years of his activity as student and schoolmaster. The events of his own time and his rôle as their interpreter demanded it; so also did his conception of the kind of preparation necessary for the writing of an epic poem: "industrious and select reading, steady observation, insight into all seemly arts and affairs." These and other related causes, coöperating with Milton's instinctive thoroughness and with his zeal for study, were calculated to be hardly less effectual than a definite intention to embrace a military career, in urging him forward to master at least the theoretical side of the art of war. The degree to which he actually did this is greatly underestimated by Masson, who speaks of the absurdity of supposing that Milton could have been considered fit for an important military office after a few months' drill under Skippon, aided by readings in Ælian, Polyænus, and Frontinus.

Masson's error in judging the proficiency of Milton as acquired from books is no doubt due to a failure to take account of the character of military science in Milton's day. The study of the military classics of antiquity, however superfluous it may be in the training of an officer at present, was then of the utmost practical importance. The application of the principles set forth in them had revolutionized the art of war in the early Renaissance and upon them the actual practice of Milton's time was based. They were therefore indispensable text-books for the soldier and as such they were edited and re-edited throughout the sixteenth and seventeenth centuries, with more or less adaptation to contemporary conditions but with little thought of their being superseded. A typical example of such application of a fundamental ancient treatise is Henri de Rohan's *Caesar,* translated into English in 1640 by John Cruso as "The Complete Captain, or an abridgement of Caesar's Warres, with observations upon them, together with a collection of the order of the militia of the ancients and a particular treatise of modern warre." John Robinson's "The Tactics of Ælian or Art of embattling an army after the Grecian manner, Englished and illustrated with figures and notes upon the ordinary motions of the Phalange," published in 1616, serves a similar purpose, the illustrative material being such as to bridge the gap between ancient and modern warfare and to enable the scholar-soldier to appropriate the skill and experience of antiquity for present use. From such standard works as these to the independent text-books of the Renaissance it is but a step. Even the most practical of them follow the classical authorities in a way which is sometimes the despair of the modern historian of military science.

It was not, however, the technical treatises alone which were considered relevant in the academic training of the soldier. All the accounts of ancient wars, descriptions and philosophies of discipline, incidents of battle, anecdotes and aphorisms of the great captains were regarded with almost superstitious veneration as essentials of knowledge for the modern man of war. Thus Robert Ward, a writer whom Milton knew and of whom I shall have much to say in a moment, while insisting on the need of experience and practice, assigns a place of first importance in the soldier's equipment to the "knowledge of the manifold accidents which rise from the variety of human actions, wherein reason and error hath interchanged contrary events of fortune." "And this knowledge," he adds, "is only to be gained in the registers of antiquity and history recording the passages of former ages, that their harms may be our warnings, and their happy proceedings our fortunate directions." That this is no mere scholar's counsel is proved by the fact that the passage is echoed by so practical a soldier as General Monk in his *Observations upon Military and Political Affairs,* published in 1671 but written some twenty-five years before. "And therefore it is not only experience and practice which maketh a soldier worthy of his name, but the knowledge of the manifold accidents which rise from the variety of human actions is best and most speedily learned by reading history." The effects of insistence on this doctrine and, in general, of the esteem in which the classical authorities were held are well summarized by Fortescue, the historian of the British army. "Every soldier steeped himself in ancient military lore, and quoted the Hipparchius of Xenophon and the Tactics of Ælian, the Commentaries of Caesar and the expeditions of Alexander, Epaminondas' heavy infantry and Pompey's discipline. In a word Europe for two centuries went forth to war with the newest pattern of musket in hand, and a brain stocked with maxims from Frontinus and Vegetius, and with examples from Plutarch and Livy and Arrian."

From the viewpoint, therefore, of his own day Milton's exhaustive study of the Greek and Latin classics would have brought him into contact with all that was most important in the theoretical equipment of the soldier. The only question would be in regard to the degree of attention which he devoted to the military elements contained in them. Fortunately we have in the preserved notes from one division of his reading, recorded in his Commonplace Book,[2] indisputable proof of the fact that knowledge of the art of war was one of the objects uppermost in his mind. There are in the notes, besides the entries on topics which relate to this subject in its more general aspect, as, for example, those under the headings "De Fortitudine," "De Duellis," "Amor in Patriam," "Astutia Politica," "Gymnastica," several pages devoted to questions more specifically military: "Disciplina Militaris," "De Bello," "De Bello Civili," "De Seditione," "De Urbe Obsidenda et Obsessa." Nearly all those notes are drawn from post-classical history, but Milton's interests would, of course, have been the same in the analogous ancient materials; if we possessed Milton's collections from Thucydides and Tacitus, and Polybius, as we do those from De Thou and Commines and the English chronicles they would probably exemplify even more strikingly the degree to which this reading was regarded by him as affording precepts and instances applicable to the requirements of military leadership in his own time.

With the ancient works more specifically devoted to the art of war Milton was probably as familiar as any man of his generation. It is a striking fact that two of the three classical works cited in the Commonplace Book, Cæsar's *Commentaries* and Frontinus' *Strategmata*, are military treatises. These authors, together with Xenophon, Ælian, and Polyænus, Milton read, as we have seen, with his nephews. His knowledge of the other military classics of antiquity may be taken for granted, as may also his acquaintance with the older post-classical writers on the art of war which were placed by the Renaissance on an equality with the ancients themselves and were often contained in the same volumes with them. Thus Milton may well have used his Ælian in the Elzevir edition

---

[2] Edited by A. J. Horwood for the Camden Society, 1877.

of 1613, in which is included the highly esteemed *Tactica* of the Emperor Leo.

Of more significance as showing that Milton's interest in these matters was technical as well as antiquarian and as furnishing sources of his knowledge of the actual practice of war in his own day is the evidence of his acquaintance with two of the outstanding modern treatises on military science, Machiavelli's *Arte della Guerra,* and Robert Ward's *Animadversions of Warre.* The *Arte* of Machiavelli, originally published about 1520, had become both because of the reputation of its author and because of its intrinsic excellence the most highly respected military document of the Renaissance. Rendered accessible in numerous reprints and translated into English by Peter Whitehorne in 1560, it continued long in use as a text-book. The interest of Machiavelli is in the organization and training of a national as opposed to a mercenary army. He looked to the creation of a military body possessed of the skill and animated by something like the spirit of Cromwell's Ironsides. Though not himself a soldier he had studied carefully the military works of the ancients and as a responsible official in the Florentine camp before Pisa he had seen some fighting, and with the result that he had acquired a surprising knowledge, not only of the broad philosophy of success in arms, but of the technical detail as well. The work is one which would have commended itself to Milton by its style, its learning and its primary concern with questions of morale and discipline. He twice cites it in the Commonplace Book,[3] and there can be little doubt that the principles and details set forth in it with such clarity and force contributed in an important way to his technical knowledge of the subject. Contemporary editions of the *Arte,* in common with most of the other military works ancient and modern published in the later Renaissance, contained an abundance of diagrams and pictures. In one large design reproduced in Whitehorne's translation, presumably from some Italian edition, there is represented stretched out over a wide and varied landscape the whole panoply of war: great masses of infantry and cavalry, marching in columns

---

[3] *Commonplace Book,* pp. 177 and 182. Both entries deal with questions of statecraft rather than of military science proper.

and engaged in evolutions, with forests of spears and pennons, the confused activity of the camp, wagons, impedimenta, artillery, castles—in one corner a scene representing the execution of a traitor, and out on the distant battle front the actual clash of arms. The whole is well calculated not only to make clear the descriptions in the text, but vividly to impress the imagination as well. Milton may or may not have seen this particular design,[4] but he certainly saw others similar to it.

In connection with this work mention should be made of Machiavelli's *Discorsi*, which Milton also read with care as is shown by the presence of numerous notes based on it in the Commonplace Book. The second and third sections of the *Discorsi* are primarily devoted to the subject of war and a majority of Milton's quotations from them concern matters of military technique and policy, as for example the statements set down on page 242 regarding the value of fortresses, the advantages of the offensive, and the superiority of foot to horse.

The other modern treatise cited by Milton in the Commonplace Book is deserving of more detailed consideration. I am not aware that it has previously been mentioned in connection with Milton.[5] The full title is as follows: "Animadversion of Warre, or A Militarie Magazine of the Truest Rules, and Ablest Instructions for the Managing of Warre, Composed of the most Refined Discipline and Choice Experiments that these late Netherlandish and Swedish Warres have Produced, with divers new inventions, both of Fortifications and Strategems, as also Sundry Collections taken out of the most approved Authors, ancient and modern, either in Greek, Latine, Italian, French, Spanish, Dutch, or English. In Two Books by Robert Ward, Gentleman and

---

[4] Milton's citations in the Commonplace Book are to a one-volume edition of Machiavelli's works which contains no diagrams: *Tutte le opere di Nicolo Machiavelli cittadino e secretario Fiorentino,* 1550.

[5] Milton cites the work simply as "Ward. militar. Sect. 7," on page 18 of the Commonplace Book under the heading "De Fortitudine." Horwood, the editor of the Commonplace Book, apparently could not identify the reference; at least he omits Ward's volume in his list of authors cited by Milton, p. 64. The fact perhaps accounts for the failure of subsequent commentators to make use of so admirable an illustrative document in editions of Milton's works.

Commander, London. Printed by Francis Eglefield at the Sign of the Marigold in Paul's Churchyard, 1639." [6] Comprehensive as this description is it is not more so than the book itself. It is indeed a military magazine, supplied with all conceivable varieties of the munitions of those days. Though overlooked by students of literature its value has long been recognized by the military historians and antiquaries. Cockle in his military bibliography describes it as the outstanding book of reference on nearly all branches of the military art, drawn from the best sources available and enriched by many excellent observations of the author. Aside from its technical and historical importance, however, Ward's work deserves a place in the annals of seventeenth century prose. The author writes in the capacity of a cultivated and learned gentleman as well as in that of skilled commander, and he has imparted to his treatise a decided literary and philosophical flavor. Several elegant dedicatory epistles to King Charles and others are followed by a seemly Latin poem entitled "Excertatus Sacer in XI Legiones et Lectiones ordinatus," by Ben Lowes, Turmae Equestris Praefectus, and then by some English verses "To our Countrymen in Foreign Service," of which the following may stand as a sample:

> Heere, may you fight by Booke, and never bleede:
> Behold a wall blown up, and yet no Breach:
> And hear the neighing of a still-borne steede:
> And startle at an engrav'n canon's speeche.

Ward begins like all good warriors with the praise of peace, but he passes quickly to the inevitability of war, descanting rather loftily on the theme of the mutability of kingdoms. In the second section he discusses the means and provisions of war—victuals, weapons, shipping, and soldiers—inveighing against the inefficiency of the English train bands and painting a vivid picture

---

[6] Copies of this work are rather rare. The one in the Library of Harvard College, which I have used, was purchased in 1646 by Robert Keayne of Boston, founder of the ancient and Honorable Artillery Company. Sold by his widow in 1656, it passed through the hands of John Leverett, President of Harvard College, whose signature on the fly leaf bears the date 1682, Edward Wigglesworth, first Hollis professor of Divinity, and the Rev. John Andrews of Newburyport, who donated it to Harvard Library in 1835.

of the unsoldierly character of the musters. Section III presents the elements of geometry, with a thorough and technical discussion of fortifications, artillery, and mines; sections VII–IX contain a fine treatment of the subject of morale and an analysis of valor and cowardice. There follow elaborate explanations of the duties of each particular office and of the regulations of drill, a discourse of "politique strategems" after the model of Frontinus and Polyænus (some of the instances are classical and threadbare, others new), and finally a detailed and curious description of all manner of engines and warlike implements. Book II is devoted to the office of general, with aphorisms drawn from Machiavelli and others, rules of march and camp, and descriptions of the various battle formations. The volume is profusely illustrated with useful diagrams and alluring prints and the text abounds in passages of genuine eloquence.

I have dwelt at some length on the characteristics of this work of Ward's because it is precisely the combination contained in it of scholarly thoroughness with philosophic breadth and largeness of utterance which would, I think, have particularly attracted Milton. He cites in the Commonplace Book but a single passage, but this is a characteristic and significant one: "the cause of valor a good conscience, for an evil conscience, as an English author noteth well, will otherwise knaw at the roots of valour like a worme and undermine all resolutions." The whole section in which this passage is included is one which would have commended itself to Milton's way of thought. The soldiers' obedience, valor, and desert are grounded, says Ward, on the principle of showing their magnanimity to the utmost in the defense of religion, king, and country, and learning with their best endeavor the military art. To fear God and keep one's powder dry is the whole duty of the man of war. It would have been with melancholy but not unsympathetic feelings that Milton read Ward's noble passage in praise of loyalty to the sovereign.

No kingdom so fortunate and happy as those where obedience flows in a clear stream; so far from the power of gusts and storms that gentle calms are perpetuated to times, and all seasons are as Halcyon days; when subjects of all conditions and in all respects sympathize with their sovereign in authority to his lawful behests and commands, as the shadow imitates the body, or as the parts of the body are ready bent to observe and execute the pleasures and intents of the heart and faculties of the mind.

One other quotation from the same part of the work may be given as an illustration of Ward's style and temper.

> If one should but draw examples of obedience from the creatures, and observe how in all things they stand conformable and obedient to the laws of nature; how the great unruly ocean observes the course of the moon in bringing in her tides, the massie earth waits the time and pleasure of the sun's revolution, to yield up the fruit and hidden treasures contained in her bowells to the uttermost of her powers, all creatures, both vegetative and sensitive, are precise and ready bent in all obedience when nature enjoins; and yet man, a rational creature, most obstinate and heterogenial in his duty, loyalty, and obedience to his superiors, which nature doth not only challenge as a right, but God claims in as his due. And how silly are men above all other creatures in making provision for their safety. Their is no creature but nature hath armed it with some defensive weapon, not so much but the poor bee hath his pike, which most valiantly and skillfully he can use for his defense and preservation. But the times we live in are such that we have neither will nor skill, but we refer all to a general Providence, thinking it sufficient if they be roughcast with riches and prosperity.

Here are ideas which would certainly have interested Milton and accorded with his general philosophy. His specific indebtedness to Ward will be discussed in the second section of this paper. I am concerned at present only to show that Milton must have found the work not unworthy of his attention, and that in reading it he was brought into contact with the best that was known of military science in his own day, both in its technical and philosophic aspects.

There were, of course, many other English works which dealt with the theory and practice of arms. With some of these certainly and with many others very probably Milton had familiarized himself. Of the older treatises we know from a note in the Commonplace Book that he had read the *Toxophilus* of Roger Ascham. He could hardly have missed seeing the contemporary publications which proceeded from the press with ever-increasing rapidity as the nation drew on toward the civil war. Fifty-seven titles of English works purely military in character are listed by Cockle as appearing between the years 1626 and 1642, eleven of them being published in the latter year alone. One of these, John Cruso's *Military Instructions for the Cavalry*, containing some fine pictures of horse formations, had been issued at Cambridge in the last year of Milton's residence there, 1632. Milton is likely enough also to have read Henry Peacham's *The Compleat Gentleman*, published in many editions throughout his lifetime, with its chapters devoted to military discipline and the regulations of drill.

Such, then, are the sources from which Milton derived his textbook knowledge of the art of war. It may now be questioned whether he made any effort or enjoyed any opportunity to gain practical experience in arms, or whether the whole subject remained for him an academic one, included in his comprehensive program of study partly because a sound classical and humanistic scholarship demanded it, partly because he felt that his projected poetry might involve it, and above all because such knowledge was a necessary part of the equipment of one who planned to play a part of statesmanly leadership in the public affairs of his own time. In spite of all Masson has said, there is not a particle of valid evidence that Milton ever underwent military training whether under Skippon at the beginning of the civil war or earlier during his school and college life. I cannot find that there was any such organization at St. Paul's as Milton projected for his own academy. At Oxford, in the crisis of 1642, there was, we know, a flare-up of military enthusiasm and the scholars deserted their books to "train up and down the streets" in preparation for the service of the king.[7] But we hear nothing of any military feature at either university in the years of Milton's residence. In the trained bands, maintenance of which in city and country was required by law during the reign of Charles I, men of Milton's status were not expected to serve except as officers. There would seem to be little likelihood of his ever having appeared in Buckinghamshire during the Horton period at one of the drunken musters described

---

[7] Anthony Cooper, *Strategmata*, 1662, quoted by C. H. Firth, *Cromwell's Army*, p. 21.

by Ward. By 1642 the military situation had become very different. In the city, indeed, there had long been a more vigorous interest in military preparation among the citizens. Little societies had been in the habit of meeting in the Artillery Garden in St. Martin's Fields to practice their drill under expert soldiers hired to instruct them, and the men thus taught became in their turn officers of the trained bands.[8] Milton may, of course, have served his apprenticeship in arms in some such way as this, but there is no proof that he did so. In the activity which began with the outbreak of hostilities I think it extremely unlikely that he had any part. The rank and file of those at first engaged in drilling were, as is well known, men of very different character from Milton and his associates. Essex's army was in large part composed of city apprentices and country laborers—"decayed serving-men and unjust tapsters," as Cromwell remarked to Hampton. Even in the New Model the majority of the troopers are said to have been unable to write their names. It was not expected that gentlemen should serve in the capacity of private. Thus the Parliamentary impressment order of August 16, 1643, exempted clergymen, scholars, students in the Inns of Court and the universities, the sons of esquires, and persons rated at five pounds goods or three pounds lands in the subsidy books. For officers there was no lack of experienced men on either side from among the thousands of Englishmen who had seen service with the Dutch or the reformed princes of Germany, or from among the London citizens who had acquired military experience at home.

There remains the passage from the *Apology for Smectymnuus* cited by Masson as evidence that Milton was drilling in the year 1642. Milton is defending himself against the charge that his days and nights are spent in dissipation.

These morning haunts are where they should be,—at home; not sleeping, or concocting the surfeits of an irregular feast, but up and stirring,—in winter often ere the sound of any bell awaken men to labour or devotion, in summer as oft with the bird that first rouses, or not much tardier,—to read good authors, or cause them to be read, till the attention be weary or memory have its full fraught; then with

---

[8] C. H. Firth, *Cromwell's Army.*

useful and generous labours preserving the body's health and hardiness, to render lightsome, clear, and lumpish obedience to the mind, to the cause of Religion and our country's liberty, when it shall require firm hearts in sound bodies to stand and cover their stations, rather than see the ruin of our Protestantism and the enforcement of a slavish life.

"This is interesting," says Masson. "Milton, it seems, has for some time been practicing drill." [9] Obviously he has been doing nothing of the sort. He has been simply taking exercise, his lifelong habit, as a relief from study and to preserve his health for the kind of service which he was then rendering and which he was later to render in his country's cause. Had he been under arms he would certainly have said so explicitly, either in this passage or in the later reviews of his creditable activities. The fact is that Milton had early concluded that the part he was to play in life was one which very definitely excluded the activity of camp or field. He carefully distinguished in his thought another soldiership and marked it from the beginning for his own.

For I did not so much shun the labours and dangers of military service as not, in another fashion, both to do work for my countrymen of a more useful kind. . . . Having from my earliest youth been devoted in a far more than ordinary degree to the higher studies, and having always been stronger mentally than in body, I disregarded camp-service, in which any common soldier of more robust frame could easily have been my superior and got means about me to the use of which I was more competent, so that I might in what I thought my own better and more effective, or at least not inferior way, be an acquisition of as much momentum as possible to the needs of my country and to this most excellent cause.[10]

This is as plain a statement as could possibly be desired. It implies not merely that Milton did not actually serve in the Parliamentary wars, but that he never intended or prepared to do so. In estimating the reasons for this decision we must give due weight to what he says of his physical condition as well as to the kind of reflection which made moral and intellectual service seem of equal or superior dignity and value to that of arms. We know, for example, not only that Milton was under middle height, but

---

[9] Masson, II, p. 402.
[10] *Second Defense,* Masson II, p. 487.

that he was weak in eyesight, that he had been subject to head-aches from his youth, and that he suffered frequent illnesses throughout his life.[11] He was not at the time in question necessar-ily unfit for military service, but he was doubtless quite right in thinking that he would have been of little value as a fighter. I am quite persuaded, therefore, that Milton did not turn out with pike and musket in 1642, nor do I feel that his failure to do so needs any further explanation or defense than he has made for himself. As to the Turnham Green sonnet, the tone of which has been a stumbling block to some biographers, it is necessary only to understand the poem in order to divest it entirely of the sort of biographical significance which has been attached to it. Of course Milton did not post it on his door, but neither did he write it as a jest in the response to the banter of his friends. The possibility of identifying his own situation with that of Pindar awoke his imagi-nation and resulted in an utterance of purely artistic significance. It is the poet in him who is speaking, with the poet's oblivion of everything except the immediate conception of his mind.

If, however, Milton was in all probability unacquainted with the practice of soldiership from actual experience it is not quite accurate to say that his sources of knowledge were wholly aca-demic. On the one hand the physical recreations of a gentleman of Milton's time were much more than at present associated with arms. The very theory of sport, inherited from the Middle Ages and confirmed by the classics, was that it should constitute a preliminary training for military service,[12] and this idea was firmly held by Milton. For the physical exercise of his academy he rec-ommends in *Of Education* "first, the exact use of their weapon, to guard, and strike safely with edge or point, as a means of making students healthy, nimble, strong, and well in breath, and to in-

---

[11] Cf. *Epistle* XI: "First, the delay was occasioned by ill health, whose disabilities I have now perpetually to combat; next by a cause of ill health, necessary and sudden removal to another house." Stomach trouble accompa-nied his disease of the eyes. Cf. *Epist.* XV. A severe sickness had preceded the writing of the *Defensio.* See introductory paragraphs of that work.

[12] Compare Peacham, *Compleat Gentleman,* Chap. XVI, where various exer-cises, as tilting, running, swimming, shooting, hunting, are commended as a means of enabling the nobility for command and the service of their country. Precedents are cited from Cicero, Sallust, Cæsar and other ancient writers.

spire them with a gallant and fearless courage." Here we know that Milton had practiced what he preached. "I was wont," he says in the *Second Defense,* "constantly to exercise myself in the use of the broadsword, as long as comported with my habit and years. Armed with this weapon as I usually was I should have thought myself quite a match for anyone, though much stronger than myself." The image of Milton practicing the young Philipses in the art of self-defense is a very pleasant one which it is surprising that Masson had not expatiated on. He had doubtless been taught fencing by some London master or at one of the fencing schools in the university,[13] and this instruction involved a certain amount of training equivalent to drill. A statement of Toland suggests that he had been taught the use of other weapons as well, though it may simply be a generalization from the passage quoted. "His recreation before his sight was gone consisted much in feats of activity, particularly in the exercise of his arms, which he could handle with much dexterity." Milton's interest in Ascham's *Toxophilus* suggests that he may have practiced archery, an act recommended by Ascham primarily for its military value and not wholly obsolete for practical purposes in Milton's time. This was perhaps the sum of Milton's actual experience in arms, but it was enough when amended by the imagination, to give the art of war a certain reality in his consciousness which it would not otherwise have had. We must remember, also, that the atmosphere of Milton's mature years was charged with the intensest interest in military matters. The preparations of the Parliamentary forces must have met his attention on every side and he must have heard constant discussion of the progress of the war. Later he was associated with many of those who had been leaders in the struggle. His acquaintance with soldiers like Sir Henry Vane would have given him opportunity to learn at first hand of the operations of the civil war. In a time of actual warfare even the civilian who is deeply concerned in the outcome is infused with the martial spirit and may speak as familiarly of

---

[13] Cf. Earle, *Microcosmographie,* xxv, *A Young Gentleman of the University.* "His father sent him thither because he heard that there were the best fencing and dancing schools."

Sallies and retires, of trenches, tents,
Of palisadoes, frontiers, parapets

as if they were his special province. These considerations should prepare us for almost any moment of military technicality in Milton's works without resorting to Masson's unfounded suppositions.

Before entering upon the discussion of this subject I wish to consider for a moment Philips's surprising statement that there was at one time a project on foot to make Milton an adjutant general in Sir William Waller's army. I am far from certain that this should be so promptly dismissed as it was by Johnson and has been by all subsequent biographers. Philips is, to be sure, somewhat guarded in his statement but he gives details which it is hard to believe he deliberately fabricated. He says that the practice of Milton's design of founding an academy according to the model laid down in the tractate *Of Education* was afterwards diverted by a series of alterations in public affairs. "For I am much mistaken if there were not about this time a design in agitation of making him adjutant-general in Sir William Waller's army. But the new modelling of the army soon following proved an obstacle; and Sir William, his commission being laid down, began as the common saying is, to turn cat in pan." The chronology here is right enough. Milton's tractate was published in 1644; the self-denying ordinance deprived Waller of his command in February, 1645; and the New Model was created immediately afterwards. The grounds on which Masson rejects the possibility of such a thing are the inexperience of Milton and his manifest unfitness for an important military office. But it is by no means clear precisely what the term adjutant-general in Sir William Waller's army implied. No adjutants whatsoever are mentioned in the complete Parliamentary army lists of 1642. Such officers appear sporadically in the later organizations with duties rather ill defined. In the New Model the adjutant-general or general adjutant was an assistant to the commander of the cavalry, a superior aide-de-camp. "The Swedish Intelligencer" [14] speaks of the office in the following terms:

---

[14] Quoted by Firth, *Cromwell's Army.*

The General adjutant, that was Leiftenant to the Commissary [i. e. the chief officers of horse—not a commissary in the modern sense] was the Leiftenant Colonel to his regiment. The General adjutant's office, is to be assistant to the Generall: That is to be sent abroad for the giving or speeding of the Generall's commands to the rest of the armie. He is commonly some able man, or some favorite at least unto the Generall. His place in the Armie, is that of a Leiftenant Colonel; of whom he hath precedence, but is behind all Colonels. A General-adjutant is the same officer which in our English discipline wee call a corporal of the field. The French call him an aide-de-camp.

Under the terms of this description there is a conceivable place for a man like Milton. But it seems more likely that Philips is using the expression to describe some important semi-civilian function on the general staff, and is dignifying it with a well sounding title. Among the officers listed as belonging to the General's train in Essex's army there are the following: Treasurer at Warres, Muster Master General, Advocate of the Army, Secretary of the Army, Auditor of the Army. Is it not possible that Milton's services and known devotion to the Parliamentary cause might have been thought to entitle him to some such appointment? His purely academic learning, his knowledge of languages, the laws of war, historical precedent, and even, theoretically, of strategy and tactics, would have constituted qualifications of no mean order for purposes secretarial, advisory, or administrative which did not involve active participation in battle. While hesitating, therefore, to accept Philip's statement at its face value I am inclined to give it some weight; in any case I should reverse Masson's conclusion that the tradition of a proposal to bring Milton in some capacity into the army of Sir William Waller is far less credible than he should have been found serving at first in one of the regiments of the London train bands.

## ii

If it were possible to reason that a man must at some time have had actual military experience on the ground that he displays in his writings a competent and even a technical knowledge of the works of war, one would have little difficulty in establishing a case for Milton. The data is, indeed, much more extensive than Masson apparently realized. Much of the battle language which animates the utterance of Milton may, of course, be ascribed to the traditional Christian habit, founded on scripture, of applying terms of physical conflict to the realm of the spirit. Beyond this, however, Milton frequently in the course of ordinary speech slips into military phraseology of a more exceptional character. This is especially apt to occur when he is speaking of the operations of the mind in acquiring or defending truth. "Militaire men," he says in illustrating a point in *The Readie and Easie Way,* "hold it dangerous to change the form of battle in view of the enemy." Elsewhere he speaks of awaiting an opponent "at his foragings and waterings," of uniting "as those smaller squares in battle unite in one great cube, the main phalanx," of the "small divided maniples" of the Protestant sectaries in their combined attack on the Church of Rome "cutting through his ill-united unwieldly brigade." Sometimes the military figure is elaborately developed, as in the following from *Of Education:*

In which methodical course it is so supposed that they [the students] must proceed by the steady pace of learning onward, as at convenient times, for memory's sake, to retire back into the middle ward, and sometimes in the rear of what they have been taught, until they have confirmed and solidly united the whole body of their perfected knowledge, like the embattling of a Roman legion.

Or in this memorable passage from the *Areopagitica:*

When a man hath been laboring the hardest labor in the deep mines of knowledge, hath furnished out his findings in all their equipage, drawn forth his reasons as it were a battle ranged, scattered and defeated all objections in his way, calls out his adversary into the plain, offers him the advantage of wind and sun, if he please, only that he may try the matter by dint of argument, for his opponent then to skulk, to lay ambushments, to keep a narrow bridge of licensing where the challenger should pass, though it be valor enough in soldiership, is but weakness and cowardice in the wars of Truth.

It is not, however, to such casual outcroppings of Milton's familiarity with the language of strategy and tactics, themselves a manifestation of the habit of technical expression characteristic of seventeenth century prose and poetry, that we must look for the really significant results of his studies in the art of war. Motivated,

as I have said, by the intellectual and cultural tradition of the
Renaissance and stimulated by the particular circumstances of the
Puritan period, these studies had for Milton in his capacity as a
public servant, as an interpreter of the events of his own time, as a
historical scholar, and as a poet a very special and highly important object. On the one hand his understanding of military detail
enabled him to follow the military history of the Commonwealth,
to deal with former campaigns not as an amateur but as an expert,
and finally to work into *Paradise Lost* and *Paradise Regained* a
body of military minutiae calculated to make them not less competent in this respect than the epics of antiquity. On the other
hand the study of war in its large significance as a phase of human
history merged with the general political, moral and philosophic
interests of Milton and strengthened his grasp on the fundamental
issues with which he was concerned both as a statesman and as a
poet. This last aspect of the subject is involved in the general
topic of Milton's philosophy and statesmanship, which is too comprehensive to admit of treatment here. What I propose to do is
simply to approach the military elements in Milton's work from
the standpoint of military science proper, illustrating them by
reference to the sources from which they are derived. It is the
poetry which primarily concerns us, but a preliminary glance may
be taken at a prose work too much neglected in the estimate of
Milton's accomplishment, the unfinished *History of Britain*.

It is a significant fact that Milton, while considerably reducing
the legendary element in his story, however picturesque, endeavors to give as nearly complete an account as possible of all the
battles and campaigns. The following passage describing the battle of the Romans under Agricola with the British at Mons Gram-
pius illustrates his occasional minute handling of military detail.

But first he orders them on this sort: Of eight thousand auxilliary
foot he makes his middle ward, on the wings three thousand horse, the
legions as a reserve, stood in array before the camp; either to seize the
victory won without their own hazard, or to keep up the battle if it
should need. The British powers on the hillside, as might best serve for
show or terror, stood in their batallions; the first on even ground, the
next rising behind, as the hill ascended. Agricola doubting to be
overwinged, stretches out his front, though somewhat of the thinnest,

in so much that many advised to bring up the legions: Yet he, not altering, alights from his horse, and stands on foot before the ensigns. The fight began aloof . . . etc.

The whole account is taken almost literally from Tacitus (*Agricola*, 36), the significance of Milton's handling lying in his incorporation of it *in toto*, and of his comprehension of the points of strategy involved. In one instance he abbreviates an expression of Tacitus "veritus ne in frontem simul et latera pugnaretur" by translating it into more technical terminology, "fearing to be overwinged." Equally explicit is the long narrative of Caesar's conquest (188 ff.), which is reproduced from the Commentaries with a full account not only of the actual fighting but of the marches, military constructions, and manoeuverings on land and sea as well. For the campaigns not reported by the Roman historians the materials available to Milton were scanty and his accounts are correspondingly so. There can, however, be no doubt that had the history been continued to a period for which definite data were to be had, the military feature would have bulked very large indeed. It is clear also that Milton would have handled the wars of his countrymen, not after the fashion of romance, but in the scientific spirit of Xenophon or Caesar. He had aimed to write history as he had read it and to embody in his work the lessons of experience from all fields of public activity. We have already seen how in the Commonplace Book he recorded among the memorabilia from his historical reading principles and exempla strictly military in character, along with those of general political and moral significance. These notes may serve to guide us in defining the purposes of the *History of Britain* and in estimating the emphasis which would have been given to various aspects of the subject.

We are now in a position to understand more exactly the significance of the military elements incorporated in the poems. They occupy, to be sure, a subordinate place in Milton's carefully thought out schemes of values, as he himself suggests in the invocation to Book IX of *Paradise Lost*, describing himself as one

> Not sedulous by nature to indite
> Wars, hitherto the only argument

Heroic deemed, chief maistrie to dissect
With long and tedious havoc fabled knights
In battles feigned (the better fortitude
Of patience and heroic martyrdom
Unsung), or to describe races and games,
Or tilting furniture, emblazoned shields,
Impreses quaint, caparisons and steeds;
Bases and tinsel trappings, gorgeous knights
At joust and tournament.

The passage is expressive of Milton's dissatisfaction with a purely chivalric and fictitious subject matter and of his sense of the superior significance of spiritual as compared with material issues. In spite of this, however, he found himself much concerned with the lower argument of physical arms and battles, and his attitude toward this material was by no means one of indifference. On the one hand it called forth his powers of pictorial imagination, while on the other it gave him an opportunity to introduce the expert knowledge which he had won by scholarly study and observation of the art of war. The result in *Paradise Lost* is an odd but on the whole successful mixture of romance and science.

The first passage of importance in this connection is the one quoted and analyzed by Masson describing the assemblage of the Satanic hosts on the shore of the burning lake. (*P. L.*, i, 530–787). The main elements in this description are purely literary and imaginative. In elaborating his picture in its larger aspects Milton has evidently laid under contribution not only material visualized from epic and romance but his recollections of the actual pageantry of war, as he had read of it in history and seen it in the embattled armies of his own time. Thus we have such universal and poetic images as the unfurling of the imperial ensign at the war-like sound of clarion and trumpet, the forest huge of spears and thronging helms, the shout that tore Hell's concave, the waving of ten thousand banners in the air. But Milton has not rested content with these generalities. He has endeavored to give the picture a more specific martial coloring by introducing touches of archeological detail and by discreetly mingling the technical terminology of ancient and of modern war. The shields are "serried," i. e. interlocked as in the Greek and Roman battle formations; the

206

troops move forward in perfect phalanx to the Dorian mood of flutes and soft recorders, the last detail being adopted from the classical descriptions of the use of these instruments for battle music among the Greeks.[15]

Then they stand "a horrid front, with ordered spear and shield" (compare the command "Order your arms," to be found in all the English text-books) before their chief who

> through the armed files
> Darts his experienced eye, and soon traverse
> The whole batallion views.

Finally, as he prepares to speak,

> their doubled ranks they bend
> From wing to wing, and half enclose him round.

A second suggestive passage (*P. L.*, IV, 766–789), also cited by Masson is the description of the angelic night-watch about the Garden. Milton has made Gabriel send out a scouting expedition in two detachments with perfect military precision, sharpening the epic particularity of the account by working in numerous technical though familiar terms applicable to such a manoeuver:

> "Uzziel, half these draw off, and coast the south
> With strictest watch; these other wheel the north;
> Our circuit meets full west." As flame they part,
> Half wheeling to the shield, half to the spear.
>
> .   .   .   .   ..   .
>
> So saying, on he led his radiant files.

The two units meet and "closing," stand "in squadron joined." Face to face with Satan,

> the angelic squadron bright
> Turned fiery red, sharpening in mooned horns
> Their phalanx, and began to hem him round
> With ported spears.

In his commentary on these passages Masson is quite right in insisting on the exactness of Milton's language. In one point,

---

[15] Xen. *Cyrop.* lib. 7, 178 A: Aelian, cap. XI etc. Cf. the discussion of Synapsmos in the English translation of the *Tactics* by John Cruso, 1616, p. 81.

indeed, the poet is more exact than the biographer. The phrase "with ported spears" Masson and subsequent commentators describe as if it were the equivalent of the modern "port arms," which would be inappropriate. The military books which Milton read give it correctly as the position intermediate between "carry" and "charge," the point of the lance or pike being held directly forward, with the shaft at an angle of 45 degrees.[16] There is, I think, one other error in Masson's exposition. He supposes the word "attention" in "Attention held them mute" to be used by Milton in the sense of the modern command. The word appears, however, in Milton's day to have been "Silence." At least, I do not find "Attention" in the orders of drill in any of the text-books. Finally, there is nothing in the first passage quoted to justify Masson's inference that the Satanic hosts order their arms at the moment of halting without word of command. These, however, are trifling points. The passages do imply, as Masson says, a considerable amount of detailed knowledge of military methods. But their significance is obscured if we labor to find in them proof that Milton had himself at one time been a soldier. His evolutions and terminology are exact because he intended that they should be so. It is entirely unnecessary to assume practical experiences on his part in order to account for any technicalities we find in *Paradise Lost*. The orders of drill are given and defined in every English handbook, often with illustrations which make them clear at a glance. The various postures of pike and musket are described with special minuteness by Ward, and it is to such sources, supplemented by observation, that we may confidently assign Milton's knowledge of the modern detail in the above passages. His hold on this material rests on exactly the same basis as his accurate information regarding ancient discipline with which he intersperses it. Thus the expression "mooned horns" is, of course, the Greek, Roman and Italian but not the English military term, and the line "half wheeling to the shield, half to the spear" echoes the

---

[16] "This posture is performed by holding the pike a half distance between advancing and charging. . . . It is the most aptest and comliest posture for a company to use in marching through a port or gate, and most readiest for to charge upon a sudden." Ward, *Animadversions*, 224.

Latin and Greek terminology "ad scutum," "ad hastam" for right and left wheel. Ælian explains these evolutions in detail, giving the classical terms, which his English commentator converts into English as follows: "Battle wheel to the pike; battle wheel to the target." The actual contemporary command, as rendered by Ward, was "Wheel your battle to the right; wheel your battle to the left."

Material analogous to that already cited is to be found in *Paradise Lost* wherever the movements of embattled hosts are mentioned. The most extensive illustration of the composite character of Milton's materials and of the real purpose for which he marshals them is to be found in the narrative of the war in Heaven. The foundation of this narrative is the Homeric battle, with its episodes of single combat and its atmosphere of individual great deeds. But Milton must have realized that in his handling of this material he would from the viewpoint of mere narrative interest fare but ill in comparison with his originals. He would have been as quick as anyone to see that the inequality of the combatants and the impossibility of killing anybody must necessarily rob the conflict of all element of suspense and make the clash of titanic opposites less thrilling, despite his best endeavor, than the conflict of two mortal heroes, fighting with poor human javelins, in the *Iliad*. To remedy this defect he has centered attention on the military spectacle and on the idea, and in elaborating his story he has, as before, combined the most striking and characteristic features of ancient, mediæval, and modern war.

First Abdiel, returning to the loyal angels, finds them full of martial preparations:

> When all the plain
> Covered with thick embattled squadrons bright,
> Chariots, and flaming arms and fiery steeds,
> Reflecting blaze on blaze, first met his view.

The element of discipline is strongly accented in the description.

> At which command the Powers Militant
> That stood for Heaven, in mighty quadrate joined

Of union irresistible, moved on
In silence their bright legions to the sound
Of instrumental harmony, that breathed
Heroic ardour to adventurous deeds
Under their godlike leaders, in the cause
Of God and his Messiah. On they move
Indissolubly firm; nor obvious hill,
Nor straitening vale, nor wood, nor stream, divides
Their perfect ranks; for high above the ground
Their march was, and the passive air upbore
Their nimble tread.

Milton very obviously has here in mind the trained armies of civilized warfare in antiquity and in his own time. The picture of the rebel host, on the other hand, is colored with the hues and trappings of mediæval chivalry:

and, nearer view,
Bristled with upright beams innumerable
Of rigid spears, and helmets thronged, and shields
Various, with boastful argument portrayed.

What follows is Homeric, chiefly, but Milton continues to present through a series of incidental touches just so much of the theory and practice of modern systematic war as was necessary to satisfy his purpose of making this an integral element in the conception. Thus the following lines are designed to suggest the harmony of individual initiative and automatic discipline which Milton had been taught to recognize as characteristic of the ideally trained fighter:

Led in fight, yet leader seemed
Each warrior single as in chief; expert
When to advance, or stand, or turn the sway
Of battle, open when, and when to close
The ridges of grim war.

The image of orderly battalions in battle formation is constantly kept before us.

While others bore him on their shields
Back to his chariot, where it stood retired
From off the files of war.

. . . . . . . . .

> Far otherwise the inviolable saints
> In cubic phalanx firm advanced entire,
> Invulnerable, impenetrably armed.

The day's fighting concludes when

> On the foughten field
> Michael and his angels prevalent,
> Encamping, placed in guard their watches round,
> Cherubic waving fires,

a picture suggestive of a passage in the *Iliad* but equally applicable to historic war.

The second battle, in the description of which Milton repeats none of the elements thus far introduced, contains the much maligned episode of the invention and first use of artillery, and here we have an even more characteristic evidence of the poet's determination to modernize and make universally representative the war in Heaven. In the description of the novel weapon he skillfully adapts his scientific knowledge to the purposes of poetry.

> These in their dark nativity the Deep
> Shall yield us, pregnant with infernal flame;
> Which into hollow engines long and round
> Thick rammed, at the other bore with touch of fire
> Dilated and infuriate, shall send forth
> From far, with thundering noise, among our foe
> Such implements of mischief as shall dash
> To pieces and o'erwhelm whatever stands
> Adverse.

The same method is followed in the account of the preparation of the guns and powder. And finally the firing of the pieces is described with full consciousness of the actual technique of artillery working in connection with infantry in contemporary war. At Zophiel's command the loyal angels move on embattled,

> when, behold,
> Not distant far, with heavy pace the foe
> Approaching gross and huge, in hollow cube
> Training his devilish enginery, impaled
> On every side with shadowing squadrons deep,
> To hide the fraud.

At the order "Vanguard, to right and left your front unfold," epic language for "Wheel off your front by divisions," [17] the cannon are unmasked.

> A triple mounted row of pillars laid
> On wheels (for like to pillars most they seemed,
> Or hollowed bodies made of oak or fir,
> With branches lopped, in wood or mountain felled)
> Brass, iron, stony mould, had not their mouths
> With hideous orifice gaped on us wide,
> Portending hollow truce. At each, behind,
> A seraph stood, and in his hand a reed
> Stood waving tipped with fire; while we, suspense,
> Collected stood within our thoughts amused.
> Not long! for sudden all at once their reeds
> Put forth, and to a narrow vent applied
> With nicest touch. Immediate in flame,
> But soon obscured with smoke, all Heaven appeared,
> From those deep throated engines belched, whose roar
> Embowelled with outrageous noise the air,
> And all her entrails tore, disgorging foul
> Their devilish glut, chained thunderbolts and hail
> Of iron globes.
>
> .   .   .   .   .   .   .   .   .   .
>
> Foul dissipation followed and forced rout;
> Nor served it to relax their serried files.

Here if anywhere we should be able to trace Milton's indebtedness to his military sources. As a matter of fact we find in Ward, not only all the necessary technical information regarding artillery itself, but also an account of substantially the evolution here described, with an accompanying diagram. Chapter xvi of the second book is entitled "A fifth way of Imbattling an Army consisting of twelve thousand Foot and four thousand Horse, the Ordinance being placed covertly in the midst and also on the wings." The first part of the analysis in the text is as follows:

In this first figure following you may perceive at the letter A, four hundred shot [i. e. musketeers] upon either flank before the main

---

[17] Cf. Ward, p. 225: "This motion is easy to be performed, for all the file leaders on the right flank are to wheel about to the right, the rest of each file following their leaders; the file leaders likewise to the left flank are to wheel about to the left and then join or close their divisions."

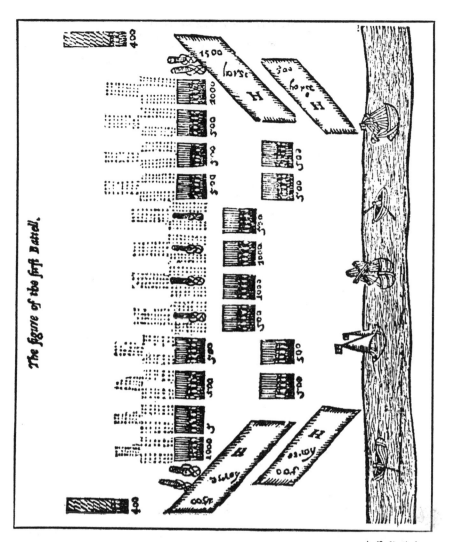

**ARTILLERY MASKED
BY INFANTRY**

(From Robert Ward's *Animadversions of Warre*, 1639. The dots
represent a plan view of the
formations, the rear rank of each
battalion being shown in elevation.)

battle; these are to surprise the enemy's ordinance which is supposed to be planted upon a hill; further you may observe sixteen batallias, the ordinance being planted in the main battle between the divisions thereof, having four hundred musketiers ordered before them, and by them obscured; and as soon as the enemy is approached within distance, those musketiers are to divide themselves on either hand, so that the shot [i. e. cannon balls] may have free passage to disorder the enemy's troops, upon which advantage the other batallias are to advance forwards, and seriously to charge the enemy in his disorders.

Of the actual employment of this evolution we have an account in Wilson's *Life of James I,* London, 1653 (p. 140. Cited by Keightley, *Paradise Lost,* p. 441) :

Anhalt used a more real stratagem that took effect. He brought his ordinance up behind his men invisibly, loaden with musquet-ball; and, when they should have charged the enemy, made them wheel off, that those bloody engines might break their ranks, which they performed to purpose, and forced them to retire into a wood, where, pursuing their advantage, they scattered their main body.

In view, however, of Milton's acquaintance with Ward's volume we may assume that he adopted from it the fundamental plan of Satan's diabolical assault on the courageous but old-fashioned army of the saints of Heaven.

In order fully to estimate Milton's reasons for introducing the artillery episode into *Paradise Lost* it is necessary to consider it, not as an isolated piece of sensationalism, a more than questionable artistic tour de force, nor yet simply as an epic convention of the Renaissance, but in its relation to the total conception of Book vi and indeed of the poem as a whole. The underlying idea of Milton's treatment of the conflict in Heaven is that it should be an epitome of war in general, or rather the archetype of war, according to the Platonic conception expressed by Raphael in his preliminary address to Adam, in which it is suggested that earth is but the shadow of Heaven, "and things therein each to other like more than on Earth is thought." In order to represent this conception to the imagination he had at the same time to be typical and concrete. Thus in describing the cannon he refuses equally to make them of any one particular metal or to leave them of no metal at all. He says they are "brass, iron, stony mould." And the same method is reproduced in the larger features of the narrative.

In defiance of archæological consistency Milton has combined in the picture the characteristic detail of all the great types of warfare among men, fusing them into a large unity of impression which is not the least of his imaginative achievements. Even the primitive combat of the titans is represented, when both armies finally desert their discipline and abandoning civilized arms hurl confusedly at each other whatever crude missiles come to hand. Milton meant to suggest that the last end of war is like its beginning, bestial, anarchic, inconclusive. The utmost refinements of scientific slaughter are but a mask of chaos and can only end in the disruption of the orderly civilization of which they are the product. The significance of the whole is definitely indicated at the close of Book VI, when the Almighty, beholding the confusion, declares that

> War wearied hath performed what war can do,
> And to disordered rage let loose the reins,
> With mountains, as with weapons, armed; which makes
> Wild work in Heaven, and dangerous to the main,

and sends forth the Son in majesty to put an end at once to evil and to strife. In the light of this controlling purpose our consciousness of the artistic improprieties of Book VI tends, I think, to disappear. By employing the legendary framework of a war in Heaven, required by his plot and already established in literary tradition, as a vehicle for a large and not unpoetic philosophical idea Milton brings this portion of *Paradise Lost* into harmony with his conception of the whole and justifies the boast that his song pursues

> Things unattempted yet in prose or rhyme.

It should be added that in introducing the use of gunpowder Milton is expressing the current feeling of his time that there was in such a weapon something peculiarly diabolic and unnatural. The Renaissance dislike of firearms on humane and chivalric grounds in comparison with the nobler weapons is suggested by the remark of Hotspur's lordling in *Henry IV*,

> And that it was great pity, so it was,
> This villanous saltpetre should be digged

215

> Out of the bowels of the harmless earth,
> Which many a good tall fellow had destroyed
> So cowardly; and but for these vile guns,
> He would himself have been a soldier.

The intrinsic hellishness of the instrument is thus alluded to by W. Neade, inventor of the combination bow and pike. "Amongst all which, Bartholdus Swart, the Franciscan friar, with his most devillish invention of gunpowder, is the most damnable, and from hell itself invented." [18] Had Milton written in our own day he would have ascribed to Satan the invention of poison gas.[19]

After the sixth Book, in which the battle in Heaven is concluded, we find no further military details in *Paradise Lost,* though the wars of the Old Testament are incidentally recorded in Michael's prophetic narrative to the repentant Adam. *Samson Agonistes,* while it resounds with the echoes of heroic deeds, is equally devoid of the elements with which we are concerned. The exploits of a giant, assailing his enemies with the jaw-bone of an ass, scarcely come under the category of the art of war. In *Paradise Regained,* on the other hand, Milton introduces material drawn from his special studies in a way which again illustrates their basic importance in the fabric of his poetry. One essential element in his design in the epic of the temptation was the representation of the civilized world in the characteristic aspects which it wore at the beginning of the ministry of Christ. In the course of the second temptation the Savior is carried by Satan to a mountain whence he beholds with sweeping view the kingdoms of the earth and the glory of them. As the culmination of the first part of this geographical and historical pageant (III, 298 ff.) attention centers on the Parthians, then engaged in a campaign against the Scythians. The spectacle is one of arms, and Milton sketches swiftly but with precision the Parthian armament and mode of war.

> For now the Parthian king
> In Ctesiphon hath gathered all his host

---

[18] *The Double Armed Man,* 1625, p. 85.

[19] [It is not hard to guess what weapon Hanford would have used for illustration if this essay had been written in 1946 instead of 1921. Hanford's point that the war in Heaven is generalized war is further supported. J. S. D.]

Against the Scythian, whose incursions wild
Have wasted Sogdiana; to her aid
He marches now in haste. See, though from far,
His thousands, in what martial equipage
They issue forth, steel bows and shafts their arms,
Of equal dread in flight or in pursuit—
All horsemen, in which fight they most excel;
See how in warlike muster they appear,
In rhombs, and wedges, and half-moons, and wings.

Here we see Milton dealing with the cavalry and exhibiting for the first time his text-book knowledge of this field. The line "In rhombs, and wedges, and half-moons and wings" is particularly significant, for the poet has chosen, whether correctly or not, to attribute to the Parthians the use of the rather fancy formations described by the Greeks and adopted, at least in theory, by the cavalry of Milton's time. The locus classicus for these formations is Ælian, who explains in detail several varieties of the rhomb and wedge, together with the square, which Milton does not mention here. The Renaissance editions regularly diagram them, and John Cruso's *Militarie Instructions for the Cavalry,* to cite but a single contemporary text, contains fine pictorial representations of these time-honored forms of battle. The half-moon is not described by Ælian as a cavalry formation but as a way of embattling infantry to encounter a rhomb of cavalry. A convex half-moon of foot is also described and pictorially represented. Ward, as a practical soldier, discusses these matters rather briefly. Milton's line presents, with beautiful condensation, the whole pageant of cavalry formation, as his imagination had reconstructed it from the technical descriptions of the authorities.

In the verses which follow the passage just quoted we have an elaboration of the picture into a splendidly comprehensive spectacle of ancient war.

He looked, and saw what numbers numberless
The city gates outpoured, light-armed troops
In coats of mail and military pride.
In mail their horses clad, yet fleet and strong,
Prauncing their riders bore.
.   .   .   .   .   .   .   .   .

217

He saw them in their forms of battle ranged,
How quick they wheeled, and flying behind them shot
Sharp sleet of arrowy showers against the face
Of their pursuers, and overcame by flight;
The field all iron cast a gleaming brown.
Nor wanted clouds of foot, nor, on each horn,
Cuirassiers all in steel for standing fight,
Chariots, or elephants indorsed with towers
Of archers; nor of labouring pioners
A multitude, with spades and axes armed,
To lay hills plain, fell woods, or valleys fill,
Or where plain was raise hill, or overlay
With bridges rivers proud, as with a yoke:
Mules after these, camels and dromedaries,
And wagons fraught with utensils of war.

It was with just scholarly discrimination that Milton introduced the military portion of his picture in connection with the rising Parthian power. Having done so he does not return to it except incidentally. The image of Rome is constructed of triumph, architectural splendor, luxury and cosmopolitan imperialism; that of Greece of intellectual and cultural dominion, as was appropriate to the time of which he was writing. But to the Parthian picture he has, against strict archeological probability, transferred the complexity and splendor of Persian, Roman, Carthaginian and Macedonian warfare, making it stand symbolically for the glamor of arms in general, an aspect of earthly glory, which, with all the other enticements—of wealth and power and the pride of human learning—Christ rejects and by rejecting teaches his faithful followers to despise.

In this way, therefore, Milton finds a place even in recounting the triumph of the Prince of Peace, for the introduction of the martial element so firmly fixed in epic tradition.

With this final illustration of the way in which Milton assimilated to the idea of poetry the technical detail given him by his studies in military science, our investigation might perhaps be brought to a close. It is difficult to go further without incurring the risk of vagueness and confusion. Yet there can in general be no question that Milton's consideration of the art of war in the large sense in which it was conceived by the ancients and by the Renaissance, exercised an influence of considerable importance on his broader thinking, entering into his conception of human character and coloring his philosophy of life. It has not, I think, been pointed out that Milton's ideas on the subject of discipline derive something of their quality from the application of this principle in the sphere of arms. "There is not," he remarks in *The Reason of Church Government*, "that thing in the world of more grave and urgent importance throughout the whole life of man, than is discipline. What need I instance? He that hath read with judgment of nations and commonwealths, of cities and camps, of peace and war, sea and land, will readily agree that the flourishing and decaying of all civil societies, all the moments and occasions are moved to and fro upon the axle of discipline. . . . Hence in those perfect armies of Cyrus in Xenophon and Scipio in the Roman stories, the excellence of military skill was esteemed, not by the not needing, but by the readiest submitting to the edicts of their commander." The quotation suggests that such passages as those already quoted from Robert Ward, together with innumerable illustrations from history, had gone home to him with full effect and had strengthened his hold on a principle which, notwithstanding the rôle which he was called upon to play of rebel against constituted authority, remained an essential element in his thought.

These studies must also have contributed to his reflection on the nature and sources of fortitude. He rejoiced to set down in the Commonplace Book Ward's affirmation that the true cause of valour is a good conscience. He would have exulted, surely, if he had read it, in Monk's chapter, brief as that on the snakes in Ireland, concerning the armor of a musketeer. "The armour of a musquetier is good courage." The entire section from which Milton's quotation from Ward is taken is a singularly fine analysis of bravery and cowardice. Though there is no detailed proof I cannot help thinking that Milton's characterization of the leaders of the infernal legions in Book II of *Paradise Lost* was influenced by it. Ward makes true valor a mean between softness and presumption, describing the extremes in terms which suggest Milton's representation of Belial and Moloch as two types of councillor and warrior. Certainly this passage and the entire body of Milton's study and reflection regarding military morale, the military character, and the qualities of military leadership enter deeply along with many other varied elements into the portrait of Satan in his capacity as generalissimo of the rebel hosts. No one, I think, having freshly in memory Xenophon's clear cut and systematic presentation of military virtue and skilled leadership in the *Cyropedia* or the anecdotes of great generals and their policies collected by Frontinus and Polyaenus or the modern discussions of Ward and Machiavelli, can read Books I, II, and VI, of *Paradise Lost* without being conscious of a significant relation between certain features of Milton's delineation and this coherent body of ideas and exempla.

In making these claims for the influence of Milton's military reading on his conception of Satan and his fellow captains I do not, of course, ignore the fact that he had also before his eyes as living models the great warriors and councillors of the Commonwealth. But these figures were themselves assimilated in Milton's thought to their ancient types and to the ideal conceptions which already dwelt in his mind as the result of meditative study. His portraits of Cromwell, Vane, and Fairfax illustrate this process and contain besides some clear reflections of Milton's specific study of the art of war. Thus in describing Cromwell's virtues and achievements as commander of the armies of the Commonwealth Milton speaks particularly of the fact that he succeeded in attracting the good and brave from all quarters to his camp and in retaining the obedience of his troops "not by largess or indulgence but by his sole authority and the regularity of his pay." "In this instance," he characteristically adds, "his fame may rival that of Cyrus, of Epaminondas, or any of the great generals of antiquity." The sonnet to Cromwell makes allusion to the importance attached by ancient writers to the enjoyment of Fortune as the qualification of a general, a principle which Milton of course disparaged.

> And on the neck of crowned Fortune proud
> Hast reared God's trophies.

Lines 7 and 8 of the sonnet to Sir Henry Vane the Younger incorporate the oft-quoted maxim that money is the sinews of war, concerning which Milton had quoted an observation of Machiavelli's in the Commonplace Book:

> Then to advise how war may best, upheld,
> Move by her two main nerves, iron and steel,
> In all her equipage.

In this poem Vane's generalship is not separated from his activity in council but is made a part of it. The lines just cited suggest his wisdom in those larger policies and principles of war in which the art military becomes one with the art of rule.

The intimate relation between Milton's military studies and his general scholarly equipment, the degree to which lessons and principles derived from the experience of man in arms are incorporated in the moral, political, and philosophical wisdom which is the common basis both of his poetry and his prose, as well as the very considerable amount of detail furnished to his imagination by the minutiae of ancient and modern war, should now be clear. It was inevitable, given Milton's essentially humanistic temper, that what most interested him in this great and characteristic department of man's activity should be its ultimate significance for human life. In the marshalling of men under the discipline of civilized armies he saw primarily the beauty and effectiveness of order. In the insistence of all wise commanders on the importance of the spirit of the individual fighter in the arbitrament of battle he saw a proof of the superiority of mind over matter. To him as to Robert Ward the real sources of the victorious spirit were moral and religious—righteousness and consciousness of a righteous cause—and this truth was confirmed by the experience of the generation in which he lived. War, then, constituted for Milton a precious illustration of the operation in man of spiritual forces and of the triumph in human affairs of the almighty will. Yet while valuing war for what it has to give of interest and beauty and insight into man's nobler nature, Milton none the less deplores it as an evidence and outcome of man's fallen state. The cause to which he was most deeply allied was the cause of peace, and we may read an eloquent expression of his point of view in the set of sonnets already cited as illustrations of his sense of the military virtues of the captains of the Commonwealth. Great as these men have been as leaders in war their greater work remains:

> O yet a nobler task awaits thy hand
> (For what can war but endless war still breed).
> Peace hath her victories
> No less renowned than those of war.

The same idea is majestically embodied in the contrast between the sixth and seventh books of *Paradise Lost*. Creation follows destruction in the order of Heaven as in that of earth. Thus the angels sing of the unimaginable activities of the Almighty as Milton himself had done of the human deeds of Cromwell.

> Thee that day
> Thy thunders magnified; but to create
> Is greater than created to destroy.

In his own studies in the larger policy of war itself Milton had been much impressed with its constructive side. Under the heading "de disciplina militari" in the Commonplace Book he notes "the justice and abstaining from spoil in the army of Henry V and the benefit thereof"; under the title "De bello" he cites Henry's conduct at Harfleur as an instance of "moderate and Christian demeanor after victory." Another section of the Commonplace Book deals with treaties. These citations suggest the point of contact between Milton's interest in war and his broader study of international relationships. He had read Grotius and must therefore have seen the importance of the restraining usages of civilized warfare as the foundation of a law of nations. For the idea of the larger unity of man Milton had as mighty an enthusiasm as the most ardent of modern internationalists. "Who does not know that there is a mutual bond of amity and brotherhood between man and man all over the world, neither is it the English sea that can sever us from that duty and relation." His hopefulness is tempered, however, both by experience and by the implications of his theology, and he sees no prospect of doing away with war while human nature remains in its present unregeneracy. In his whole attitude toward war Milton is as far removed as possible from the position of the Quakers, with whose ideas in other respects he had much sympathy. His point of view, already made apparent throughout the course of the present study, is, from the theological angle, explicitly set forth in the treatise *Of Christian Doctrine.* "There seems no reason why war should be unlawful now, any more than in the time of the Jews: nor is it anywhere forbidden in the New Testament." The "duties of war," as Milton in his curious way inferred them from the relevant scriptural texts, are said to be, first, that it be not undertaken without mature deliberation; secondly, that it be carried on wisely and skillfully; thirdly, that it be prosecuted with moderation; fourthly, that it be waged in a spirit of godliness; fifthly, that no mercy be shown to a merciless enemy; sixthly, that our confidence be not placed in human strength but in God alone; seventhly, that the booty be distributed in equitable proportions. Regarding which trim reckoning one can only say, in his own words, "This is gospel, and this was ever law among equals."

# 6

## The Dramatic Element in
*Paradise Lost*[1]

Among the literary influences which inspired and guided the genius of Milton critics have never failed to accord a large measure of importance to Elilabethan drama. His early enthusiasm for the English stage is well known. His initial imaginative kinship with Shakespeare and Fletcher and Jonson is admitted and made much of. The obvious fruit is *Comus,* wherein Milton blends a philosophical idealism and a moral seriousness which are peculiarly his own with the imaginative spirit of Elizabethan drama in its more lyric aspects. Commonly, however, the poetic inspiration of the Elizabethans is felt to be in Milton a steadily decreasing factor, giving way more and more to the domination of classical standards and to the requirements of a sterner moral and theological purpose, lingering to a measurable degree in *Paradise Lost* and imparting to it much of its poetic glory, fading into grayness in *Paradise Regained,* and suffering all but complete eclipse in *Samson Agonistes.* So in a sense it is. But a distinction which criticism has tended to neglect must here be carefully maintained. What passes out of Milton is but the more sensuous and aesthetic essence of Elizabethan poetry, the spirit of the masque and the lyric, of *The Faithful Shepherdess* and *A Midsummer Night's Dream.* Milton's sympathy with the English Renaissance in its moral, philosophical, and human phases deepens with advancing years. Classicism moulds and modifies the Elizabethan

---

[1] Reprinted by permission from *Studies in Philology,* xiv, 1917.

influences; Puritanism makes them wear a special expression which though not new is intensified by the circumstances of the later time. But neither classicism nor Puritanism can efface them. They form the ground work of Milton's imagination in his greatest period; and *Paradise Lost* not less but rather more than *Comus* and *L'Allegro* must be explained and interpreted in the light of Elizabethan literature. In the present article I wish to consider some important effects of the dramatic tradition on the form and substance of Milton's epic.

i

If the consequences of Milton's dramatic heritage have never received full recognition it is because of certain facts and assumptions which have tended to draw critical attention in other directions. Chief among these are, first, his disparagement of modern drama and his often expressed preference for the antique; secondly, the fact that his greatest achievement is in epic, whence it is assumed that he is an "epic genius" and that whatever dramatic qualities may be observed in his work are relatively unimportant, an accidental outcome of his subject, and not the product of his more vital inspiration; finally, the notorious Miltonic self-consciousness, which has led critics to regard all his work, from *Lycidas* to *Samson,* as essentially autobiographical and non-dramatic.

But Milton's critical disapproval of modern as opposed to ancient drama is not conclusive with regard to his instinctive sympathies. That Aeschylus, Sophocles, and Euripides are "as yet unequalled of any" was the conviction of a scholar. The fact that his plans for drama show that he contemplated only tragedy on severely classical lines means simply that his classical conscience forbade him to stoop below his critical and conscious ideal. There is no evidence that Milton ever outgrew his early love of Elizabethan drama. Though the masque and comedy which had charmed his youthful fancy ceased to claim him as serious interests became more dominant, the dynamic appeal of the profounder drama of the preceding age would naturally, if he remembered it at all, become stronger in his maturer years and the deep impression of the "Delphic lines" of Shakespeare was not so easily effaced. Frequent echoes in *Paradise Lost* of *Hamlet, Othello, Macbeth,* and the histories show how intimate was Milton's knowledge of these plays.[2] In *Eikonoklastes* he points out a verbal parallel between a passage in *Richard III* and a phrase in one of Charles's prayers, and he comments on the historic truth of Shakespeare's picture of Richard's hypocrisy. More important evidence of the continued relation with Elizabethan tragedy is to be found in his blank verse, which is borrowed as a medium from the English drama though justified by classical and Italian precedent as well, and which in its special Miltonic character is deeply impregnated with the influence of Marlowe.[3]

Finally Milton's very fondness for Greek tragedy above all other ancient forms may perhaps be regarded as itself an evidence of the persistence of tastes first developed under the influence of the Elizabethans. Inheriting from them the dramatic interest and habit but disapproving critically of the modern stage Milton turned to ancient drama where his natural instinct, his scholar's judgment, and his demand for a superior moral significance could find equal satisfaction. It was as natural that Milton should always have had a leaning toward drama as it was that he should have followed the classical model in his own dramatic plans. The ancient plays are too remote to give rise to an enthusiasm for drama as such, though they may mould and develop such enthusiasm when it is of native growth. The essentially Elizabethan character of Milton's dramatic inspiration is recognizable through the classical draperies of *Samson Agonistes* not less than in the more palpably romantic *Comus.*

Unguarded acceptance of the second and third of the traditional assumptions which I have mentioned above, the fallacies,

---

[2] Compare Verity's notes in his Cambridge edition of *Paradise Lost* to II. 662, 911, 1033; III. 1, 60, 606; V. 285; VI. 306, 586; VII. 15; XI. 496; XII. 646, etc.

[3] For specific recollections of Marlowe's *Dr. Faustus* see Verity on *P. L.* I. 254; IV. 20, 75; V. 671, etc. The geographical survey of the kingdoms of the east in *Paradise Regained* is suggestive of Tamburlaine's dying enumeration of his conquests. Part II, scene v. But the kinship of Milton's verse and Marlowe's does not rest on verbal parallels.

namely, of the "epic genius" and of the dominance of self-portraiture, have, I believe, considerably distorted the current Miltonic criticism. To the relation of the autobiographic and the objective elements in Milton's imagination I shall return. The other issue is squarely put in Sir Walter Raleigh's *Milton.* "He is an epic, not a dramatic poet," says Raleigh; "to find him at his best we must look at those passages of unsurpassed magnificence wherein he describes some noble or striking attitude, some strong or majestic action, in its outward, physical aspect." But to claim for Milton a genuine though limited dramatic faculty is not to deny him the epic faculty as well. Why must his genius be so strictly classified? Can we, indeed, be sure of the validity of hard and fast distinctions of the sort apart from the demands of a particular theme and the limitations imposed by a traditional form? With the literary judgment which Raleigh's statement carries with it regarding the relative power and excellence of different portions of Milton's work I find myself in flat opposition. If Milton is an "epic genius" and nothing else, then *Comus* and *Samson Agonistes* and the lyrics are somehow a mistake; but who shall say that Milton was more within his special province in the narrative of Satan's flight through Chaos than he was in the wrathful denunciation of the clergy in *Lycidas* or in the dramatic portrayal of the inner agony of *Samson?*

## ii

The true battle ground of these opinions is *Paradise Lost,* for it is here that the epic and the dramatic impulses meet, as I believe in equal strength. And it is in their meeting that I find the explanation of much that is puzzling in the structure of the poem. Before considering the more fundamental operation of the dramatic principle in *Paradise Lost* I may point to certain outward evidences of the fact that Milton's habit of dramatic expression led him to a far-reaching modification of the epic form.

The way to the extensive use of the more typically dramatic devices was made easy by the character of the epic tradition itself, with its liberal use of dialogue and its tendency toward the visual representation of action. But Milton goes beyond all previous epics in his approximation to dramatic form. With regard to the use of dialogue the question is not primarily one of the actual number of lines in direct discourse but rather of the character of the speeches. The utterances in *Paradise Lost* are, on the whole, less static than is common in earlier epics and more responsive to the situation. The setting is more often brought before us, not in the narrative, but through description put into the mouths of the characters in the scene.

> With first approach of light, we must be ris'n,
> And at our pleasant labour, to reform
> Yon flourie Arbors, yonder Allies green.

> and sweet the coming on
> Of grateful Ev'ning milde, then silent Night
> With this her solemn Bird and this fair Moon,
> And these the Gemms of Heav'n, her starrie train.

> But see the angry Victor hath recall'd
> IIis Ministers of vengeance and pursuit
> Back to the Gates of Heav'n.

There is epic precedent for this, as, for example, in the first book of the *Aeneid,* where Venus refers to a flight of eagles hitherto unmentioned; but reference to the setting is, for the most part in earlier epics, mere allusion, having little or none of the picturesque effect of the lines just quoted. Closer parallels to Milton are to be found in Elizabethan drama, in such passages, for example, as *Romeo and Juliet,* III, 1 ff.

> The grey-eyed morn smiles on the frowning night,
> Chequ'ring the eastern clouds with streaks of light,
> And flecked darkness like a drunkard reels
> From forth day's path and Titan's fiery wheels.
> Now, ere the sun advance his burning eye,
> The day to cheer and night's dank dew to dry,
> I must fill up this osier cage of ours
> With balefull weeds and precious-juiced flowers.

The extension of this device in *Paradise Lost* to the indication of the entrance of a new character may be even more definitely associated with dramatic practice. Thus Gabriel announces the coming of the angelic guard with Satan:

> O friends, I hear the tread of nimble feet
> Hasting this way, and now by glimps discerne
> And with them comes a third of Regal port,
> But faded splendor wan.[4]

The formula is identical with that used for entrances in *Comus, Arcades,* and *Samson.*

> Break off, I feel the different pace
> Of some chaste tread.

> For I descry this way
> Some other tending.

Further evidence of Milton's resort to typically dramatic method is to be found in his transformation of two traditional epic devices, the soliloquy and the relation. They are not, with him, as they are in the main with the earlier epic writers, merely a means of varying the narrative method or of giving rhetorical expression to emotion;[5] they are rather revelations of character and motive and constitute an integral element in the plot. This will be clearer upon a consideration of the dramatic purposes which they arise to serve. We may notice here, as an evidence of Milton's ever present sense of the immediate situation, the pains with which Raphael adapts his narrative to the experience of Adam. We are not allowed to forget that the story is told to him. Thus in seeking for a comparison to express the number of God's hosts he recalls to Adam's memory a scene from his own life:

> as when the total kind
> Of Birds in orderly array on wing
> Came summoned over *Eden* to receive
> Their names of thee.

---

[4] Compare Adam's description of the coming of Michael, Book XI, 192 ff.

[5] Milton has one example of the typical epic soliloquy, Book VI, 113 ff. The nearest approach in ancient epic to the Miltonic character-soliloquy is in the soliloquies of Dido, *Aeneid* IV, 534 ff. and 590 ff. But, aside from the fact that the whole Dido story is episodic, one feels that these utterances are, like the Ovidian suasoria, dominantly rhetorical rather than dramatic. The soliloquies in *Paradise Lost* are, as I shall show later, strikingly analogous in purpose and effect to those in Elizabethan drama.

There has been, as I have said, a tendency among critics to pass over the psychological and dramatic aspects of *Paradise Lost* as nonessential or to consider them even as interfering with his true and epic purpose. Thus Raleigh speaks slightingly of those who "treat the scenes he portrays as if analysis of character were his aim and truth of psychology his touchstone." But psychology and analysis are his aim in so far as the merely human aspect of the story is concerned. The earthly events in the life of Adam and Eve could not be treated with epic externality and bear comparison with the stupendous action of the revolt of Lucifer or the victory of Christ. Regarded otherwise than as a mere episode in the epic whole they must be dignified by emphasis on the psychological factors preparatory to and attendant upon the fall. Nor can it be said that the exigencies of Milton's subject forced him into an emphasis which was alien to his genius. Such a judgment finds its confutation in the consistency and inner truth with which Milton has elaborated the drama of the fall. It is not quite a fact that Adam and Eve, as Stopford Brooke remarks, "are not intended in any sense to represent men and women as we know them, worn with the wars of thought and passion." They do represent man and woman as essentially we know them with all the deeper emotions and the more universal motives of humanity; they have, moreover, a keen, if somewhat limited, experience of life, and a knowledge of many things, which coheres in their consciousness, however unnaturally imparted. The very uniqueness of their situation has bred in them a kind of special character, which, though strange, is not beyond the bounds of the intelligible in human nature. Above all they have the capacity for suffering, for a suffering the more intense because they have once been happy beyond the happiness of men since born. It is only the Satan-blinded critic who will say that their story does not claim us. Involving as it does the elements of human strength and human weakness, the machinations of the power of evil, resistance, fatal error, misery and death, it is the type of all subsequent tragic experience, and Milton has realized as fully as was possible under the limitations of the epic form its tragic value.

He marks with a distinctness unknown in epic the precise weaknesses in both Adam and Eve which lead them to destruction. Eve's intellectual inferiority, which seems at first to be dwelt on with gratuitous and spiteful emphasis, prepares us for the easy blinding of her eyes by the subtle tempter. It is indicated not only by reiterated warning to Adam from on high, but in more dramatic fashion by her words and acts. At the moment of her creation she mistakes the shadow for reality and all her life she is a prey to dreams. She exhibits inferior wisdom in her proposal to work for a day apart from Adam; and she is still shown to be thinking weakly, though with the mental fertility of woman and the radical boldness sometimes manifested by the sex in desperate straits, when after the fall she suggests violent measures in a vain hope to escape the inevitable doom. Curiosity and vanity, the positive defects in her nature, are no less consistently and purposefully brought out. Instinctive desire for admiration, the woman's portion, subsequently increased by Adam's adulation, is unconsciously revealed by her in the narrative of her earliest experiences. It is this which gives to her relation a strongly dramatic as well as an epic character. Thirst for a new experience prompts her to desire the fatal separation from her husband. And the workings of the two motives are subtly portrayed in soliloquy as she resolves, first to taste, and then to share the apple.

With Adam the tragic flaw is simpler but since attention focuses on him it receives proportionally larger emphasis. His superior mentality, his stronger self-control, his greater freedom from the petty human weaknesses render him inaccessible to danger through the channels by which it comes to Eve. The contrast between the two is carefully maintained throughout. Intellectual curiosity of the higher sort he has, but at a word from Raphael he is able to curb it safely within bounds. A nobler and more masculine weakness yet remains in his love for Eve. Here is the one spot of vulnerability in the glorious armor otherwise so flawless. His relation of his first view of Eve has a dramatic purpose correlative to her own. It reveals the ominous and overmastering power of his passion. The angelic visitation is designed to satisfy no idle curiosity but to apprize him of the forces which are ranged against him and to warn him against allowing his passion to control his judgment. Raphael's narrative becomes, therefore, like the others, an integral portion of the dramatic plan. His sin itself is the logical outcome of the motives thus consistently elaborated in the account of his life in Eden. He falls through passion,

> not deceived
> But fondly overcome with female charm.

And as his nature is nobler and more steadfast than Eve's so his fall is greater and more tragic. The "sense of tremendous waste" is here, of power and goodness brought to ruin through the seeming accident of fatal excess in what might have been a best endowment, an effect analogous to that of *Dr. Faustus* or *Macbeth.*

The portrayal of the effects of sin in Adam and Eve is not less worthy of the highest traditions of serious drama than the motivation. In Book IX, which is almost wholly dialogue, Milton all but forgets the larger movement of the poem for the time in his absorption in the human situation. Adam confronted with the terrible fact of Eve's transgression is a genuinely tragic figure. The swiftly changing moods which follow his resolve to share the fate of the beloved Eve are portrayed with the subtlety and power of the greatest of the Elizabethans. False exultation and a renewal of passion are the first results. Then comes mutual recrimination, anger, and revulsion. There is an interruption of the dramatic movement in the interests of the epic action at the beginning of Book X, but in line 720 Milton picks up the earlier scene with a renewed intensity. Adam, "in a troublous sea of passion tost," is tortured with remorseful thought. When Eve addresses him he turns upon her fiercely. Her infinitely pathetic appeal, the panic of the woman who sees the passion of her lover turned to hate, marks one of the intensest moments in the human action.

> Forsake me not thus, Adam, witness Heav'n
> What love sincere, and reverence in my heart
> I beare to thee, and unweeting have offended,
> Unhappilie deceav'd; thy suppliant
> I beg, and clasp thy knees.

From this point on the two actions blend, the repentance of Adam and Eve belonging properly to the larger theme. But there

is a renewal of the tragic note at the pronouncement of the decree
of banishment, and again in the prophecy of Michael, when Adam
beholds the consequences of his sin in his descendants. The mur-
der of Abel, enacted before Adam's eyes, gives the true climax of
the story of the fall. Adam turns in dismay to Michael for explanation of the deed which he has witnessed, and when he learns that
he has at last come face to face with the mysterious and dreaded
Death he starts back in tragic horror at the work of his own hands.

> Alas, both for the deed and for the cause!
> But have I now seen Death? Is this the way
> I must return to native dust? O sight
> Of terrour, foul and ugly to behold,
> Horrid to think, how horrible to feel!

So Othello and Œdipus and Lear reach the pitch of their inward
agony when the film of sin and error is removed from their vision
and they behold for the first time clearly the ruin they have
wrought. The actual catastrophe—be it blindness or banishment
or death—is but the outward consummation of this tragic experience of the soul.

It is not my intention, in thus reading the story of the fall as
tragedy, to minimize the importance of all other elements and
motives. The "tragedy" is tragedy in solution. Its intensity is
necessarily lessened by the requirements of the broader narrative
and by the co-existence of a didactic and philosophic purpose. But
it is truer to Milton's aims to see essential tragedy in *Paradise Lost*
than it is to regard it as a sermon, far truer than to distort it into a
kind of appendage to Miltonic biography. Determination to regard Milton's treatment of the relations of Adam and Eve as a
record of personal experience, to see in Eve, particularly, "the
embodiment of a doctrine," has led to a criticism which is blind
to certain real artistic values in the account. It is no law of
dramatic genius that it must be untouched by individual bias,
must hold no creed but that of artistic sympathy with its creations.
Milton found it possible to reconcile the objective necessities of
his subject with the data of his own experience as many another
artist has done. Personal conviction gave emphasis to, it did not
determine the handling of his theme, and to insist on the personal

element to the exclusion of the objective and dramatic is to do a
serious injustice to his art. A fair example of the fruits of the
autobiographical fallacy is Raleigh's remark that "Milton's disap-
pointment in marriage, which had inspired the early Divorce
Pamphlets, finds renewed expression in Adam's prophecy of un-
happy marriages." [6] Quite aside from the doubt whether Milton's
twenty-year-old memory of his first marriage was poignant enough
to have inspired this passage, one protests against ignoring the
dramatic justification of Adam's words. Whether Milton was disil-
lusioned or not, Adam certainly was, and with good reason. He is
like Antony bursting out in wrath at Cleopatra,[7] or, if a more
exact dramatic parallel is sought, like Jason, expressing his loath-
ing for Medea in a denunciation of all woman kind.[8] Raleigh
believes that Milton "passionately resented" the susceptibility of
man to the attractions of feminine beauty and grace, and that
Raphael, in his remark, "Love hath his seat in reason and is
judicious," "committed himself to a statement which longer experience of the world would have enabled him to correct." But
surely Milton preaches no such doctrine. Adam's love is an evil
not absolutely but only in its excess. Raphael speaks no less than
the truth of love in its proper and ideal essence. The tirade of
Adam, the angelic warnings, the insistence on the comparative
inferiority of Eve constitute no fifth tractate on divorce but are, as
we have seen, in entire consistency with Milton's artistic purpose.

## iii

That the actual literary traditions which most affected Milton
in the portrayal of the inner aspects of the fall were dramatic and
not epic is almost self-evident. For drama alone had hitherto dealt
with the problems of human destiny in its relation to human
character, powerfully and with artistic completeness. We have
already observed Milton's debt to the special method of drama in

---

[6] The passage beginning "Out of my sight, thou Serpent!" *P. L.* X, 867 ff.
[7] *Antony and Cleopatra* IV, 30 ff. "Ah, thou spell! Avaunt!"
[8] Euripides, *Medea*, 573 ff. The language is definitely echoed in Adam's
speech. Cf. also *Hippolytus*, 616 ff.

his modification of epic soliloquy and dialogue. The influence of actual dramatic practice is more deeply felt in the distinctness with which he embodies in *Paradise Lost* the tragic principles of irony and ὕβρις.

There is a strong and pervasive irony in the expectation by Adam and Eve of unbounded happiness as a result of their transgression.

> but I feel
> Far otherwise th'event, not Death but Life
> Augmented, op'nd Eyes, new Hopes, new Joyes.

The touch of madness in their utterances is too clearly marked to have been unconscious. It is ὕβρις in its most essential character —the irrational exaltation which precedes the downfall, the blindness, which drives its victims headlong to destruction, the belief, in short, that they have become as gods. It becomes profoundly ironical when we know the inevitable outcome.

> On my experience, Adam, freely taste,
> And fear of Death deliver to the Windes . . . .
> As with new Wine intoxicated both
> They swim in mirth, and fansie that they feel
> Divinitie within them breeding wings
> Wherewith to scorn the Earth.

A similar ironical emphasis marks the exultant return of Satan to Hell, in a false triumph soon to be dashed by his transformation to a serpent. The ὕβρις motive is present in the portrayal of Satan from the first, coloring perceptibly the purely theological conception of his sinful pride. His defiant spirit, as Verity remarks, recalls Prometheus. He exemplifies the truth of Enobarbus's words concerning Antony:

> I see men's judgments are
> A parcel of their fortunes, and things outward
> Do draw the inward quality after them.

For his logic, even with himself, is sophistry. He falls, like many of Ate's victims,[9] into the error of fatalism and becomes a sceptic of God's power.

---

[9] E.g. Julius Caesar, Macbeth, and Jonson's Sejanus, to name only three Elizabethan instances.

> To mee shall be the glorie sole among
> The infernal Powers, in one day to have marr'd
> What he Almightie styl'd, six Nights and Days
> Continu'd making.[10]

Both Adam and in a higher degree Eve are touched in their sin with the same philosophy:

> The Gods are first, and that advantage use
> On our belief, that all from them proceeds;
> I question it, for this fair Earth I see,
> Warmed by the Sun, producing every kind,
> Them nothing.[11]

In his conscious employment of the ὕβρις motive in *Paradise Lost,* as later in *Samson Agonistes,* Milton was undoubtedly strengthened by its prominence in ancient drama; but on the whole his conception and conduct of the story of the fall are more Shakespearean than Greek. The adoption of the epic plan gave scope for a more complete and essential human drama than was possible under the original dramatic plan. The classical bias of the early drafts, with their elaborate allegory, their emphasis on choric utterance, and their restricted action made necessary by the preservation of the unities, precluded the possibility of any such psychological evolution as we have found in *Paradise Lost.* The adoption of the epic plan brought the poem infinitely nearer to *Hamlet* and *King Lear.* Thus the actual temptation and fall, which in the drama were to have been narrated, could in the epic be represented, with adequate emphasis on motive and with full dramatic effect as in Elizabethan tragedy.

A host of analogies might be pointed out between the more dramatic parts of *Paradise Lost* and the scenes and situations of Elizabethan drama. J. W. Hales has described with convincing distinctness the kinship in theme and purpose of *Paradise Lost* and Shakespeare's *Macbeth.*[12] He forgets, however, to indicate the parallel between the relations of Adam and Eve and those of

---

[10] Cf. I. 116: "Since by Fate the strength of Gods And this Empyreal substance cannot fail." Also Belial's doubt whether God can give annihilation if he will, etc., etc.

[11] Cf. also IX, 806, 928 ff., and X, 799 ff.

[12] "Milton's 'Macbeth.'" *Folia Litteraria,* pp. 198 ff.

Macbeth and his lady. Milton's adoption of romantic love as an essential motive in his story is in itself sufficient to mark his nearness to the Elizabethans.

And it is not only to *Macbeth* that *Paradise Lost* is closely akin. The situation of Adam and Eve in relation to Satan is an essential repetition of that of Othello, Desdemona and Iago,—innocence and love assailed and broken by a villain utterly evil and of superhuman ingenuity. Adam's last parting with Eve in innocence recalls, in its tender pity and poignant irony, Othello's farewell to Desdemona in Act III, scene ii:

> Perdition catch my soul
> But I do love thee! and when I love thee not,
> Chaos is come again.

There is much in Satan to suggest Iago. The jealousy, the malignity, the "motive-hunting," the ironical half-pity, the machination, of Satan's great soliloquy as he first contemplates the hapless human pair amid their bliss make him seem like a reincarnation of the clovenhoofed adversary of *Othello*.

He is of the lineage, too, of other Elizabethan villains. The explicit avowal of an evil intent—"Evil, be thou my good"—made keener by his inability to partake of the delights which he sees around him, ally him closely with Richard III.

> the more I see
> Pleasures around me, so much the more I feel
> Torment within me, as from the hateful siege
> Of contrarieties; all good to me becomes
> Bane.

So Richard:

> And therefore, since I cannot prove a lover
> To entertain these fair well-spoken days,
> I am determined to prove a villain
> And hate the idle pleasures of these days.

Compare also the ironical

> League with you I seek,
> And mutual amity so streight, so close,
> That I with you must dwell, or you with me
> Henceforth.

with Richard's grimmer but less tragic words of Clarence:

> Simple, plain Clarence! I do love thee so,
> That I will shortly send thy soul to Heaven.

The self-torturing remorse of Satan is foreign to both Richard and Iago. It is, on the other hand, the one characteristic which he has in common with the Mephistophilis of Marlowe, and there can be little doubt that Milton received the first suggestion for his conception of Satan in this aspect from his Elizabethan predecessor. The parallel between the two passages in *Dr. Faustus* [13] in which Mephistophilis reveals the hell within and Satan's "Which way I flie is Hell; myself am Hell" is well-known. An almost equally striking likeness between the soliloquy in which this line occurs and the fruitless prayer of Claudius in *Hamlet* has not, I think, been pointed out. Satan's speech itself is, amazingly enough, a kind of frustrated prayer, addressed not directly to the deity, but to the Sun, "that with surpassing glory crownd, Look'st from thy sole dominion like the God Of this new world." He almost longs, like Claudius, for a reconciliation which is made impossible by the persistence of the sin itself.

> O then at last relent; is there no place
> Left for Repentence, none for Pardon left?
> None left but by submission; and that word
> *Disdain* forbids me.

So in *Hamlet*

> What then? what rests?
> Try what repentance can; what can it not?
> Yet what can it when one cannot repent?

Phillips, in his Life of Milton, says that the opening lines of Satan's address were originally composed as the exordium of the drama which Milton had at first designed. If so, it may well be that the tragedy of *Paradise Lost* would have been written much

---

[13] Scenes iii and v.

"For where we are is hell.
And where hell is there must we ever be."
Compare also the earlier words of Faustus:
"Whither should I fly?
If unto God, he'll throw me down to hell."

238

more directly under Elizabethan influences than the dramatic drafts would indicate.

A final instance of the reproduction in *Paradise Lost* of the profounder moods of Elizabethan tragedy is to be found in Adam's self-communion after the fall.

> how gladly would I meet
> Mortalitie my sentence, and be Earth
> Insensible, how glad would lay me down
> As in my Mothers lap? there I should rest
> And sleep secure . . .
> Yet one doubt
> Pursues me still, lest all I cannot die,
> Least that pure breath of Life, the Spirit of Man
> Which God inspir'd, cannot together perish
> With this corporeal Clod; then in the Grave,
> Or in some other dismal place, who knows
> But I shall die a living Death? O thought
> Horrid, if true!

The yearning for death is expressed in language obviously inspired by the Book of Job; but the weighing of the problem, the shrinking on the brink of the unknown, the sense of a mystery which "puzzles the will"—"to die, to sleep! To sleep! perchance to dream!"—all this is *Hamlet*.

But matters of specific and conscious debt to Shakespeare or Marlowe are not here primarily in question. The parallels given above are significant only as evidences of the great impulse of the spirit which passed from the dramatists to Milton and led him to conceive his theme in the light of their creations. If the tragic ideal which he was consciously or unconsciously endeavoring to realize had been attained more artistically and distinctly by the Greeks, it had been attained more powerfully and with an underlying philosophy more in accord with Milton's own by the Elizabethans. It was to them, therefore, that Milton inevitably turned for guidance in the fulfillment of a kindred inspiration.

## iv

The exact position of the tragic element in the economy of *Paradise Lost* and its relation to the other motives in the poem may best be made clear by a consideration of the known facts regarding the growth of Milton's literary plans. His earliest intention was to write an epic, as Spenser had done before him, with King Arthur as the hero. The story, which was as we may infer from *Mansus* and the *Epitaphium Damonis* to have moved toward the defeat of the Saxons as its climax, fell easily and naturally within the traditional epic scope. It could have been plotted on lines exactly parallel to the *Aeneid* or the *Jerusalem Delivered.* Alfred's victory over the Danes at Edlingsby, the only subject set down as heroical in the list drawn up by Milton about the year 1641, is specifically indicated to be like the actions of Odysseus. By this time, however, Milton shows a decided preference for dramatic themes. Of these some thirty are British, and the subjects—murders and the like—are such as would have led Milton to the composition of pure tragedy, presumably on the model of the Greek though doubtless with an underlying Elizabethan content. The remaining sixty odd are scriptural. They are not, like the British themes, specifically designated as tragedies, and some, for example "Samaria liberata," suggest the epic form. Others were clearly intended to be dramatic, but their treatment would obviously have differed from that of the "British tragedies," for the human catastrophe, as in *Christus Patiens* or *Sodom,* would have been enveloped in a wider religious theme. Milton's increasing preference for such material is the inevitable outcome of the religious bias which compelled him to see in all human events the hand of Providence, punishing the wicked and shaping through evil itself the ultimate triumph of its purposes. Yet the human and dramatic aspects of these themes would have remained a vital and original element in their appeal. It was too late in the day for a great poet to revive the religious mystery pure and simple and Milton could not have wished or planned to do so. In the four successive dramatic drafts of *Paradise Lost* the human possibilities of the theme are not lost sight of. They are, however, sorely straightened by the machinery of angels and allegorical figures. Adam and Eve do not appear on the scene until after their fall, the representation of their love and marriage being entrusted to the chorus. On the other hand the wider sweep of the divine action would have been even more imperfectly represented. Milton's ultimate decision to adopt the epic form must have resulted from a perception that neither the one element nor the other could receive its full development within the contracted limits of tragedy. In epic there was ample scope for all. But the epic which should include them would differ radically from any that Milton had previously contemplated on typically heroic themes. For it would retain a core of drama inherited from the original conception and would be subject to the influence of the dramatic quite as much as of the epic tradition.

That Milton was ready enough to accept the transformation of the epic type in which his materials were to involve him is indicated by a passage in the *Reason of Church Government* (1641), where, speaking of his literary plans, he questions whether in epic "the rules of Aristotle are to be strictly kept or nature to be followed, which in those that know art and use judgment is no transgression but an enrichment of art." Consciousness of a radical difference between his epic and others is shown in the invocation at the beginning of Book IX:

> I now must change
> Those notes to tragic . . . . .
> Not sedulous by nature to indite
> Wars, hitherto the only argument
> Heroic deemed.

His own theory of the respective provinces of epic and drama was extremely liberal, the distinction existing in his mind being a merely formal one. Thus he speaks of the Book of Job as a brief epic and of the Apocalypse and the Song of Solomon as drama. In his later work the encroachment of drama on epic is apparent in *Paradise Regained,* which is a series of scenes in dialogue, with a narrative framework almost as slight as that of Job, while *Samson Agonistes,* as Moody remarks, "holds in solution a large amount of narrative" and is, indeed, a "kind of epic drama."

Availing himself of the epic form thus loosely conceived Milton poured into it the materials which so obviously transcended his dramatic plan. He preserved the story of the fall, with much fuller elaboration of its inner and human meaning. He developed also

241

the wider theme, of the general problem of evil and of God's plan for the redemption. The blending of the two elements is accomplished with the highest skill. From man's first disobedience as a center we pass back to the origin of that event in the revolt of Satan and forward to its nullification in the atonement. The poem has a unity of design more apparent than the *Iliad* or the *Aeneid* since the action is less episodic. But within the unity there exists a fundamental duality of motive. The fall of man refuses to be treated as an incident or as a mere exemplum; its tragedy will not be obliterated and lost in a theological triumph of the good. Milton's sense of it, made keen by the experience of life and definite by his inheritance of classic and Elizabethan tragedy, remains to plague us with its poignancy, and he was too great an artist to wish it away. The tragic, therefore, claims its place in the interpretation of the poem. It is deeply inwrought in Milton's fundamental conception and constitutes as essential an element therein as does the noble philosophical ideal of Professor Greenlaw's exposition or the theological doctrine which is the more ostensible goal of Milton's thought.

It is only by recognizing and giving due weight to all the elements which are held in balance in *Paradise Lost* that we can do full justice to Milton's greatness. The criticism which makes him a mere poetic voice, speaking gloriously of irrational or petty things, is as outworn as the Calvinistic system by which his outlook is supposed to have been so strictly bound. The view of life in *Paradise Lost* is one which far transcends the limits of the Puritan theology while it includes its ideal faith. Maintaining a firm hold on spiritual reality and finding in Christianity philosophically considered the guide and hope of man, Milton yet retains a consciousness of the inexplicable mystery of human life. Out of the puzzle of character and destiny springs a sympathy for struggling, taxed humanity which no mere theologian can have. Milton cannot be simply angry with Adam in spite of the enormity of his offense. Nor can he merely rejoice in his repentance and salvation. There remains in his story a residuum of tragedy which outlives the promise of eternal bliss. Death, to the eye of faith, is swallowed up in victory,

Yet tears to human suffering are due,
And mortal hopes defeated and o'erthrown
Are mourned by man.

If Milton thus conceived his theme in a manner more lastingly true to our human experience than is the Calvinistic theology in its rigid and uncompromising clearness, it is because he had drunk deep at the fountains of the Renaissance. The very duality of Milton's epic is an evidence of the high lineage of which he comes. Such complexity of consciousness is as deeply characteristic of *King Lear* [14] as it is of *Paradise Lost,* and it survives the strong assaults of Puritanism and classicism alike in *Samson Agonistes.*

---

[14] The spiritual victory of Lear finds its counterpart in the repentance, the strengthening, and the salvation of Adam. But in *King Lear* as in *Paradise Lost* the triumph of the good does not wipe out the tragic impression or resolve the mystery of evil. For evil is in a sense triumphant too. As Goneril and Regan and Edmund have their partial victory in the wrecking of the earthly happiness of Lear and Cordelia, so Satan has his partial victory in "the fruit whose mortal taste brought death into the world and all our woe." The sudden plunge into tragedy in the fifth act, following the happy consummation toward which the play has moved, is exactly analogous to the stern exile of Adam and Eve, which brings us back to sorrow after the angelic prophecy. The tranquil but saddened closing lines of *Paradise Lost* and *Lear* represent a similar blending into harmony of the opposing principles.

# 7

# The Temptation Motive in Milton [1]

Milton, like all Puritans, was prone to detect in almost every phase of human experience the presence of a moral conflict, to interpret even those aspects which to other men raise no moral questions, in terms of the eternal struggle of good and evil. Victory or defeat in this struggle is the crucial issue in the lives of men as Milton read them, and accordingly temptation, yielded to or overcome, is a dominant motive of his creative art. It is the purpose of this paper to illustrate the application of this principle, not merely to those poems in which it is obvious and universally recognized, but to the whole body of his imaginative work. Such an application, though suggested everywhere in Milton criticism, has never been fully made. The investigation involves a classification of the chief aspects in which the lure of evil presented itself to Milton's consciousness and raises some important questions of interpretation. It serves to throw into strong relief the conflict between the Puritan and the merely human sides of Milton's nature and to emphasize in a new way the well recognized relation between his personal character and the objective creations of his imagination.

i

It was inevitable that Milton should have dealt largely with the subject of temptation. It was no less inevitable that the phases of

---

[1] Reprinted by permission from *Studies in Philology*, xv, 1918.

temptation which he depicts should have been those which presented themselves most characteristically to his own experience. Of these the most obvious is what may be called the temptation of the sense. Milton's strongly sensuous nature and his Renaissance inheritance of appreciation of the absolute value of the life of sensation found themselves in conflict with the inherent asceticism of the Puritan ideal. In his earliest works there is but slight trace of such a conflict. The love of moral purity and the love of beauty, which were the dominant passions of his youth, exist side by side without contradiction. Most of the Latin poems are frank in their avowal of delight in the senses. So also are the Italian sonnets and the English sonnet, *O Nightingale!* In *L'Allegro* and *Il Penseroso* the choice presented is simply between two refined ideals of sense enjoyment, and that choice is presented without committal to either one. The attitude is naive and semi-pagan, an Epicureanism modified only by the ideal of temperance present in Milton's consciousness from the first. In *Lycidas* and the *Sixth Elegy* an opposition is created between the principle of sense indulgence and that of a tempered asceticism, not, however, on strictly moral grounds. The choice comes to Milton as a seeker after the highest poetical achievement. Those who devote themselves to light elegy, he writes to Diodati, may freely indulge in the enjoyments of the Christmas revels; the great serious poet must live sparely, after the manner of Pythagoras. So, with an added suggestion of the difficulty of the course, in *Lycidas,*

> Fame is the spur that the clear spirit doth raise
> (That last infirmity of noble mind)
> To scorn delights, and live laborious days.

In *Comus* the issue is clear cut between sensuality and virtue, but, in accordance with the mediæval temper of Milton's mind and art at this period, he represents the opposition in purely abstract terms. The poem is an allegory rather than a picture of temptation, and the conflict seems remote and unreal. It is as if Milton foresaw rather than actually felt it.

In *Paradise Lost,* on the other hand, the struggle is within the soul. The poem represents the culminating point in Milton's consciousness of danger from this source. It is unnecessary to emphasize the primarily sensual character of Adam's temptation and sin or the relation of the dramatic portrayal to Milton's personal experience. The subject has been comprehensively discussed in Professor Greenlaw's article, "A Better Teacher than Aquinas," and in my own on "The Dramatic Element in *Paradise Lost*," in the preceding essay in this volume; it is also treated in such standard works on Milton as that of Raleigh. In both *Paradise Lost* and *Comus* the doctrine of temperance makes possible a partial reconciliation between the ascetic and the sensuous ideals, the legitimacy of restrained enjoyment being duly defended and the real temptation in *Paradise Lost* being interpreted simply as that of sinful excess. The same characteristic point of view is represented in the sonnet to Lawrence:

> He who of those delights can judge, and spare
> To interpose them oft, is not unwise.

In *Paradise Regained* and *Samson Agonistes* the ascetic point of view has triumphed, but the immediate sense of the reality of the temptation has disappeared. The motive clearly appears in Belial's proposal to tempt Christ with female beauty and in Dalila's endeavor to reawaken passion in the heart of Samson, incidents which seem like distant echoes of the supreme crisis in the life of Adam. In neither poem is there any suggestion of a compromise or of a conflict in Milton's mind between the two ideals. Thus Satan scornfully rejects the idea that any such lure will be of avail with Christ, and Samson proves by his lack of response to Dalila's blandishments how completely free he is from all trace of his former weakness. Milton retains a vivid memory of the temptation,

> Yet beauty, though injurious, hath strange power,
> After offense returning, to regain
> Love once possessed,

but he has, presumably, like Samson ceased himself to feel its power.

246

## ii

No less essential an element in Milton's personal makeup than
the love of sensuous beauty was the abstract love of knowledge; in
like manner the intellectual passion and the pride of intellectual
achievement, indulged in for their own sake and without reference to moral ends, came to be felt by him, under the Puritan
spell, to contain an element of danger. The opposition here is not,
perhaps, so sharp as in the former case. Intellectual curiosity and
the pursuit of fame are less patently associated with the thought of
sin, and the line of demarcation between knowledge sought for its
own sake and knowledge which looks toward the securing of the
soul's salvation is more difficult to draw, especially for a disciple of
the Reformation and a Platonist. The *Areopagitica* shows how
liberal was Milton's interpretation of the permissible in intellectual activity, but it also shows that the subordination of such
activity to moral and religious uses was constantly in his thought.
Truth, which is the goal of all thought and study, is for him
religious truth, "which came once into the world with her Divine
Master." So, also, in the tract on Education the end of learning is
"to know God aright, and out of that knowledge to love him, to
imitate him, to be like him." The supplementary idea that we can
most clearly arrive at such knowledge "by orderly conning over
the visible and inferior creature," and the later definition of a
complete and generous education as "that which fits a man to
perform justly, skilfully and magnanimously all the offices both
private and public, of peace and war," is where Milton parts
company with the Middle Ages and the strictest Puritanism and
joins the Renaissance. Yet the absolute "nihil humanum," though
as strong an instinct in Milton as in any man, could not be
accepted by him as a principle, however much in actual practice
he lived and wrought in the spirit of this creed. Not frequently,
perhaps, in his own zeal for knowledge was he checked by the
consciousness of sin, but it was inevitable, even with a man so
assured of the rightness of his ways as Milton, that the question

should sometimes have intruded itself upon his thoughts. Certainly his theory remained fixed; and, recognizing the presence of a temptation even here, he more than once incorporates it as a motive in his works.

In *Paradise Lost* Adam, seeking for more knowledge than the angel has vouchsafed him, is met with the warning to ask no further:

> Heaven is for thee too high
> To know what passes there; be lowly wise;
> Think only what concerns thee and thy being;
> Dream not of other worlds.

It is not without astonishment that we read these words from Milton's pen. They seem like the most violent contradiction of the whole spirit of his life and jar strangely with the impassioned plea for free inquiry in the *Areopagitica*. Yet the utterance is not insincere. It is the stern Puritan who speaks, chastening as with a rod the unregenerate spirit of intellectual curiosity, which, like passion, is instinctive in the human heart. Both tendencies are, in Milton's view, weak spots in the armor of the natural man, even in Adam living without sin. They are, however, equally innocent *per se;* and here the doctrine of temperance comes again to Milton's rescue, though not without a subtle contradiction. Though all knowledge which is not "for use" is sin (Milton does not quite call it sin but folly) we may freely seek if we seek not to know too much.

> But knowledge is as food, and needs no less
> Her temperance over appetite, to know
> In measure what the mind may well contain;
> Oppresses else with surfeit, and soon turns
> Wisdom to folly, as nourishment to wind.

As for Adam he can willingly content himself within the limits set by his angelic guest. He even elaborates the point.

> To whom thus Adam, cleared of doubt, replied:—
> "How fully hast thou satisfied me, pure
> Intelligence of Heaven, Angel serene,
> And, freed from intricacies, taught to live

The easiest way, nor with perplexing thoughts
To interrupt the sweet of life, from which
God hath bid dwell far off all anxious cares,
And not molest us, unless we ourselves
Seek them with wandering thoughts and notions vain!
But apt the mind or fancy is to rove
Unchecked; and of her roving is no end,
Till, warned, or by experience taught, she learn
That not to know at large of things remote
From use, obscure and subtle, but to know
That which before us lies in daily life,
Is the prime wisdom; what is more is fume,
Or emptiness, or fond impertinence."

Clearly it is not through this gateway that sin will find access to Adam's soul. With Eve, however, the case is different. She had sought, in innocence, to learn by listening unperceived that which concerned her not to know, and vain curiosity to try the experience of good and evil is one of the co-operating motives in her fall.

In *Paradise Regained* the issue comes up again and that in a form which seems to bring us nearer to a real debate in Milton's mind. In the highly elaborate second temptation Satan shows Christ "the kingdoms of the world and the glory of them." Milton interprets the temptation progressively. The power of wealth is offered first, as a means of satisfying physical appetite and as a means by which Christ may accomplish his purpose. When the Lord rejects both wealth and the power of wealth Satan proposes fame; lastly he actually exhibits empire before his eyes, passing from the spectacle of mere material power illustrated by Parthia and Rome to the more glorious one of intellect and culture embodied in the literature and thought of ancient Athens. The representation is from one point of view historical and dramatic. The issue between the specious and the true means of accomplishing his mission is such a one as might be supposed actually to have presented itself to Christ. But we feel that the tempter, while ostensibly submitting these things as an aid to Christ's messiahship, relies also on their attractiveness for their own sakes. The connection with a special and divine mission, though representative of the way in which men of high ideals may be seduced from their true course, is in the main peculiar to the historical Christ, but the elaborate review of the things of this world considered as objects of desire applies to all mankind. The extension and emphasis of the account can hardly be explained except on the supposition that Milton was aiming chiefly at this broader application. The tempter who rejects female beauty as an instrument of temptation would little deserve his reputation for subtlety, so completely does he forget Christ and his situation in passage after passage, if he were not directing his appeal through Christ to humanity at large. Milton slightly masks his purpose by insisting on the human rather than the divine aspect of Christ. Considered as Son of God his experience is unique; considered as man it is universal; as mankind fell through Adam's weakness, it stands again in Christ's firm resistance of the characteristic temptations of human life. Such, as I conceive, it is the true theme of *Paradise Regained*. The poem is a majestic piece of symbolism, expressing in objective and historical terms a subjective and universal content. The criticisms which have been levelled at Milton's handling of the second temptation fail to take into account the author's wider purpose. He is charged with having falsified the biblical account by elaborating the simple phrases of Scripture and making Christ argue with his enemy. But how else could he have contrived to reveal the pageant of this world, displaying, as he does to the full extent of his powers, on the one hand its glamor of attractiveness, and on the other its vanity? It is, indeed, this object which justifies Milton in writing at all on the temptation. Whether true or false to the psychology of Christ the poem has a universal validity as a great debate between the good and evil principles, a modern *"de contemptu mundi,"* written by a man who could, in his own phrase, "apprehend and consider vice with all her baits and seeming pleasures, and yet abstain, and yet distinguish, and yet prefer that which is truly better."

In this interpretation *Paradise Regained* gives us a more complete insight than any of the earlier works into Milton's thought concerning the nature and aspects of temptation. The lure of the senses is here, in the description of the banquet, which, as Mr. A.

H. Gilbert has conclusively shown,[2] is a part of the second temptation, not a repetition of the first. The feast is calculated not
merely to satisfy hunger, but to satisfy it in a sumptuous manner
and with an appeal to the æsthetic sense.

> And at a stately sideboard, by the wine
> That fragrant smell diffused, in order stood
> Tall stripling youths rich clad, of fairer hue
> Than Ganymed or Hylas; distant more,
> Under the trees now tripped, now solemn stood,
> Nymphs of Diana's train, and Naides
> With fruits and flowers from Amalthea's horn,
> And ladies of the Hesperides, that seemed
> Fairer than feigned of old, or fabled since
> Of faery damsels met in forest wide
> By knights of Logres, or of Lyones,
> Lancelot, or Pelleas, or Pellenore.
> And all the while harmonious airs were heard
> Of chiming strings or charming pipes; and winds
> Of gentlest gale Arabian odors fanned
> From their soft wings, and Flora's earliest smells.

The whole marvellous passage has been blunderingly assailed by
an illustrious line of Milton critics, who begin by confounding it
with the temptation to turn the stone to bread and assert that
Milton has lowered the moral tension of the original and has
failed in his artistic aim because "given Christ's nature, the temptation is not tempting." The answer is obvious.

The banquet stands for luxury. If Christ, after forty days of
fasting in the wilderness would not have been moved by such a
scene, most men would find in it no small degree alluring.

As for Milton himself his point of view toward the merely
material side of the temptation, the banquet, perhaps, in its grosser
aspects, certainly the thirst for worldly power and the glory of
conquerors and princes, is wholly impersonal. He knows that
these things move men; him they do not move. He grows enthusiastic, it is true, as he pictures the grandeur that was Rome, but it

---

[2] "The Temptation in *Paradise Regained*," *Journal of English and Ger-
manic Philology*, 1916.

is because that grandeur appeals to him as an object of knowledge and contemplation. Rome as a material fact had ceased to be, but the Rome of the imagination, "with towers and temples proudly elevate," lived on and powerfully appealed to Milton's interest. This consideration serves to lead us to that element in the temptation which comes closer to his personal sympathies and inclinations.

In a memorable passage in Book IV (238–284) Milton gives the most eloquent of pleas for ancient culture. He speaks in his own person as a man of the Renaissance; yet in putting the plea in the mouth of Satan and in making Christ reject it all as vanity he reveals the obstinate Puritanical questioning, the same that dictated the angel's rebuke of Adam for considering too curiously what concerned him not to know. Nor can it be said that the poet was led simply by dramatic probability to make Christ condemn all ancient wisdom as

> Conjectures, fancies, built on nothing firm;

to dismiss even Plato, who had so dominated Milton's own best thought, as but a master of "fabling and smooth conceit." It is from the depths of his conviction that Milton speaks in Christ's pronouncement,

> He who receives
> Light from above, from the fountain of light,
> No other doctrine needs.

Even here, however, the old contradiction still remains. In the midst of his disparagement of classical philosophy Milton weakens.

> But these are false, *or little else but dreams.*

And of these dreams he cannot bring himself to say quite flatly that Jesus Christ was ignorant.

> Think not but that I know these things, or think
> I know them not.

He hedges again in making Christ modify his position and condemn, not the reading of many books, but mere reading "without a judgment equal or superior" to what is read. Finally he effects a half reconciliation between his love of learning and his Puritanism by opposing Hebrew literature at all points to pagan and contending for its superiority (IV, 331–364).

In his treatment of fame Milton again encounters the problems raised by his own instinct strengthened by the traditions of the Renaissance. Unmoved as he was by vulgar fame of worldly power Milton had been from his youth a devotee of that fame which comes from glorious achievement in the kingdom of the mind. But even this nobler ambition was in conflict with his Puritan view of what is and what is not the true object of man's earthly sojourn. Confronted with this conflict Milton again contrives, while preserving the moral issue, to reconcile the aspiration of the natural man with the claims of his higher theological existence. Satan praises fame and glory,

> glory the reward
> That sole excites to high attempts the flame
> Of most erected spirits.

Christ's reply is a rejection of vain or earthly glory, of glory for its own sake, but an implied acceptance of the higher glory, which comes from virtue.

> This is true glory and renown, when God
> Looking on the earth, with approbation marks
> The just man and divulges him through Heaven.

The whole passage is an echo, in very similar terms, of *Lycidas*. Milton's thought on the subject apparently had not changed in all the intervening years.

> Fame is no plant that grows on mortal soil,
> Nor in the glistering foil
> Set off to the world, nor in broad rumour lies,
> But lives and spreads aloft by those pure eyes
> And perfect witness of all judging Jove;
> As he pronounces lastly on each deed,
> Of so much fame in Heaven expect thy meed.[3]

---

[3] The same opposition of earthly and heavenly glory is made in the following passage from the Second Defence: "I considered that many had purchased a less good by a greater evil, the meed of glory by the loss of life;

The pursuit of fame is a phase of the great sin of pride. It was this "last infirmity of noble mind" which had prompted Satan himself to rebellion and attended him even as a spirit damned, as Milton fittingly recalls in connection with Christ's ordeal:

> So spake the Son of God; and here again
> Satan had not to answer, but stood struck
> With guilt of his own sin—for he himself,
> Insatiable of glory, had lost all.

The true aim of man is God's glory, not his own:

> For why should man seek glory who of his own
> Hath nothing.

Satan had sought his own and fallen. Christ said

> I seek not mine, but His
> Who sent me.

Such then is Milton's ascetic view of fame. But into both *Lycidas* and *Paradise Regained* there intrudes, in contradiction to the idea that fame is a thing which lives from man to God alone, the recognition of a worth in earthly glory. We feel that the passage in *Lycidas* is after all the result of a human rather than a religious aspiration. The really vital and essential contrast there is between the shortness of man's life and the eternity of fame:

> But the fair guerdon when we hope to find . . . .
> Comes the blind Fury with the abhorred shears,
> And slits the thin-spun life. "But not the praise,"
> Phoebus replied, and touched my trembling ears.

In *Paradise Regained* the distinction is drawn between a temporary blaze of fame and the lasting recognition of true merit. The one, the portion of conquerors and princes, is cut short by death:

> Till conqueror Death discover them
> Scarce men.

The other, attained without ambition, war or violence—in men like Socrates or Job, "by deeds of peace, by wisdom eminent"—

---

but that I might procure great good by little suffering; that though I am blind, I might still discharge the most honorable duties, the performance of which, as it is something more durable than glory, ought to be the object of superior admiration and esteem."

conflict is
the sonnet
he form of
ring of his
, had been
grew older
dly in large
t, the great-
rsists in his

spirit that Milton had determined to
to after times, as they should not
had sought, for *Paradise Lost,* "fit
d, as he was, not to seek glory "as
l," yet scarcely accepting in its full
classed all pursuit of earthly fame

## ii

ain in some-
a promising
ty hopes and
oubled by the

ptations springing from men's
tive desire to know all things,
earthly immortality—tempta-
e classed them, of the flesh and
ent and his practical conduct
deal. His true philosophy is
emperance, not asceticism, is
ard to temptation in another
ty of compromise. The dan-
self, and not merely in its
air, the temptation to yield
confidence in one's self and
himself is the very embodi-
e against all the shocks of
ely think of him as being
that his moral and spirit-
lict. To say, for example,
, thinking it "base to be
his fellow-citizens were
e put aside his dearest
did so "without much
l to his real humanity.
ilton himself affirms in
l greatness of Milton's
rolonged and heroic
n other respects it is
man ever had more

ade.

liate and firm,
estion was not
depths of Mil-

new and almost
which is written
iliar passage in
and again does
unting even to a
ways with him:

ied,"

nd lay hold again
ing

fate,
own!)

compelling reasons for despair and doubt, and the
everywhere implicit in his life and works. It appears in
*On His Being Arrived at the Age of Twenty-three* in t
a slight bewilderment at the unexpectedly slow matu
talents, a moment of self-questioning if, after all, he
right in expecting of himself great things. As Milton
this lack of confidence in his own genius was undoubte
part dispelled by the facts of his actual accomplishmer
ness of which he fully recognized, but a trace of it p
fear lest

> an age too late, or cold
> Climate, or years, damp my intended wing

In *Lycidas* the temptation to despondency appears a
what altered form. Startled by the untimely death o
youth Milton turns his thoughts upon his own lof
aspirations. In the face of such a catastrophe he is tr
sense that all high effort is in vain:

> Alas! what boots it with uncessant care
> To tend the homely, slighted shepherd's tr

Here, as elsewhere, the response of faith is immed
but the moment of doubt is not less real. The qu
asked merely to be answered. It springs from the
ton's consciousness.

The coming of blindness brought to Milton a
overwhelming impulse to despair, the record of
in the two sonnets on his blindness, in a fam
*Paradise Lost* (iii, 21–55) and elsewhere. Again
the persistent murmur rise within his heart, amo
protest against the apparent injustice of God's

> "Doth God exact day labour, light den
> I fondly ask.

But as often does he school himself to patience a
on faith and hope. He does so, now by remember

> Those other two equalled with me in
> (So were I equalled with them in ren

256

> Blind Thamyris and blind Mæonides,
> And Tiresias and Phineus, prophets old;

or by noting how much the more heavenly light of inspiration shines inward; or by recalling that he had lost his eyesight "overplied in Liberty's defense"; or by taking to heart the sustaining thought,

> They also serve who only stand and wait.

The variety of the response of faith shows how great was Milton's need of it. The failure of the Puritan cause and the isolation of his later days added immeasurably to his weight of gloom. Surely if we enquire after the great ordeal of Milton's personal experience it was this inward struggle with the Giant Despair, a foe more subtle than the flesh, more deadly than the pride of intellect or the quest for fame. It would be surprising if Milton had not embodied it in his more objective work.

He had done so repeatedly and with great distinctness. We may note first its early appearance, incidentally, in *Comus* (331–489), where the pessimism of the younger brother is met by the firm confidence of the elder, who voices Milton's faith in the security of virtue against real harm. The two characters are, after the allegorical manner of this piece, the symbols of fear and hope, as Comus and the Lady are of sensuality and purity. In *Paradise Lost* the moral conflict centers in the temptation of pride and passion, but after their transgression Adam and Eve fall into a deep despair, from which they must be rescued by the angelic vision, with its promise of redemption. It is not with them a sin but the inevitable consequence of sin. So also is the more hopeless despair of Satan. In the great soliloquy in Book IV of *Paradise Lost* (32–113) and elsewhere we see him engaged in an effort, rendered vain by the persistence of his pride, to throw it off. In the soliloquy of Adam in Book X (721–844), with its longing for oblivion and its questioning of divine Providence, we may perhaps see in some degree a reflection of Milton's darker hours, but the main emphasis, as I have maintained elsewhere, is certainly dramatic.

In *Paradise Regained* the trial of faith becomes essential. It constitutes, indeed, the substance of the first and third temptations, thus fulfilling the significance of the poem as the human victory over all temptation, whereby man shall regain the happier inner paradise of moral freedom promised to Adam and his descendants as the reward of their own efforts. In Milton's interpretation Satan's "command this stone that it be made bread" is not a hunger temptation.[4] Milton's attention is fixed on the words "If thou be the Son of God" and on Christ's reply "Why dost thou then suggest to me distrust?" which reveal the true nature of the trial. The third temptation (IV, 500 ff.) is essentially a repetition of the first. Satan returns to the insinuation that Christ is not the son of God in any special sense,

> For Son of God to me is yet in doubt,

and bids him test his belief by a rash act. But here there is the added element of futile violence—

> Another method must I now begin,—

and Christ's victory is given finality by the manifestation of God's approval:

> He said, and stood.
> But Satan, smitten with amazement, fell. . . .
> . . . . . . . . . and straight a fiery globe
> Of Angels on full sail of wing flew nigh,
> And on their plumy vans received him soft
> From his uneasy station.

Milton is, of course, following the Scriptural account with strict adherence to what he conceived to be its inner meaning, inventing the miracle on the suggestion afforded by the temptation itself: "For it is written, He shall give the angels charge over thee." But the first and third temptation, like the second, were certainly more to Milton than a mere historical encounter between Christ and Satan. R. D. Miller, writing on the temptation,[5] seems to me utterly to mistake the import of the work. It is true that Christ is not shown to have been inwardly moved by doubt, but to say that Milton therefore shows himself blind to the spirit-

---

[4] See Bk. II, ll. 243 ff. and A. H. Gilbert, *op. cit.*
[5] *MLN*, vol. xv, pp. 202 ff.

ual significance of the Scriptural incident is absurd. In no case, except in that of Adam and Eve, who actually sin, is temptation represented in the modern way as operating within the soul. The method in *Paradise Regained* is, as it had been in *Comus,* symbolical, with this important difference, that while the Lady is an abstract representation of virtue, Christ is a man, sharing the experience of men. We must remember that for Milton, all temptation was in a sense external, a direct suggestion of the devil. He would so interpret a conflict of conscience within himself and he so interprets the experience of Christ. He may well have believed in the physical appearance of Satan in the biblical temptation scene, but such belief does not impair the spiritual meaning of his treatment of the event in its wider application.

In the final work of his imagination Milton deals again with the temptation to distrust, which now becomes a dominant and controlling motive. *Samson Agonistes* has not ordinarily been recognized as a temptation drama. It has indeed been felt to be lacking in the essential element of dramatic conflict. This is the substance of Johnson's complaint that the play has a beginning and an end but no middle. Milton's object has been held to have been the representation in semi-epic fashion, by cumulative incident, illustration, and comment, of the character and life of Samson. The various incidents are "provocative," tending to rouse Samson from the listlessness into which he has fallen to the pitch of his last and greatest act. According to this view the true drama of Samson's life lies in the past, in his crucial experience of temptation by Dalila, a sensual temptation of which mention has already been made.

To read the play, however, from this point of view alone is to miss an essential part of Milton's conception of his subject. It is not simply that the poet transfers to his hero the gloom and pathos of his own last days. He portrays him as a great man, who in the midst of failure and personal affliction, is definitely tempted to surrender his trust in Providence because of his inability to understand its dealings with himself. Samson has lived and wrought under the conviction, approved by the miracle attending his birth and by the unmistakable voice within, that he was a chosen vessel of God's purposes. Now he has fallen on evil days, and his deeds for Israel's freedom have come to nothing. The obvious conclusion is that he was wrong; but the assurance of God's favor had been too profound to be thus easily discarded. It had been his personal evidence of the care of God for his people, and that gone, his faith in Providence itself would fail. Hence, though the dealings of God with him are become dark, Samson resists to the uttermost the suggestion of distrust.

The temptation is emphasized, not only by the logic of circumstances, but by the insinuations of the Chorus and Manoa. They are the antagonists of the drama, however much they may come ostensibly to comfort and sustain. The Chorus first raises the point of Samson's marriages:

> Why should'st thou wed Philistine women rather
> Than of thine own tribe fairer or as fair?

Samson's reply is an appeal to the validity of the inward voice: [6]

> They knew not
> That what I motioned was of God; I knew
> From intimate impulse, and therefore urged
> The marriage on.

The Chorus acquiesces, but insinuates a new distrust:

> In seeking just occasion to provoke
> The Philistine, thy country's enemy,
> Thou never wast remiss, I bear thee witness;
> *Yet Israel still serves with all his sons.*

At Samson's firm declaration that the fault rested not on him but on Israel's governors the Chorus apparently is convinced and breaks into the great ode,

> Just are the ways of God,
> And justifiable to men. . . .
> Down, Reason, then; at least vain reasoning down.

---

[6] Samson's "intimate impulse" corresponds with the "interior light, more precious and more pure" with which Milton felt himself to be illuminated.

> So much the rather, thou, Celestial Light,
> Shine inward.

So also does his sense of special consecration. Compare the Second Defence: "And, indeed, in my blindness, I enjoy in no inconsiderable degree the favour of the deity."

Then comes Manoa and straightway falls to deploring "man's ever failing trust in mortal strength." His questioning of God's purposes is more explicit:

> Oh, wherefore did God grant me my request,
> And as a blessing with such pomp adorned?
> Why are his gifts desirable, to tempt
> Our earnest prayers, then, given with solemn hand
> As graces, draw a scorpion's tail behind?
> For this did the angel twice descend? for this
> Ordain thy nurture holy, as a plant
> Select and sacred? glorious for a while,
> The miracle of men; then in an hour
> Ensnared, assaulted, overcome, led bound,
> Thy foes derision, captive, poor and blind,
> Into a dungeon thrust, to work with slaves!
> Alas! methinks whom God hath chosen once
> To worthiest deeds, if he through frailty err,
> He should not so o'er whelm.

But Samson still rings true:

> Appoint not Heavenly disposition, Father
> Nothing of all these evils hath befallen me
> But justly; I myself have brought them on.

Again Manoa renews the assault, this time raising the question whether the inner impulse was indeed of God:

> I cannot praise thy marriage-choices, son—
> Rather approved them not; but thou did'st plead
> Divine impulsion prompting how thou might'st
> Find some occasion to infest our foes.
> I state not that; this I am sure—our foes
> Found soon occasion thereby to make thee
> Their captive and their triumph.

And he reveals in the Philistine proposal to make Samson exhibit himself in honor of Dagon the depths of his degradation and failure. The circumstance intensifies Samson's misery, but only brings forth a more confident utterance of his faith. For himself he has no hope, but God will triumph over Dagon. There follows (606–651) a new outburst of wretchedness prompted by the goad of Manoa's comfort, but through all his agony Samson does not question whether God be God or doubt the evidence of his former favor.

Here, then, is the "middle" of the drama for which Johnson sought. The crisis comes at this point, technically at the end of the second act. The trial is over and Samson has emerged from it unscathed. He is soon to be rewarded for his faith by being made the very instrument of God's triumph over Dagon. The remaining incidents in the drama are devoted to preparation for the event and to the gradual shaping of Samson's purposes toward his final act. Even the Chorus and Manoa, though they are mistaken as to the nature of Gods' proposed deliverance, have come to share the lofty confidence of Samson.

> Go, and the Holy One
> Of Israel be thy guide
> To what may serve his glory best, and spread his name
> Great among the Heathen round:
> Send thee the Angel of thy birth, to stand
> Fast by thy side.

The play is thus the exact counterpart of *Paradise Regained*, the work to which it is most closely related in style and art, and the connection between the two poems is emphasized by their common relation to the Book of Job, which may, indeed, be said to have been in a general way Milton's model in his interpretation of the experiences both of Christ and Samson. That the book was much in Milton's thoughts at this time is evident from the references in *Paradise Regained*, where the case of Job, tempted by Satan, is repeatedly paralleled with that of Christ. The situation in *Samson Agonistes* is even more strikingly analogous with that of Job. In each the counsel of the comforters is the counsel of despair. In each their suggestions encounter an inward conviction, firmly held against the present evidence of God's disfavor. In each the hero goes through a spiritual crisis, from which, after intense suffering he comes forth with a clearer faith. In each the maintenance of this faith against all assaults is rewarded by a triumphant manifestation of God's approval.

In its relation to Milton's personal life *Samson Agonistes* is not only an embodiment of his own sorrows and an allegory of his

fortunes and those of the Puritan party. It is a living representation of the assault of temptation, bred after the subtle manner of the tempter, upon the fortress of the soul. In that heroic
Samson, wrestling, not alone with the outward ills of blindness
and captivity, but against a subtler foe within the breast, the true
Milton stands revealed, no alien figure dwelling like a star above
the reach of human weakness, but a man, struggling as he had
from youth in the arena of life, "where that immortal garland is to
be run for, not without dust and heat." The passage in the *Areopagitica* from which these words are taken gives his mature ap-
praisal of the value of the conflict. His was no "fugitive and
cloistered virtue, unexercised and unbreathed." It had met its
adversary in many forms and had been purified and strengthened.
The rugged steep which he had climbed was the same which he
had seen, as it were, from a distance, in *Comus,* the same which
the angel had pointed out to repentant Adam, the same which
Christ had traveled in the wilderness, the same which Samson had
ascended to the peace of soul which came to him only with his
death.

# 8

## *Samson Agonistes* and Milton in Old Age [1]

*Paradise Lost,* the "monumentum aere perennius" which Milton had planned in youth but whose execution he perilously delayed till beyond his fiftieth year, stood complete and glorious by the summer of 1665. Before its publication in 1667 its author had probably finished the second masterpiece of his maturity, *Paradise Regained.* The composition of *Samson Agonistes* presumably fell within the immediately succeeding years. The two poems appeared together in 1671. Were these later works really afterthoughts, as Thomas Ellwood's well-known anecdote regarding the first of them suggests? Despite the gentle Quaker's unquestionable candor I cannot think so. At his comment, "Thou hast said much here of Paradise lost, but what hast thou to say of Paradise found?", the poet sat in silence and seemed to meditate. We are under no compulsion to believe that he was struck dumb by the novelty of the idea! There is, to be sure, the later very explicit statement, quoted by Ellwood as made when Milton showed him in London the manuscript of *Paradise Regained* "This is owing to you, for you put it in my head at Chalfont which before I had not thought of," but is it not quite possible that Ellwood is here innocently twisting some merely polite or even ironical remark of Milton's into conformity with his own self-flattering opinion that he was the "fons et origo" of an epic poem?

---

[1] Reprinted by permission from University of Michigan *Studies in Shakespeare, Milton and Donne,* New York: Macmillan, 1925.

However this may be, there is a kind of inevitability in these last two works which makes it difficult to accept the idea that a chance suggestion in any very important way determined either of them. In form and general character, at least, we may regard them as predestinate. The evidence goes back to a passage in the *Reason of Church Government,* written in 1641, where Milton takes the reader into his confidence regarding his literary ambitions. He is in doubt, he tells us, whether to adopt the form of an extended epic like the *Aeneid,* or of the brief epic which he says is illustrated by the Book of Job, or of drama, "in which Sophocles and Euripides reign." Since life and energy endured he did all three, taking thereby a triple bond of fame. *Paradise Lost* is the new *Aeneid,* exhibiting all the recognized technique of the full and perfect epic; *Paradise Regained* is something more unusual, a heroic poem composed entirely of dialogue, save for a narrative introduction and conclusion and a few links. Its formal precedent is obviously the Book of Job, regarded not as a drama but, more strictly, as a modification of the epic type. *Samson Agonistes,* finally, is Hellenic tragedy restored.

With his plan of life endeavor thus beyond expectation fulfilled, it seems unlikely that Milton would ever have considered a further addition to his poetical works. The lengthy list of dramatic subjects in the Cambridge manuscript (which includes a "Samson Agonistes" under the title "Dagonalia" and a kind of "Paradise Regained" under that of "Christus Patiens") together with the corresponding one of epic themes which Professor Gilbert supposes him to have drawn up at the same time [2]—these lists were not in any sense a program. Milton was not given, like the dreamer Coleridge, to projecting vaguely a host of works which he could never write. The manuscript materials are notes taken in the process of canvassing the whole range of available materials before making a final choice. Had Milton enjoyed twenty more years of life and had there been twenty Ellwoods to urge him on, we should never have had at his hands the suggested epic on the deeds of Alfred, or the drama of "Sodom Burning" or the new

---

[2] "The Cambridge Manuscript and Milton's Plans for Epic," *Studies in Philology,* 16 (1919). 172–176.

Macbeth. To write any one of them would have been to mar the antique symmetry of his achievement.

It is not, however, from the standpoint of outward form alone that Milton had reason to regard his contemplated work as done. The three poems are complementary in theme and in ethical idea. Taken together they constitute a complete and unified embodiment of Milton's Christian humanism, the full working out of the didactic purpose which he had accepted as a responsibility implied in his abandonment of the office of preacher for the more congenial one of poet. Let us, as an approach to the present object of giving sharper definition to the significance of *Samson Agonistes* as a work of the poet's last years, consider first the relation of the two companion epics. This relation is clearly not the mechanical one which their contrasting titles might at first suggest, and which, had *Paradise Regained* been named but never written, we should naturally have inferred from Milton's initial statement of his theme:

> Of man's first disobedience and the fruit
> Of that forbidden tree whose mortal taste
> Brought death into the world and all our woe,
> With loss of Eden till one greater man
> Restore us, and regain the blissful seat.

These lines appear to promise a scheme of salvation, according to the ideas of traditional Christianity, and for such a scheme we do not have to await a second work. It is already amply given in the first. But the truth is that Milton pays little more than lip honor to the theological system which his work bears in its superscription. His deeper interest is to be sought elsewhere. At the close of *Paradise Lost* the Archangel Michael, after revealing to Adam at somewhat wearisome length the history of redemption, instructs him in quiet but thrilling words how he may regain what he has lost and build for himself "a paradise within thee happier far." The program is that of all humanity, for Adam is the representative of man. Mere repentance and the sacrifice of Christ are but the form of salvation. The thing itself involves the coöperating will as manifested in the successful meeting of future trial. It is the work of no vicarious and of no single act, but of patient moral discipline in a world of evil, according to a pattern from above. The actual exhibition of the process is not included in *Paradise Lost*. The unique situation of Adam made it impossible for him to serve as an illustration of the struggles and triumphs which raise man from his degraded state. His story is of a fall. It remained for Milton to embody in another work its counterpart, to set forth in detail the successful encounter of humanity with the manifold forms of evil which present themselves in the complexities of a developed civilization. In this view *Paradise Regained* becomes a necessary sequel of *Paradise Lost*. Its theme, in its ethical as distinct from its theological aspect, is, indeed, already foreshadowed in the earlier poem, where the Christian virtues of faith, hope, love, humility, patience are indicated by the angel for Adam's attainment. Their exemplification is in Christ, who becomes for Milton the second Adam, protagonist of a humanity confronted with choices which the first Adam in the freshness of the world could not have known. This is the key to the development of the temptation scenes in *Paradise Regained*.[3] The first and third temptations are special, having to do with the peculiar character and mission of Christ. The second—the kingdoms of the world and the glory of them—is universal, implying all human moral issues. Milton accordingly elaborates it into a "survey of vice with all its baits and seeming pleasures," for which Christ's calm answers afford the antidote of reason. The critical objection that the temptations, given the nature of Christ, are not tempting, is beside the point. They are such temptations as experience shows to be the characteristic ones of men at large—luxury, wealth, power, fame, the pride of knowledge. By his indifference to these allurements and by his Socratic exposition of their emptiness Christ instructs all men how they may despise them. It is no mere piece of biblical commentary that Milton is composing, nor is it an attempt at portraiture of the historic Christ (though this motive from time to time appears). It is rather a pictorial map of the moral universe, a representation of the happier inner Paradise

---

[3] This view of the theme of *Paradise Regained* and the corresponding interpretation of the conflict in *Samson Agonistes* are set forth in "The Temptation Motive in Milton," the preceding essay in this volume.

of life according to right reason, an image of redemption in the only sense in which Milton in his maturer years could even pretend to understand redemption.

The theme was one which commanded the full resources of a life of meditative study, not in the dubious realms of demonology and Christian myth, but in the sun-clear walks of moral and religious wisdom, in history and political philosophy, in the biography of good men and great, in the exalted teachings of poet and seer, most of all in the gospels taken in their plain historical and moral sense, and such a theme gave Milton the opportunity to be altogether his humanistic self. In *Paradise Lost* he had been committed to a more or less inflexible story and to a traditional system of ideas which his best endeavor could not wholly rationalize or adopt to his own more individual thought, with the result that though his imagination was stimulated to unexampled activity, the work is but an imperfect and distorted image of his philosophical point of view. In *Paradise Regained* he was largely free. It is no wonder that he resented the suggestion that the second work was inferior to the first. Though lacking in color and vivid outward incident, it had even its points of superority. Its drama was of an inward intensity like that of the Book of Job. Its truth was unmixed with the accessory element of fiction. To Milton, in the severity of his age, this was argument of excellence. He knew, moreover, that the poem was more harmonious than *Paradise Lost,* simpler if less sensuous, and woven more close in "matter, form, and style."

It is now possible to consider the less obvious position of *Samson Agonistes* in Milton's poetic scheme. Formally and theologically the poem has no relation at all to its predecessors. For Milton does not, in his interpretation of the Old Testament material, adopt the point of view of the medieval religious drama, which built everything it treated into a single structure, regarding the events and characters of Hebrew history as episodes in an action which proceeded logically from the creation of the angels to the day of judgment. The story of Samson has for him an independent human value, neither implying nor prefiguring the life of Christ. For this very reason it adapts itself more naturally to his purposes, and affords the means of completing his representation of the state of man. The function of Christ we have already seen. He is, besides being the redeemer, the second Adam and the model man. But unlike Adam, Christ is without sin. Hence while he is the pattern and guide of human life, his victory is not, as ours must be, a recovery of something lost. The full account of man in his relation to the forces of good and evil demands another picture— the representation of frail humanity, burdened with the memory of former sin, but now repentant, restored to strength, and wrestling successfully with further trial. To what extent can *Samson Agonistes* be shown to fit this ideal prescription? The question raises some points of interpretation which appear to have been neglected by the numerous critics who, since Samuel Johnson, have discussed the merits of the work as drama.

When Milton, in 1641, first considered the life of the great but erring Hebrew champion as possible literary material and set down five subjects from it in the Cambridge manuscript, he was doubtless prompted chiefly by the coincidence of the story with characteristic themes of ancient drama. Samson was blind through his own guilt like Oedipus. In all other respects he was a Hebraic Herakles—the performer of incredible labors, enthralled by woman, sealing his baffled strength by a final destructive act. Such circumstances meant much in Milton's predisposition to a literary theme. More influential, however, in his final decision in favor of the subject was his perception of the parallel between Samson's sin and that of Adam. The point had already impressed itself upon him when he wrote of Adam's fall in the Ninth Book of *Paradise Lost,*

> So rose the Danite strong,
> Herculean Samson from the harlot lap
> Of Philistean Dalila, and waked
> Shorn of his strength, they desolate and bare
> Of all their virtue.

In the tragedy itself he is concerned with the fallen Samson's recovery of God's lost favor. The process involves his punishment and repentance, and the facing of new trials with a firmness won of experience and faith. It involves also a reward in the consciousness of God's having again accepted him as a worthy instrument of his purposes.

The trial itself is, I believe, the real center of the inward action, providing the play with such vital dramatic conflict as it exhibits. The Chorus and Manoa continually suggest distrust and compromise. They imply, in their attempted consolation, that Samson has been deceived in his belief that he once enjoyed God's special favor and was his chosen vessel. His marriages were not, as he had supposed, of a divine suggestion. God's dealings in sending the angel of his birth and apparently electing him as the champion of Israel, only to desert and leave him impotent, are unintelligible, if not unjust, for all has been turned to the glory of the Philistines. Against this Samson opposes, on the whole, the attitude of faith. He resists the suggestion that God was not really with him in the past. He reiterates the cry that nothing of all his evils has befallen him but justly. He meets the challenge of Manoa's

> Yet Israel still serves with all his tribes,

with the rejoinder that it is they themselves who through their own weakness have neglected God's proposed deliverance. For himself he knows that he has forfeited all hope, but he remains unshaken in the belief that God will not

> Connive, or linger, thus provoked,
> But will arise, and his great name assert.

Throughout the dialogue there are marked similarities to the Book of Job. Manoa and the Chorus have a function analogous to that of the friends who sharpen Job's agony by their mistaken comfort. Samson's resistance of the attempt to shake the convictions of his innermost experience has its counterpart in Job's passionate denial of the imputation of unrighteousness. There is, of course, a formal contrast between the two, in that Samson, unlike Job, is afflicted by a sense of sin, but both are loyal to truth and both maintain their positions against the apparent facts. Both, finally, are rewarded for their consistency by a manifestation of God's approval. With Job it is the voice out of a whirlwind, with Samson the renewal of "rousing motions" of innermost impulse, which have stirred and guided him to great deeds before his fall.

Of these motives there is in the Scriptural account of Samson not the slightest hint. The hero of the Hebrew chronicle is a naïve and semi-humorous märchen figure, whose sluggish intellect is far removed from any capability of spiritual conflict. Milton preserves the traits of his impulsiveness of temper and his original simplicity of spirit, but endows him, after his disillusionment, with extraordinary force of mind and with penetrating insight. The infusion into this mighty champion of old, of the complex emotions of the maturest and most profound creation of Hebrew thought, is the last masterful stroke of Milton's genius. For it, he had, to my knowledge, no precedent in literary tradition.

But if Milton is indebted to Job for the most essential elements in his conception of Samson's character, it is to his own constructive imagination, working within the artistic forms provided by occidental drama, that he owes the development of his theme. In the Book of Job there is little outward action and no clear progression. In *Samson* there are both. The framework of the plot is that of a Greek play. It is simple even to meagerness. Samson is consoled by the Chorus, worried by Dalila, insulted by Harapha, summoned before the Philistines by an officer. Old Manoa is busy meanwhile with misguided plans for his release, the moment of his success ironically coinciding with that of Samson's death. A messenger relates the catastrophe. The Chorus sings of Samson's fate and triumph.

Within this formal action the spiritual movement is richer than one at first observes. At the opening Samson is a spectacle of tragic misery and debasement. Out of his intense depression there rises higher and higher the note of active pain. At first his utterance concerns chiefly his physical and outward state:

> O loss of sight, of thee I most complain!
> Blind among enemies! O worse than chains,
> Dungeon or beggery, or decrepit age!

The first chorus, unheard by the protagonist, echoes and interprets his lament, with emphasis on the contrast between what once he was, is now. In the ensuing dialogue Samson's attention is diverted from his present wretchedness to its causes and significance. The memory of his fault is more bitter than the punishment wherewith it has been visited.

> Ye see, O friends,
> How many evils have enclosed me round;
> Yet that which once was the worst now least afflicts me,
> Blindness, for had I sight, confused with shame,
> How could I once look up, or heave the head,
> Who, like a foolish pilot, have shipwracked
> My vessel trusted to me from above.

The sight of Manoa wakes "another inward grief," and his words are as a goad to Samson's bitter remembrance. His proposal to treat with the Philistine lords serves only to reveal his son's indifference to his outward fate. The scene culminates in a spiritual outburst, expressive no longer of the hero's physical misery and obvious disgrace,

> Ensnared, assaulted, overcome, led bound,
> Thy foes' derision, captive, poor, and blind,

but of the inner agony of soul which springs from full contemplation of his sins, "and sense of Heaven's desertion." The opening words of the passage clearly indicate the forward movement:

> Oh, that torment should not be confined
> To the body's wounds and sores,
> With maladies innumerable
> In heart, head, breast, and reins,
> But must secret passage find
> To the inmost mind,
> There exercise all his fierce accidents,
> And on her purest spirits prey,
> As on entrails, joints, and limbs,
> With answerable pains, but more intense,
> Though void of corporal sense!

The conclusion is one of unrelieved despair and marks the darkest moment of Samson's suffering, corresponding precisely to Adam's remorseful misery as he meditates upon his sin:

> Hopeless are all my evils, all remediless.
> This one prayer yet remains, might I be heard,
> No long petition—speedy death,
> The close of all my miseries and the balm.

Henceforth we have recovery. By confronting his own guilt without evasion, and by resisting the temptation to doubt God's ways are just, or to fear for the ultimate triumph of his cause, Samson has won the right to be put to proof a second time. His firmness is subjected first to the insidious approaches of Dalila, whose visit, however doubtfully motivated in itself, is essential to the idea of the drama. Her plea is specious, but Samson remains unmoved, the significance of his victory being pointed out in the choric comment,

> Yet beauty, though injurious, hath strange power,
> After offence returning, to regain
> Love once possessed, nor can be easily
> Repulsed, without much inward passion felt
> And secret sting of amorous remorse.

He next confronts physical force in the person of Harapha, who collapses, like all brute menace, before the champion's indifference to fear, and the chorus, participating for the moment in Samson's strength, sings the great ode,

> O how comely it is, and how reviving,
> When God into the hands of their deliverer
> Puts invincible might,
> To quell the mighty of the earth, the oppressor,
> The brute and boistrous force of violent men.

They are, of course, like Samson himself, still blind to what is to come, and they go on to sing of patience as the final crown of saints.

The coming of the officer creates a problem. Samson's refusal, at first, to do his bidding illustrates his uncompromising allegiance to the God of his fathers and his contempt of personal safety. The Chorus suggests the easier way of yielding, pointing out the fact that he has already served the Philistines (with the old implication that he cannot regard himself as a being set apart). Their reasoning is met with a clear distinction between compromise in

273

things indifferent and the surrender of a point of conscience. Then, as if in answer to this final proof of Samson's single devotedness to God's service, comes again the inner prompting, "disposing to something extraordinary my thoughts." He obeys it unhesitatingly and goes forth under divine guidance as of old. He has, in a sense, regained his own lost Paradise, and in his story Milton, by vindicating the power of a free but erring will to maintain itself in obedience and be restored to grace, has again asserted eternal Providence and justified the ways of God to man.

The fact that Samson is an Old Testament figure and achieves his triumph before the time of the Redeemer shows the true place of Christ in Milton's system. The blood of his sacrifice is plainly no necessary instrument of salvation; even his example may be dispensed with by those who enjoy a direct and special relation with the Divine. Yet the Hebrews did have Christ in prophecy, and for the men of later time he is the way. By his present example the path is open, not for chosen heroes alone, but for all, to

> love with fear the only God, to walk
> As in his presence, ever to observe
> His providence, and on him sole depend,
> Merciful over all his works, with good
> Still overcoming evil, and by small
> Accomplishing great things—by things deemed weak
> Subverting worldly-strong, and worldly-wise
> By simply meek;

Such is Milton's final teaching and the ethical goal of his poetic art. The desire expressed in the introduction to Book IX of *Paradise Lost* to sing "the better fortitude of patience and heroic martyrdom," is fulfilled by the portrayal of a divine pattern in *Paradise Regained. Samson Agonistes* is its nearest possible fulfillment in the life of mortal man. To embody it more completely by representing the humbler trials and victories of daily life would have been incompatible with the tradition of Milton's literary allegiance—incompatible, too, with the memory of the heroic struggle in which he himself had been engaged.

Of this experience and this struggle I have as yet said nothing. How deeply it enters into the bone and sinew of *Samson Ago-*

*nistes* no one can doubt. That Milton felt the parallel between his own situation and that of Samson and that he in some way identified himself with his hero is obvious and has been emphasized by the biographers. I have myself elsewhere pointed out that in making Samson wrestle with despair Milton was championing his own faith assaulted by inward murmuring and challenged by the apparent failure of his cause.[4] It remains to enquire as to the extent and nature of this personal identification and to analyze more exactly the psychological reactions, conscious and unconscious, which are implied in the composition of the play.

Let us recognize at once that *Samson Agonistes* is a work of art and not a disguised autobiography. To a reader unacquainted with Milton's life the poem would seem as monumentally independent as *Prometheus Bound*. It deserves to be so judged and would, perhaps, stand higher as a masterpiece of art if it had been less often used as an illustration of Milton's personal life and temper. It should not, however, suffer from interpretation in the light of the poet's characteristic moods and thoughts, if we clearly recognize the conditions of their operation in his creative work. His most intimate emotions are invariably sublimated by the imagination and so far depersonalized. The process enables him to project himself with sympathy into characters and situations which have only a partial analogy with his own. So it is with his representations of Comus, or of Satan and Adam in *Paradise Lost*. In other cases, as in those of Dalilah, Eve, or Mammon he is capable, within a limited range, of being as objective as any artist of essentially romantic temper.

In the representation of Samson, Milton has undoubtedly put more of himself than in any other of his imaginative creations. The sense of power and dignity, the "plain heroic magnitude of mind," the will toward championship are Milton. So too is the noble self-pity, expressed in the consciousness of deprivation in the loss of sight ("The sun to me is dark, and silent as the moon"), and, the feeling of physical helplessness ("In power of others, never in my own"). But all this is heightened and ideal-

---

[4] In "The Temptation Motive in Milton."

ized for purposes of art. The tragic gloom and flat despair of Samson, the wretchedness of pain, the distaste of life, are the embodiments of an aesthetic mood which owes quite as much to literature as to personal experience. As a matter of fact the impression left by such direct biographical records as we have of Milton in old age is quite the reverse of this, suggesting the persistence in him to the end of a temper unspoiled by tribulation. The "cheerful godliness" of Wordsworth's sonnet appears to be an entirely appropriate description of the poet's habitual outward mood in the last years of his life.

With regard to his blindness it is worth noting that the most poignant allusions to it were written longest after the event itself. At the actual moment of the catastrophe Milton was silent. His poetical occupation in the immediately succeeding years was the translation of Psalms, a literary and religious discipline. In 1654 he gives expression in prose, not to his sense of irrecoverable loss, but to the consciousness of spiritual compensation in "an interior illumination more precious and more pure." [5] in 1655, on the third anniversary of his loss of sight, he allows himself to consider how his "light is spent ere half his days," and to give voice to the pathos of his condition, only, however, as a preparation for the expression of acquiescence and of the consolations which come from the sense of having sacrificed himself in a noble cause. The utterances in *Paradise Lost* are touched with a deeper pathos, but it is first in *Samson,* where they are no longer directly personal, that they become a tragic cry:

> Dark, dark, dark, amid the blaze of moon,
> Irrecoverably dark, total eclipse,
> Without all hope of day.

A similar account might be given of the poet's antifeminism. It is entirely absent from the sonnets which belong to the days of his estrangement from Mary Powell. Indeed the two poems written at that time, *To a Virtuous Young Lady* and *To the Lady Margaret Ley,* are sincere though sober tributes to female virtue. The general indictment of the sex begins with Adam's words to Eve in

---

[5] *Defensio Secunda, Prose Works* (Bohn), I, p. 239.

Book X of *Paradise Lost* and reaches a strain of unrelieved bitterness in *Samson Agonistes*.

Such are the facts, as we read them in the chronological consideration of Milton's works. One cannot fail to be struck by the analogy which exists between the processes of the poet's expression of certain phases of his inmost experience in this last epoch of his literary life and the youthful development which we have studied in the preceding essay. The position of *Samson Agonistes* in its relation to the complex of emotions and ideas which centered in the poet's blindness is singularly like that of *Comus* with reference to the conflict of sensuous and ideal impulses in his adolescence. Each represents the culmination of a train of introspective thoughts which may easily be conceived to have been disturbing to Milton's mental equilibrium. In each work he appears to achieve for the first time a full expression of these emotions, and in achieving it to obtain a spiritual mastery of them. The result is one which is always, perhaps, in some degree present in the intenser activity of the creative imagination, and it has received general recognition from the critics and philosophers of literature. The most luminous statement is the following by Croce in his *Aesthetic*.[6] "By elaborating his impressions man frees himself from them. By objectifying them, he removes them from him and makes himself their superior. The liberating and purifying function of art is another aspect and another formula of its character as activity. Activity is the deliverer, just because it drives away passivity. This also explains why it is usual to attribute to artists both the maximum of sensibility and the maximum of insensibility or Olympian serenity. The two characters are compatible, for they do not refer to the same object. The sensibility or passion relates to the rich material which the artist absorbs into his psychic organism, the insensibility or serenity to the form with which he subdues and dominates the tumult of sensations and passions."

It is scarcely possible to determine the degree to which Milton, in recreating and transforming emotions which in their rawer

---

[6] Chapter 2. Douglas Ainsley's translation, 1922.

form made inroads upon his carefully cherished serenity, experienced a similar deliverance. Some light may be gained, however, by a consideration of certain neglected aspects of the play itself, the indications, namely, which the poet has given of what he himself thought of its function as a work of art. These indications refer mainly, to be sure, to what he looked for in its effect upon the reader or spectator, but they are not without application to the artist as well and it seems to me quite clear that Milton must have been guided in his interpretation of the power of tragedy to effect spiritual benefits upon others by what he had himself experienced in creating it.

The question centers in his understanding of the formula for tragedy and its purgative effect as given in the famous Aristotelian definition. The importance of this formula in Milton's thought and the degree to which he must have been conscious of it in constructing his drama are suggested by the fact that he quotes it in Latin on his title page and devotes the first part of his prose preface to its elaboration. His opening statement is as follows: "Tragedy as it was anciently composed hath been ever held the gravest, moralest, and most profitable of all other poems; therefore said by Aristotle to be of power by raising pity and fear, or terror, to purge the mind of those and such like passions, that is to temper and reduce them to just measure with a kind of delight, stirred up by seeing those passions well imitated."

In considering the application of this principle to *Samson Agonistes* we must observe, first of all, that, by representing a clearly marked triumph of the human will over its own weakness, and by the substitution of Providence for blind fate as the power which overrules the action, the play provides material for a different understanding of catharsis from that contemplated by Aristotle, an understanding which falls in with the first part of Milton's description—that tragedy is the gravest, moralest, and most profitable of poetic forms—rather than with the last—that it transforms painful emotions into pleasurable. On a superficial view we might, indeed, be tempted to regard the purgation, as Milton actually worked it out, as a purely ethical and religious process, the result of a consciously didactic purpose by which our faith is strengthened and our sympathy with Samson's pain swallowed up in our exultation in his triumph. It is the function of Manoa's last speech and of the final chorus to emphasize this motive:

> Come, come, no time for lamentation now,
> Nor much more cause; Samson hath quit himself
> Like Samson, and heroicly hath finished
> A life Heroic. . . .
> With God not parted from him as was feared,
> But favouring and assisting to the end.
>
> .  .  .  .  .  .  .  .  .
> All is best, though we oft doubt,
> What the unsearchable dispose
> Of highest wisdom brings about
> And ever best found in the close.

To some critics [7] these quotations have seemed an adequate formula for the poem as a whole, and a mark of the failure of *Samson Agonistes* to embody the genuinely tragic motive of the unsuccessful struggle of man with fate. Such a judgment is obvious and in part correct. It fails, however, to take account of the actuality of the tragic impression which the drama must leave upon every reader who comes to it unhampered by definitions and comparisons. The pain of the earlier scenes is something which cannot be so easily displaced. Sealed as it is with the hero's death, it outlives all consolation, as the tragic suffering of Hamlet outlives the accomplishment of his purpose, the choric benediction of Horatio, and the restoration of a wholesome commonwealth by Fortinbras. The pronouncement "All is best" is of scarcely more avail than the identical formulae which bring Greek plays to their conclusion and from which this one is derived. The consolation which is offered of "what can quiet us in a death so noble" is not enough. Samson should have gone on from one glad triumph to another and emerged unscathed. Outward circumstance, the treacheries of others, and his own conspiring fault have brought him low, and have constrained him to wear, however gloriously,

---

[7] See Paull F. Baum, "Samson Agonistes Again." *Publications of the Modern Language Association,* XXXVI (1921) , pp. 365 ff.

the crown of martyrdom. Here surely is tragedy enough. Though Providence is proclaimed, its ways are dark and its face, at times, is hardly to be distinguished from the countenance of Fate herself. The secret is that there remains an irreducible element in the midst of Milton's faith—a sense as keen as Shakespeare's of the reality of suffering which neither the assurance of God's special favors to himself nor his resolute insistence on the final triumph of his righteousness can blot out. The antique strain in Milton's experience and thought stands side by side with the Christian, and the two alternate or combine in their domination of his artistic moods. It is in vain that he repudiates stoicism as a futile refuge and a false philosophy; he is betrayed by the vehemence of his declarations against it, and he instinctively adopts its weapons.

These considerations prepare us to examine the operation in *Samson Agonistes* of catharsis in its strict Aristotelian sense. Milton's effort to demonstrate in his drama the truth of Aristotle's pronouncement is part and parcel of a thoroughgoing conscious classicism, which extends far beyond such matters as the ordering of the incidents and the employment of ancient devices like the messenger. It is shown in a more philosophic and intrinsic way in the subtle turns which the poet gives to the interpretation of his theme in order to bring it more nearly into conformity with the spirit of ancient tragedy. Paull Baum counts it a major defect of *Samson Agonistes* that the hero's tragic fault is undignified and sub-heroic. But observe the means which Milton takes to dignify it. He associates it with the most dignified of all tragic faults— rebellious pride. Intoxicated by success Samson forgets to refer his victories to their source, and so becomes, in Milton's interpretation, an instance of classical hybris. Like Shakespeare's Mark Antony he "struts to his destruction."

> Fearless of danger, like a petty God,
> I walked about, admired of all, and dreaded
> On hostile ground, none daring my assault.
> Then swollen with pride, into the snare I fell
> Of fair fallacious looks, venereal trains.

This is somewhat forced, one must confess, and Milton appears to be aware of it. Witness the shading he is compelled to give to the idea in the following:

> But I
> God's counsel have not kept, his holy secret
> Presumptuously have published, impiously,
> *Weakly at least and shamefully*—a sin
> That Gentiles in their parables condemn
> To their Abyss and horrid pains confined.

The cloak of Prometheus and Tantalus evidently refuses to fit the less majestic Hebrew Titan. The conception of hybris and Ate applies more perfectly to the Philistines and is accordingly invoked in the triumphant semi-chorus beginning in line 1669:

> While their hearts were jocund and sublime,
> Drunk with idolatry, drunk with wine
> And fat regorged of bulls and goats,
> Chaunting their idol, and preferring
> Before our Living Dread, who dwells
> In Silo, his bright sanctuary,
> Among them he a spirit of phrenzy sent,
> Who hurt their minds,
> And urged them on with mad desire
> To call in haste for their destroyer.
> They, only set on sport and play,
> Unweetingly importuned
> Their own destruction to come speedy upon them.
> So fond are mortal men,
> Fallen into wrath divine,
> As their own ruin on themselves to invite,
> Insensate left, or to sense reprobate,
> And with blindness internal struck.

Both passages, however, are illustrative of the degree to which Milton had grasped the central motive of Greek tragedy and the pains he was at to bring his own material under the ethical, religious, and artistic formulae afforded by it.

A more vital result of his assimilation of the point of view of his ancient models is to be found in the great chorus which follows Samson's deeper expression of despair, in lines 608–650. If anything in Milton or indeed in all modern literature deserves to be called a reproduction of antiquity it is this passage. It is as perfectly representative as Milton could have wished of "Aeschylus, Sophocles, Euripides, the three tragic poets unequalled yet by any, and the best rule to all who endeavor to write Tragedy," and it comes little short of their noblest choral odes in the grandeur and intensity of its tragic feeling. In the majestic rhythms of the opening the Chorus sings of the vanity of consolation in the ears of the afflicted and expostulates with Providence in its uneven course with men. Thoroughly Greek and as thoroughly Miltonic is the centering of attention on the woes, not of the common rout of men who grow up and perish like the summer fly, but on those of heroic mould, "with gifts and graces eminently adorned." The ensuing lines embody the idea of the excess of evil which rains down on the head of the tragic hero according to Aristotle's description in the *Poetics:*

> Nor only dost degrade them, or remit
> To life obscured, which were a fair dismission,
> But throw'st them lower than thou didst exalt them high—
> Unseemly falls in human eye,
> Too grievous for the trespass or omission;
> Oft leav'st them to the hostile sword
> Of heathen and profane, their carcasses
> To dogs and fowls a prey, or else captived,
> Or to the unjust tribunals, under change of times,
> And condemnation of the ungrateful multitude.
> If these they escape, perhaps in poverty
> With sickness and disease thou bow'st them down,
> Painful diseases and deformed,
> In crude old age;
> Though not disordinate, yet causeless suffering
> The punishment of dissolute days. In fine,
> Just or unjust alike seem miserable,
> For oft alike both come to evil end.

The personal note here is too distinct to be mistaken. "Unjust tribunals under change of times," "their carcasses to dogs and fowls a prey" are certainly echoes of the Restoration, with its brutal trials of men like Henry Vane, and the indignities to which the bodies of Cromwell and Ireton were subjected. The parallel and not less wretched fate of poverty and disease is Milton's own. He goes so far as almost to specify the rheumatic ills from which we know him to have suffered—"painful diseases and deformed" —with the bitter reflection that these afflictions, justly the fruit of dissipation, may come also to those who, like himself, have lived in temperance. Nowhere else in his works, not even in the laments of Adam, does Milton permit himself to indulge in so unrelieved an expression of pagan sentiment. He does so under the shield of dramatic objectivity, yet none of his words spring from deeper sources in his consciousness. Here momentarily he faces the world with no other arms than those of pure humanity, giving utterance to a view of life directly opposed to that to which he had subdued his thinking as a whole.

It is in such a mood as this and in such an utterance that Milton must, if ever, have felt, in his own emotional experience, the reality of the Aristotelian catharsis, and the need of it. The question of the means whereby affliction may be soothed is one which had always interested him, and his works contain numerous suggestive utterances on the subject. It is prominent in the discussion of the case of Samson. Thus, contemplating, at this point, his hero's misery, he makes the Chorus tell how useless for the sufferer in his pangs are those wise consolations of philosophy, "writ with studied argument, lenient of grief and anxious thought." It is only, they affirm, by "secret refreshings from above" that the afflicted wretch can be restored. But such refreshings are obviously not always to be commanded. To prepare for their benign influence the mind must first be emptied of its pent-up bitterness, and for such a process tragedy, in the Aristotelian conception, supplies the means. So, one would suppose, might Milton have thought and felt. And if such was his experience it is not surprising that he should have dwelt with such insistence on the rationale of the process in his prose preface.

His initial statement I have already quoted. Pity, fear, and like passions, it implies, are, in their raw state, dangerous and painful. Objectively represented, they are tempered and reduced to just measure by a kind of delight. "Nor is Nature," adds Milton, "wanting in her own effects to make good his assertion; for so, in

283

Physic, things of melancholic hue and quality are used against melancholy, sour against sour, salt to remove salt humours." This passage has often been cited with approval by classical scholars as expressing the soundest modern interpretation of the dark oracle of Aristotle's pronouncement, and there has been discussion of Milton's priority in employing the medical analogy. No one, I think, has called attention to his application of this conception to the analysis of Samson's spiritual ills in an outstanding passage in the play itself. The hero has just expressed his indifference to the efforts proposed in his behalf and his expectation of an early death. Manoa replies:

> Believe not these suggestions, which proceed
> From anguish of the mind, and humours black
> That mingle with thy fancy.

There follows the great lyric outburst of Samson's spiritual woe, which must now be given at greater length.

> O that torment should not be confined
> To the body's wounds and sores,
> With maladies innumerable
> In heart, head, breast, and reins;
> But must secret passage find
> To the inmost mind,
> There exercise all his fierce accidents,
> And on her purest spirits prey,
> As on entrails, joints and limbs,
> With answerable pains, but more intense,
> Though void of corporal sense!
> My griefs not only pain me
> As a lingering disease,
> But, finding no redress, ferment and rage;
> Nor less than wounds immedicable
> Rankle, and fester, and gangrene,
> To black mortification.
> Thoughts, my tormentors, armed with deadly stings,
> Mangle my apprehensive tenderest parts,
> Exasperate, exulcerate, and raise
> Dire inflammation, which no cooling herb
> Or medicinal liquor can assuage,
> Nor breath of vernal air from snowy Alp.

Sleep hath forsook and given me o'er
To death's benumbing opium as my only cure;
Thence faintings, swoonings of despair,
And sense of Heaven's desertion.

The idea which Milton here develops with somewhat shocking explicitness is obviously the same as that which underlies his conception of catharsis—the idea, namely, that the passions operate in precisely the manner of bodily poisons, which, when they find no outlet, rage destructively within. Samson is given over to pity and fear, and there is no apparent prospect of relief, no cooling herb or medicinal liquor to purify the "black mortification" of his thoughts. It is quite clear, then, that Milton intends to suggest a kind of Aristotelian diagnosis of Samson's tragic state, parallel to the more obvious religious interpretation which I have previously expounded. But if he partly identified himself with his hero, then such a diagnosis would serve also to that extent to describe his own. As, however, he draws a sharp distinction on the religious side between Samson's spiritual darkness and his own illumination by an inner light, so here he must have been conscious of a difference in the manner of their deliverance from the morbid introspection to which they are equally subject. The intensity of Samson's pain lasts only so long as he remains inactive. His lyric elaboration of his inward woe is immediately followed by the unexpected visits of his foes. His attention is thus distracted from his suffering to a series of situations which confront him and he finally loses himself in glorious though disastrous action.

For Milton, in the impotence of his situation after the Restoration, there can be no such deliverance. He is enrolled perforce among those "whom patience finally must crown." But he has in his possession a recourse without which the way of patience is at times too hard. The purgation which the untutored champion of Israel must find in deeds is available to the man of culture through the activity of the mind and spirit. It offers itself to Milton in a dual form, corresponding to his twofold inheritance from the Reformation and the Renaissance. As the play draws to an end the two motives are subtly balanced and as nearly reconciled as, perhaps, it is within the power of human skill to reconcile them. The champion's final deed and the triumph of God's uncontrollable intent promote in us a sense of exultation and confirm our faith, but the greatness of his suffering and the pathos of his death produce a different effect, making possible the serene dismission of the close:

> His servants he, with new acquist
> Of true experience from this great event,
> With peace and consolation hath dismissed
> And calm of mind, all passion spent.

It is characteristic of the critical self-consciousness which Milton carries with him even in his moments of highest creative inspiration and suggestive also of the vital uses to which he turned aesthetic as well as religious doctrine that the last word of all should be an almost explicit reference to the tragic formula which he had derived from the authority of "the master of those who know."